W9-ADM-899

Register for Free Membership to

solutions@syngress.com

Over the last few years, Syngress has published many best-selling and critically acclaimed books, including Tom Shinder's *Configuring ISA Server 2000*, Brian Caswell and Jay Beale's *Snort 2.0 Intrusion Detection*, and Angela Orebaugh and Gilbert Ramirez's *Ethereal Packet Sniffing*. One of the reasons for the success of these books has been our unique **solutions@syngress.com** program. Through this site, we've been able to provide readers a real time extension to the printed book.

As a registered owner of this book, you will qualify for free access to our members-only solutions@syngress.com program. Once you have registered, you will enjoy several benefits, including:

- Four downloadable e-booklets on topics related to the book. Each booklet is approximately 20-30 pages in Adobe PDF format. They have been selected by our editors from other best-selling Syngress books as providing topic coverage that is directly related to the coverage in this book.

- A comprehensive FAQ page that consolidates all of the key points of this book into an easy to search web page, providing you with the concise, easy to access data you need to perform your job.

- A "From the Author" Forum that allows the authors of this book to post timely updates links to related sites, or additional topic coverage that may have been requested by readers.

Just visit us at **www.syngress.com/solutions** and follow the simple registration process. You will need to have this book with you when you register.

Thank you for giving us the opportunity to serve your needs. And be sure to let us know if there is anything else we can do to make your job easier.

SYNGRESS®

SYNGRESS®

Cyber Adversary

Characterization

AUDITING THE HACKER MIND

Tom Parker

Matthew G. Devost

Marcus H. Sachs

Eric Shaw

Ed Stroz

Syngress Publishing, Inc., the author(s), and any person or firm involved in the writing, editing, or production (collectively "Makers") of this book ("the Work") do not guarantee or warrant the results to be obtained from the Work.

There is no guarantee of any kind, expressed or implied, regarding the Work or its contents. The Work is sold AS IS and WITHOUT WARRANTY. You may have other legal rights, which vary from state to state.

In no event will Makers be liable to you for damages, including any loss of profits, lost savings, or other incidental or consequential damages arising out from the Work or its contents. Because some states do not allow the exclusion or limitation of liability for consequential or incidental damages, the above limitation may not apply to you.

You should always use reasonable care, including backup and other appropriate precautions, when working with computers, networks, data, and files.

Syngress Media®, Syngress®, "Career Advancement Through Skill Enhancement®," "Ask the Author UPDATE®," and "Hack Proofing®," are registered trademarks of Syngress Publishing, Inc. "Syngress: The Definition of a Serious Security Library"™, "Mission Critical™," and "The Only Way to Stop a Hacker is to Think Like One™" are trademarks of Syngress Publishing, Inc. Brands and product names mentioned in this book are trademarks or service marks of their respective companies.

KEY	SERIAL NUMBER
001	HV764GHJ82
002	PO5FG2324V
003	82JH2776NB
004	CVPLQ6WQ23
005	C3KLC542MK
006	VBT5GH652M
007	H63W3EBCP8
008	29MK56F56V
009	629MP5SDJT
010	IMWQ295T6T

PUBLISHED BY
Syngress Publishing, Inc.
800 Hingham Street
Rockland, MA 02370

Cyber Adversary Characterization: Auditing the Hacker Mind

Copyright © 2004 by Syngress Publishing, Inc. All rights reserved. Printed in the United States of America. Except as permitted under the Copyright Act of 1976, no part of this publication may be reproduced or distributed in any form or by any means, or stored in a database or retrieval system, without the prior written permission of the publisher, with the exception that the program listings may be entered, stored, and executed in a computer system, but they may not be reproduced for publication.

Printed in the United States of America
1 2 3 4 5 6 7 8 9 0
ISBN: 1-931836-11-6

Acquisitions Editor: Christine Kloiber
Technical Editor: Tom Parker
Page Layout and Art: Patricia Lupien

Cover Designer: Michael Kavish
Copy Editor: Darren Meiss and
 Darlene Bordwell
Indexer: Rich Carlson

Distributed by O'Reilly Media in the United States and Canada.

Acknowledgments

We would like to acknowledge the following people for their kindness and support in making this book possible.

Jeff Moss and Ping Look from Black Hat, Inc. You have been good friends to Syngress and great colleagues to work with. Thank you!

Syngress books are now distributed in the United States and Canada by O'Reilly Media, Inc. The enthusiasm and work ethic at O'Reilly is incredible and we would like to thank everyone there for their time and efforts to bring Syngress books to market: Tim O'Reilly, Laura Baldwin, Mark Brokering, Mike Leonard, Donna Selenko, Bonnie Sheehan, Cindy Davis, Grant Kikkert, Opol Matsutaro, Lynn Schwartz, Steve Hazelwood, Mark Wilson, Rick Brown, Leslie Becker, Jill Lothrop, Tim Hinton, Kyle Hart, Sara Winge, C. J. Rayhill, Peter Pardo, Leslie Crandell, Valerie Dow, Regina Aggio, Pascal Honscher, Preston Paull, Susan Thompson, Bruce Stewart, Laura Schmier, Sue Willing, Mark Jacobsen, Betsy Waliszewski, Dawn Mann, Kathryn Barrett, John Chodacki, and Rob Bullington.

The incredibly hard working team at Elsevier Science, including Jonathan Bunkell, Ian Seager, Duncan Enright, David Burton, Rosanna Ramacciotti, Robert Fairbrother, Miguel Sanchez, Klaus Beran, Emma Wyatt, Rosie Moss, Chris Hossack, and Krista Leppiko, for making certain that our vision remains worldwide in scope.

David Buckland, Daniel Loh, Marie Chieng, Lucy Chong, Leslie Lim, Audrey Gan, Pang Ai Hua, and Joseph Chan of STP Distributors for the enthusiasm with which they receive our books.

Kwon Sung June at Acorn Publishing for his support.

David Scott, Tricia Wilden, Marilla Burgess, Annette Scott, Geoff Ebbs, Hedley Partis, Bec Lowe, and Mark Langley of Woodslane for distributing our books throughout Australia, New Zealand, Papua New Guinea, Fiji Tonga, Solomon Islands, and the Cook Islands.

Winston Lim of Global Publishing for his help and support with distribution of Syngress books in the Philippines.

Author

Tom Parker is one of Britain's most highly prolific security consultants. Alongside providing integral security services for some of the world's largest organizations, Tom is widely known for his vulnerability research on a wide range of platforms and commercial products. His more recent technical work includes the development of an embedded operating system, media management system and cryptographic code for use on digital video band (DVB) routers deployed on the networks of hundreds of large organizations around the globe.

In 1999, Tom helped form Global InterSec LLC, playing a leading role in developing key relationships between GIS and the public and private sector security companies. Tom has spent much of the last few years researching methodologies aimed at characterizing adversarial capabilities and motivations against live, mission critical assets. He also provides aid in identifying adversarial attribution in the unfortunate times when incidents do occur. Currently working as a security consultant for NetSEC, a provider of managed and professional security services, Tom continues to research practical ways for large organizations to manage the ever-growing cost of security by identifying where the real threats exist.

Contributors

Matthew G. Devost is President and CEO of the Terrorism Research Center, Inc., overseeing all research, analysis and training programs. He has been researching the impact of information technology on national security since 1993. In addition to his current duties as President, Matthew also provides strategic consulting services to select international governments and corporations on issues of counter terrorism, information warfare and security, critical infrastructure protection and homeland security. Matthew also cofounded and serves as Executive Director of Technical Defense, Inc., a highly specialized information security consultancy. Prior to that, he was the Director of Intelligence Analysis for Infrastructure Defense (iDefense), where he led an analytical team identifying infrastructure threats, vulnerabilities and incidents for Fortune 500 and government clients including Microsoft and Citigroup.

Matthew is certified in the operation of numerous security tools and in the National Security Agency's INFOSEC Assessment Methodology and is an instructor for the Threat, Exposure and Response Matrix (TERM) methodology. He is a member of the American Society for Industrial Security, the Information Systems Security Association, and the International Association for Counterterrorism & Security Professionals. He has appeared on CNN, MSNBC, FoxNews, NPR, CBS Radio, BBC television, NWCN, Australian television and over five dozen other domestic and international radio and television programs as an expert on terrorism and information warfare. He has lectured or published for the National Defense University, the United States Intelligence and Law Enforcement Communities, the Swedish, Australian and New Zealand governments, Georgetown University, American University, George Washington University, and a number of popular press books, magazines, academic journals and over 100 international conferences. Matthew holds an Adjunct Professor position at Georgetown University, has received a B.A. degree from St. Michael's College, and a Master of Arts Degree in Political Science from the University of Vermont.

Marcus H. Sachs is the Director of the SANS Internet Storm Center and is a cyberspace security researcher, writer, and instructor for the SANS Institute. He previously served in the White House Office of Cyberspace Security and was a staff member of the President's Critical Infrastructure Protection Board. While a member of the White House staff, Marcus coordinated efforts to protect and secure the nation's telecommunication and Internet infrastructures, leveraging expertise from United States government agencies, the domestic private sector, and the international community. He also contributed to the National Strategy to Secure Cyberspace, upon his joining of the National Cyber Security Division of the US

Department of Homeland Security. While working for DHS, he developed the initial concept and strategy for the creation of the United States Computer Emergency Response Team. Marcus retired from the United States Army in 2001 after serving over 20 years as a Corps of Engineers officer. He specialized during the later half of his career in computer network operations, systems automation, and information technology.

Eric Shaw is a clinical psychologist who has spent the last 20 years specializing in the psychological profiling of political actors and forensic subjects. He has been a consultant supporting manager development and organizational change, a clinician aiding law enforcement and corporate security, an intelligence officer supporting national security interests and a legal consultant providing negotiation and litigation assistance. He has also provided cross-cultural profiling for the U.S. Government on the psychological state and political attitudes of figures such as Saddam Hussein, Iranian revolutionary leaders under Khomeini, senior Soviet military commanders, as well as Yugoslav, Laotian, Cuban and other military and political leaders. In 2000 he helped develop a tool designed to help analysts identify political, religious and other groups at-risk for terrorist violence. This approach examines the group's cultural context, its relationship with allied and competitive actors in the immediate political environment, their internal group dynamics and leadership. It utilizes a range of information on the group, including their publications, web sites and internal communications. Eric has recently published articles on cyber terrorism examining the likelihood of the use of cybertactics by traditional and emerging forms of terrorist groups.

Ed Strotz (CPA, CITP, CFE) is President of Stroz Friedberg, LLC, which he started in 2000 after a sixteen-year career as a Special Agent for the Federal Bureau of Investigation (FBI). Stroz Friedberg performs investigative, consulting, and forensic laboratory services for the most pre-eminent law firms in the country. Ed has advised clients in industries including banking, brokerage, insurance, media, computer and telecommunications, and has guided clients through problems including Internet extortions, denial of service attacks, hacks, domain name hijacking, data destruction and theft of trade secrets. He has supervised numerous forensic assignments for criminal federal prosecutors, defense attorneys and civil litigants, and has conducted network security audits for major public and private entities. Stroz Friedberg has pioneered the merging of behavioral science and computer security in audits of corporate web sites for content that could either stimulate or be useful in conducting an attack by a terrorist or other adversary.

In 1996, while still a Special Agent, he formed the FBI's Computer Crime Squad in New York City, where he supervised investigations involving computer intrusions, denial-of-service attacks, illegal Internet wiretapping, fraud, money laundering, and violations of intellectual property rights, including trade secrets. Among the more significant FBI investigations Ed handled were: Vladimir Levin's prosecution for hacking a US bank from Russia; the hack against the New York Times web site; the Internet dissemination by "Keystroke Snoopers," a hacking group responsible for a keystroke capture program embedded in a Trojan Horse; Breaking News Network's illegal interception of pager messages; the denial of service attack against a major business magazine; efforts to steal copyrighted content from the Bloomberg system; and the hack of a telecommunications switch. Ed and his squad were also participants in the war game exercise called "Eligible Receiver."

Ed is a member of the American Institute of Certified Public Accountants, the Association of Certified Fraud Examiners and the American Society of Industrial Security. He is a graduate of Fordham University, a Certified Information Technology Professional, and a member of the International Association for Identification. He is an active member of the United States Secret Service's Electronic Crimes Task Force, Chairman of the Electronic Security Advisory Council and former Chairman of the New York chapter of the FBI's Ex-Agents Society.

Special Contribution

(The fictional story, "Return on Investment," at the conclusion of this book was written by Fyodor and was excerpted from Stealing the Network: How to Own a Continent, *ISBN 1931836051).*

Fyodor authored the popular Nmap Security Scanner, which was named security tool of the year by Linux Journal, Info World, LinuxQuestiosn.Org, and the Codetalker Digest. It was also featured in the hit movie "Matrix Reloaded" as well as by the BBC, CNet, Wired, Slashdot, Securityfocus, and more. He also maintains the Insecure.Org and Seclists.Org security resource sites and has authored seminal papers detailing techniques for stealth port scanning, remote operating system detection via TCP/IP stack fingerprinting, version detection, and the IPID Idle Scan. He is a member of the Honeynet project and a co-author of the book Know Your Enemy: Honeynets.

Preface

A book about hacking is a book about everything.

First, the meaning of *hacker*.

The word "hacker" emerged in an engineering context and became popular at The Massachusetts Institute of Technology (MIT), among other places, as a way to talk about any ingenious, creative, or unconventional use of a machine doing novel things, usually unintended or unforeseen by its inventors. A hacker was someone involved in a technical feat of legerdemain; a person who saw doors where others saw walls or built bridges that looked to the uninitiated like planks on which one walked into shark-filled seas.

The mythology of hacking was permeated with the spirit of Coyote, the Trickster. Hackers see clearly into the arbitrariness of structures that others accept as the last word. They see contexts as contents, which is why when they apply themselves to altering the context, the change in explicit content seems magical. They generally are not builders in the sense that creating a functional machine that will work in a benign environment is not their primary passion. Instead, they love to take things apart and see how machines can be defeated. Their very presuppositions constitute the threat environment that make borders and boundaries porous.

In their own minds and imaginations, they are free beings who live in a world without walls. Sometimes they see themselves as the last free beings, and anyone and anything organizational as a challenge and opportunity. Beating *The Man* at his own game is an adrenalin rush of the first order.

The world of distributed networks evolved as a cartoon-like dialogue bubble pointing to the head of DARPA. Hackers sometimes missed that fact, thinking they emerged whole and without a history from the brow of Zeus. The evolution of the "closed world" inside digital networks began to interpenetrate, then assimilate, then completely "own" the mainstream world of business, geopolitical warfare, intelligence, economics, ultimately everything. Hackers were defined first as living on the edge between the structures evolving in that new space and the structures defined by prior technologies. That liminal world requires a fine balance as the perception of the world, indeed, one's self, one's very identity, flickers back and forth like a hologram, now this and now that.

When the closed world owned the larger world in which it had originally formed, it became the Matrix, a self-enclosed simulated structure of intentional and nested symbols. Once that happened, hackers as they had been defined by their prior context could no longer be who they were.

During transitional times, it must be so. The models of reality that fill the heads of people defined by prior technologies stretch, then make loud ungodly screeching sounds as they tear apart and finally explode with a cataclysmic pop. Instead of their annihilation yielding nothing, however, yielding an empty space, the new world has already evolved. And like a glistening moist snakeskin under the old skin, scraped off in pieces on rocks, defines the bigger bolder structure that had been coming into being for a long time. Hierarchical restructuring always includes and transcends everything that came before.

Inevitably, then, the skills of hackers became the skills of everybody defending and protecting the new structures; the good ones, at any rate. If you don't know how something can be broken, you don't know how it can be protected.

Inevitably, too, the playful creative things hackers did in the protected space of their mainframe heaven, fueled by a secure environment that enabled them to play without risk or consequences, were seen as children's games. The game moved online and spanned the global network. Instead of playing digital games in an analogue world, hackers discovered that the world was the game because the world had become digital. Creativity flourished and a hacker meritocracy emerged in cyberspace, in networks defined by bulletin boards and then web sites. In, that is, the "real world" as we now know it.

But as the boundaries flexed and meshed with the new boundaries of social, economic, and psychological life, those games began to be defined as acts of criminal intrusion. Before boundaries, the land belonged to all, the way we imagine life in these United States might have been with Native Americans roaming on their ponies. Once dotted lines were drawn on maps and maps were internalized as the "real" structure of our lives, riding the open range became trespass and perpetrators had to be confined in prisons.

The space inside mainframes became the interconnected space of networks and was ported to the rest of the world; a space designed to be open, used by a trusted community, became a more general platform for communication and commerce. New structures emerged in their image; structures for which we still do not have good name; structures we call distributed non-state actors or non-government global entities. Legal distinctions, which it seemed to hackers and those who mythologized cyberspace as a new frontier, cyberspace hanging in the void above meat space, all legal distinctions would cease to exist in that bubble world, because hackers thought they were obliterated by new technologies. Instead they were reformulated for the new space in which everyone was coming to live. First the mountain men and the pioneers, then the merchants, and at last, the lawyers. Once the lawyers show up, the game is over.

A smaller group, a subset of those real hackers—people who entered and looked around or stole information or data—became defined as "hackers" by the media. Now the word "hacker" is lost forever except to designate criminals, and a particular kind of criminal at that—usually a burglar—and the marks of hacking were defined as breaking and entering, spray painting graffiti on web site walls or portals, stealing passwords or credit card numbers, vandalism, extortion, and worse.

When we speak of the hacker mind, then, we have come to mean the mind of a miscreant motivated by a broad range of ulterior purposes. We don't mean men and women who do original creative work, the best and brightest who cobble together new structures of possibility and deliver them to the world for the sheer joy of doing so. We mean script kiddies who download scripts written by others and execute them with the click of a button, we mean vandals with limited impulse control, we mean thieves of data, and then we mean all the people who use that data for extortion, corporate or industrial espionage, state-level spy craft, identity theft, grand larceny, blackmail, vicious revenge, or terror.

That's lots of kinds of minds, needing to be understood, needing to be profiled, needing to be penetrated, needing to be known inside and out.

As security experts like Bruce Schneier are fond of saying, it takes one to know one. The flip side of a criminal is a cop and the flip side of a cop is a criminal. Saints are sinners, and sinners are always latent saints. Hackers have hearts full of larceny and duplicity and if you can't, at the very least, mimic that heartset and mindset, you'll never understand hackers. You'll never defend your perimeter, never understand that perimeters in and of themselves are arbitrary, full of holes, and built for a trusting world, the kind in which alas we do not and never will live. A perimeter is an illusion accepted by consensus and treated as if it is real.

Hackers do not live in consensus reality. Hackers see through it, hackers undermine; they exploit consensus reality. Hackers see context as content— they see the skull behind the grin. Hackers do not accept illusions. The best hackers create them and lead the rest of us in circles by our virtual noses.

So if you do business, any kind, any how, or if you are entrusted with the functions of government, or if you understand that distinctions between for-eign-born and native are amorphous moving targets, then you had better understand how the digital world has delivered new opportunities for mayhem and mischief into the hands of mainstream people who appropriate the know-how of hackers for their own nefarious purposes.

You had better understand how difficult security really is to do, how as one gets granular and drills down, one finds more and more opportunities for breaking and entering and taking and destroying the way electron microscopes let you see the holes between things you thought were solid.

You had better understand that nested levels of fractal-like social and eco-nomic structures make deception necessary, identity fluid, and the tricks and trade of the intelligence world available to anybody who learns how to walk through walls. You had better understand why many exploits and flaws are never fixed, because state agencies like it that way and use them to monitor their enemies. You had better understand that "friend" and "enemy" is an arbi-trary designation, that the digital world is a hall of mirrors, and, therefore, "secure boundaries" will depend on your definitions and the limits of what you know. You had better understand risks and how to manage them; what a loss means or does not mean. You had better understand the real odds. You had better understand the meaning of the implied and actual use of power in the digital world, how networks change the game, how the project addressed by this book is only the beginning of difficult decisions about securing your enter-prise, your organizational structure, the flow and storage of critical information, in fact, your life—your very digital life.

That's why books like this are written. Because we had all better under-stand. "There is no inevitability," Marshall McLuhan said, "so long as there is a willingness to contemplate what is happening."

Becoming conscious is not an option. But the digital world turns the pro-ject of consciousness into a multi-level twitch-fast game.

So ... let the games begin

— *Richard Thieme*

Contents

Chapter 6 Bringing It All Together: Completing the Cyber Adversary Model 137

Chapter 7 WarmTouch: Assessing the Insider Threat and Relationship Management 145

Chapter 8 Managing the Insider Threat 171

Foreword

The systematic approach to the issue of adversaries in the on-line world is not new, but the detail and breadth of this book's effort is. Cyber-crime has become an all too real threat with the rapid growth and increased reliance on computers and the Internet. From a "hacktivist" concerned with worldly politics and agendas, to a script kiddie looking for a little fun, criminal hackers are as varied, as they are skilled. Recognizing and understanding these adversaries and the potential threats they pose is key to securing any network. *Cyber Adversary Characterization: Auditing the Hacker Mind* answers: Who is the hacker, what do they want to hack, and why do they want to hack it. More than just a collection of anecdotes and speculation, the authors provide recent case studies and profiling of cyber-terrorists including attacks from state-sponsored groups to unhappy employees on the inside.

The ever-increasing emphasis and reliance on the use of computers and the Internet, has come in hand with the increased threat of cyber-crime. Many systems and infrastructures are exceedingly vulnerable to attacks, as the complexity of computer networks is growing faster than the ability to understand and protect them. Heightened vigilance is not enough, but needs to be coupled with active defensive measures to guarantee the best protection. This book provides the reader with understanding of and an ability to anticipate that "cyber adversary" silently waiting in the wings to attack.

Hackers are in the business of attacking things. They may not be doing it for money or advancement, but that doesn't mean they are any less skilled or dangerous. Just like a cat burglar, the hacker needs a good tool box, and accurate information to be successful. The burglar needs to know when the occupants of the target house are gone, as well as what kind of safe is inside so they can select the right safecracking tools. The tools are to help perform the technical aspects of defeating any mechanisms set in place to stop them, and the information is to help decide how to best achieve the goal. Both tools and information are critical to a successful attack. Without the right exploits and tools the knowledge of a vulnerability is of no use, and vice versa. You have to have the knowledge of a vulnerability in the target system, have the tools and the skills to take advantage of it, be in both a physical and logical position to perform the attack, and if all goes well, get away without a trace.

That is technically what must happen to claim victory. What this does not address is the motivation of the attacker, which is critical to the defense of the systems being attacked. Because of the economics of defense, it is simply not possible to defend against all threats all of the time. Smart defenders therefore want to spend their limited resources defending against the *most likely* attackers and threats. This requires them to step back from the purely technical aspects of their job, and to play psychologist and risk manager. How likely is it that an angry employee will try and steal a customer database? That a drunk driver will run into, and destroy the power lines to your facility? That a political opponent deface your website? Each of these threats requires a completely unique defense.

Security professionals generally group attacks into several categories. Natural disasters, un-intentional attacks, and intentional attacks. While all of these attacks have the potential to disrupt business, people generally understand and accept the risks of mother nature (In contracts you see this referred to as "Acts of God") and accidents. What people have a hard time dealing with is the last type, the intentional attack. What I am getting at is that if you don't know who is attacking you and why, it gets very expensive and time consuming to cover every possibility. These intentional attacks comprises the majority of this book, and are normally comprised of some combination of technical attacks, physical attacks, and social engineering.

Purely technical attacks rely on software, protocol, or configuration weaknesses exhibited by your systems, and these are exploited to gain access. These attacks can come from any place on the planet, and they are usually chained through many systems to obscure their ultimate source. The vast majority of attacks in the world today are mostly this type, because they can be automated easily. They are also the easiest to defend against. Physical attacks rely on weaknesses surrounding your system. These may take the form of dumpster diving for discarded password and configuration information or secretly applying a keystroke-logging device on your computer system. In the past, people have physically tapped into fax phone lines to record documents, tapped into phone systems to listen to voice calls, and picked their way through locks into phone company central offices. These attacks bypass your information security precautions and go straight to the target. They work because people think of physical security as separate from information security. To perform a physical attack, you need to be where the information is, something that greatly reduces my risk, since not many hackers in India are likely to hop a jet to come attack my network in Seattle. These attacks are harder to defend against but less likely to occur. Social engineering (SE) attacks rely on trust. By convincing someone to trust you, on the phone or in person, you can learn all kinds of secrets. By calling a company's help desk and pretending to be a new employee, you might learn about the phone numbers to the dial-up modem bank, how you should configure your software, and if you think the technical people defending the system have the skills to keep you out. These attacks are generally performed over the phone after substantial research has been done on the target. They are hard to defend against in a large company because everyone generally wants to help each other out, and the right hand usually doesn't know what the left is up to. Because these attacks are voice-oriented, they can be performed from anyplace in the world where a phone line is available. Just like the technical attack, skilled SE attackers will chain their voice call through many hops to hide their location. When criminals combine these attacks, they can truly be scary. Only the most paranoid can defend against them, and the cost of being paranoid is often prohibitive to even the largest company.

Those who know me know that I love telling stories, and I am going to tell you one to illustrate how hard it is from the defenders standpoint to understand the motivations of an attacker. It was the mid-90s and someone didn't like the French. They thought they would be doing the world a favor if they made it so the French were not on the Internet at all. To accomplish this, they started an exhaustive undertaking of breaking into as many routers and servers as possible in France to gain control of them. After many months, they had managed to own over 1,100 boxes, about half way to their target of 2,500. By the time I learned of this endeavor it had become a full time job for two people. When not drinking, sleeping, or playing Nintendo they would be hacking. When I asked them what the goal was they said, to paraphrase, "We want France to wake up one morning and not be on the net." To do this they were going to coordinate all the boxes they had owned to delete themselves all at the same time. As you have probably guessed, this never happened. It became too much of a management nightmare to keep root on all the machines, and they were spending more time covering their tracks than compromising more machines. They didn't own enough machines to drop France from the net, and in order to achieve their goal they would have to involve more people. And, that meant more risk they were, understandably, not prepared to take. They just walked away and never went back to any of the machines they had compromised.

Now, take a minute and think about how that would have looked to France. How could they tell that the adversary was some disgruntled European with an axe to grind against the "pretentious" French, as opposed to some hostile government or terrorist group?

As a Criminal Justice Major in college and later on as a law student, the motivations of the attacker have always interested me. But, I must admit that when I was asked to write this foreword I was a bit skeptical. I was not skeptical of the authors' qualification, but of what practical knowledge could be produced by a book looking at adversaries. I have seen talks on this subject at security conferences, but was unsure if there was really enough compelling information for a full book. It is often too easy to fall back on stereotypes, "soft" explanations, and speculation when it comes to hackers and their motivations. The authors approach this problem head on, and whether you agree with their conclusions or not, you have to acknowledge their effort to explore this area in an objective way. From the theoretical to group behavior to state sponsored threats, it is refreshing to read something that is not full of buzzwords, acronyms, and subjective statements.

The wonders and advantages of modern age electronics and the World Wide Web have ushered in a new age of cyber-crime. The growing connectivity among secure and insecure networks has created new opportunities for unauthorized intrusions into sensitive or proprietary computer systems. Some of these vulnerabilities are waiting to be exploited, while numerous others already have. Everyday that a vulnerability or threat goes unchecked greatly increases an attack and the damage it can cause. Who knows what the prospects for a cascade of failures across US infrastructures could lead to. What type of group or individual would exploit this vulnerability, and why would they do it? *Cyber Adversary Characterization: Auditing the Hacker Mind* sets the stage and cast of characters for examples and scenarios such as this, providing the security specialist a window into the enemy's mind—necessary in order to develop a well configured defense.

Written by leading security and counter-terrorism experts, whose experience include first-hand exposure in working with government branches & agencies (such as the FBI, US Army, Department of Homeland Security), this book sets a standard for the fight against the cyber-terrorist. It proves that at the heart of the very best defense is knowing and understanding your enemy.

—Jeff Moss
Black Hat, Inc.
www.blackhat.com
June, 2004

## Chapter 1

Introduction

Topics in this Chapter:

- Introducing Adversary Characterization
- Cyber Terrorist: A Media buzzword?
- Failures of Existing Models
- An Introduction to Characterization Theory

Cyber Adversary Characterization

When you picked this book from the shelf, chances are you did it for one of two reasons: from mere curiosity about the subject matter or because you felt that it will give you a better understanding of whom you are protecting your assets against and how you can do a better job at that task. Systems administrators and other IT professionals often find ourselves looking for a better understanding of who it is that we are protecting our assets against; this often creates a feeling of insecurity or vulnerability—the "not knowing" factor.

The "not knowing" feeling can be introduced into the equation at multiple levels, and not always directly related to the administration of computer networks. Perhaps you're a member of your firm's human resources department, unsure whether the young systems administrator you just hired may one day turn on the firm, causing damage to company assets on a massive scale. And whose fault would it be if that were to happen? So perhaps you should not take the risk and just find another candidate. Does his young age and lack of experience on a large corporate network make it more likely that he constitutes an insider threat to your organization? That perhaps one day he will turn against the company, giving systems access to his so-called friends on an Internet Relay Chat channel he frequents, because he is upset over a salary dispute? Or is he likely to leak sensitive company intellectual property to a competitor when offered a bribe?

Perhaps you *are* that systems administrator, concerned that the systems it is now your task to protect are at risk, but you aren't sure from whom or what. What does your adversary look like? What kind of attacks will he or she use in trying to compromise the network? Indeed, what is it that's motivating your adversary? You are also concerned that a mission-critical application has not been designed in a secure manner; what factors should the development team consider when designing attack countermeasures?

These examples make up a minute percentage of the questions employees of organizations large and small are asking themselves on a daily basis—but with what authority are they answering them? What courses have they studied that enable them to accurately identify a threat to their organization and mitigate in an effective manner? The truth is, in the public sector, there is little data available to average employees to enable them to answer these questions. Government organizations and law enforcement are a little better off, given the threat-modeling systems many of them use on a daily basis.

There is a clear need for a better understanding of the cyber adversary of today and tomorrow, from what it is that motivates an adversary to the threat that said adversary poses to your organization's assets. Of course, with hindsight it is easy to make sweeping statements, such as a greater awareness of computer security-related issues within your organization would have mitigated the repercussions of many of recent history's computer security-related incidents, or perhaps even prevented the incident in the first place.

But as you'll know if you're a systems administrator, persuading management that a threat exists, attempting to identify the nature of that threat, and expressing it in a way that even a CEO will understand, especially when it involves budgetary considerations, is not so easy. Even in the case where an incident has occurred, how do we learn from the incident? Sure, you can run around patching systems that will probably be vulnerable again in a few months anyway, but what can we learn from the adversary who has, in spite of what we admit in public, outmaneuvered you?

It is clear that we need a better understanding of an adversary's core properties and a set of proven threat characterization metrics to measure these properties and determine how any given adversary would behave in a defined situation—or more important, against a specific asset. Throughout this book, you will find various characterization metrics and theories, with each chapter designed to focus on the differing applications of characterization theory. We characterize the threat from adversaries inside your organization to the threat your company may be exposed to from so-called high-end cyber adversaries, such as members of terrorist organizations and well-funded rogue states.

The following pages document several case studies, either based on real events containing partially fictitious information or accounts of actual incidents. Although these case studies do not alone scope out the full extent of the characterization problem, they set the scene nicely for what's to come.

The first case study is the infamous Kevin Mitnick's first-person account of an attack against a small technology company based in the San Fernando Valley. The story was taken from Kevin during an interview with the author and details his 1987/1988 attempt to gain unlawful entry to Digital Equipment Corporation materials. The story exemplifies one of the many motivations of cyber adversaries—the retrieval of additional capabilities, in this case, source code. In the concluding chapter, we will use the characterization theory we cover in the intervening chapters to examine Kevin's attack and the ways it could have been prevented through a better understanding of the cyber adversary.

Case Study 1: A First-Person Account from Kevin D. Mitnick

"Over a decade ago, I had compromised a number of systems owned by Digital Equipment Corp. [DEC], located on the corporation's wide area network named *Easynet*," Kevin Mitnick recalls. "My ultimate goal was to gain access to the systems within DEC's engineering department in order to retrieve the source code for VMS—DEC's flagship operating system product. The aim of getting the source code for VMS and other operating systems was so that I could analyze the extremely well-commented [documented] code, written by DEC developers, to determine where security-related modifications had been made. DEC engineers would often document the details of a fixed vulnerability next to the previously vulnerable code segment. A generally unknown fact, my ultimate objective goal as a hacker was to become the best at circumventing security systems, and overcome any technical obstacles that would get in my way; whatever the objective, I possessed enough persistence to always succeed."

"I Put My Freedom on the Line for Sheer Entertainment ..."

"Although I had already acquired access to the DEC Easynet network, none of the systems to which I had access resided on the VMS development cluster. One information-gathering method was to install network sniffers on the systems I had previously compromised in hopes that I could intercept interesting information, like user authentication credentials. My goal was to eventually gain access to the VMS development cluster—complete with development tools and the latest release of operating system source code. Unfortunately, back in those days, many operating system vendors had yet to standardize the use of TCP/IP as the network transport protocol of choice. Most, if not all, of the systems on Easynet primarily used the DECNET/E protocol. I installed sniffers on certain compromised nodes (systems) which allowed me to gain access to additional computing resources. The targeted resources were other nodes on the network with a sufficient amount of unused disk storage, and any system which had direct connectivity to the Internet. The source code files were so large, even when compressed, that it would have taken months to download over dial-up. I needed a way to transfer the code outside DEC so I could analyze it without the fear of being detected.

And so, I began to research the possibility of writing or acquiring a sniffer that worked with the DECNET/E protocol. After a few of hours researching, a few names of vendors came up. These vendors sold expensive products that would have been useful in my endeavor to intercept traffic. Sometime later, I stumbled across a network diagnostics program designed to analyze and monitor DECNET/E protocols, written by a company in the San Fernando Valley named Polar Systems. A feature of the network diagnostics suite was the ability to collect and display packets collected from a DECNET interface. The tool was just what I needed—I just had to figure out how I was going to borrow it.

My initial attempts to retrieve the software from Polar Systems consisted of using my knowledge of the telephone system to identify which phone numbers also terminated at the likely address where the product was developed, sold, or supported. After every telephone number terminating at the Polar Systems address, I proceeded to identify which of the lines were data, fax and voice. It turned out that Polar Systems was actually run out of someone's residence which made my reconnaissance much easier. I identified two numbers that answered with modem breath. I dialed into both, discovering the all-too-familiar beep, indicating the box was waiting for me to enter the system password.

A security feature allowed the operator to require a password before the system would prompt for a username and password. The telltale sign was a distinctive beep after hitting the return key on my VT100 terminal. I guessed that Polar Systems used these numbers to remotely dial into their system—perhaps if I could get access through their dial-in mechanism, I could access their development system, complete with sniffer software, and if I got lucky, source code! I promptly disconnected from my dial-in session, as I did not want to raise suspicions if they happened to be watching the lights blink on the dial-up modem. After all, the business was run out of someone's home.

After much thought, I decided that the easiest way in was going to be through a blended attack using both social engineering and technical expertise. I remembered that DEC was under intense pressure to release security patches for some newly discovered vulnerabilities that were recently publicized. Accordingly, DEC set up a special toll-free number so anyone could call in and request the latest security patch kit on magnetic or cartridge tape. As luck would have it, the telephone operator at the toll-free number did not bother verifying whether the customer was a legitimate customer. This meant that pretty much anyone with a telephone line and the guile to call DEC could get themselves a free tape critical security patch kit for the cost of calling a toll-free number—absolutely free.

I placed several telephone requests for patch kits to be delivered to several addresses in the Los Angeles area. After receiving the patch kits, I proceeded to carefully remove the tape and written materials, wearing a pair of latex gloves to ensure that my fingerprints would not be left on the tapes. I knew they would eventually be in the possession of my target, and possibly thereafter, law enforcement. After extracting the files from the special VMS formatted back-up (saveset), I decided the best way to meet my objective was to backdoor the patch kit with some extra code that would covertly modify the VMS login program, which was responsible for authenticating users at the operating system level, which stood between me and Polar Systems IPR.

Figure 1.1 An Assembler Dump of the Target VAX Binary

```
 44  A    =       1
 45  B    =       2
 46       MOVL    A+1(R2),2(R3)
 47       MOVL    UNKN(R1),R2
 48       MOVL    WS+2,R2
 49  C    =       .
 50       MOVL    A+1(R2),4(R3)
 51       MOVL    WS+2,R2
 52       MOVL    A+2(R2),2(R3)
 53       MOVL    WS+2,R2
 54       BRW     .+4
 55       MOVL    A+1(R2),2(R3)
 56       MOVL    WS+4,R2
 57  .    =       1000
 58       MOVL    #WS+4,R
 59       MOVL    UNKN(R1),R2
 60       NOP
 61       NOP
 62       NOP
 63  WS:  .BLKW   1
```

After a number of hours of analysis I identified a segment of the binary which could be used to inject my own instructions—in this case several jump instructions to unused areas within the image of the login program, which would include several "special" features that would give me full control of the system once installed. To aid my work, I acquired a similar patch written by the Chaos Computer Club (CCC) which did essentially the same thing on an earlier version of VMS. After a few days researching, programming and testing, I decided that the patch was ready to be incorporated into the security patch kit.

I rolled up my patch with all the other legitimate files into a new VMS formatted backup; I wrote it to tape, and carefully repackaged the box just like it arrived from DEC. I even went to the trouble of shrink-wrapping the cartridge tape with the packing slip to give it that extra dose of authenticity.

I carefully repackaged the newly shrink wrapped tape into the DEC-labeled box—the one I had originally received it in—taking care to ensure that no fingerprints, skin cells or hair was deposited on the tape or into the box.

My next step was figuring out the best way to get my target to install the update from my "special" tape. I thought about mailing it from Los Angeles, but that may have raised a red flag—the real tape was mailed from Massachusetts. I had to think of a better way.

Once the target installed the "security" update on their systems, I would be able to sneak in over their dial-in and retrieve the programs I needed to assist my further penetration of DEC's Easynet.

All was going to plan—I opted to become a UPS delivery man for a day and hand-deliver the package to the residence where Polar Systems ran its operations. After purchasing a UPS delivery outfit from a costume shop (Hollywood is a great place to buy costumes), I made an early morning visit to the address for Polar Systems. I was greeted at the door by some guy who looked like he needed a couple more hours of sleep. I hurriedly asked the gentleman to sign for the package as I complained about being late for another delivery. The gentleman cooperatively signed for the package and took it into the house, closing the door behind him."

You may be wondering why I distracted him by acting in a hurry. Well, although I did not want to raise suspicion by coming across in an unnatural manner, I was lacking one vital object, possessed by all UPS delivery folks—a UPS truck. Luckily, the inert gentleman did not notice anything out of the ordinary."

The following day, I dialed into Polar Systems' modems, entering the secret phrase required to activate my backdoor. To my disappointment, the attempt failed—I figured that they must have not installed the security patch yet. After some 10 days, Polar Systems finally installed the critical update, allowing me to bypass the authentication on the dial-up line, and yielding access to both the source tree and binary distribution of the Polar Systems DECNET monitoring tool."

Case Study 2: Insider Lessons Learned

In May 1999, Kazkommerts Securities, a small company based in Almaty, Kazakhstan, entered into a contract with Bloomberg L.P. for the provision of database services to the firm. Shortly afterward, an employee at Kazkommerts named Oleg Zezov (purportedly Kazkommerts' chief information technology officer) discovered that he could use his newly acquired access resulting from the acquisition of Bloomberg services to escalate his privileges on Bloomberg's network to exploit software flaws and steal various user login credentials, including those of Michael Bloomberg, the founder and then head of Bloomberg L.P.

After accessing the accounts of various Bloomberg employees and retrieving data from those accounts, including Michael Bloomberg's credit card details, Zezov sent a threatening e-mail to Michael Bloomberg, demanding a substantial amount of money. In return, Zezov offered to disclose the ways he had compromised the Bloomberg computer systems and retrieved the necessary authentication credentials to compromise the account and data of the company head. After realizing the nature of the compromise, Bloomberg quickly remedied the software flaw that allowed Zezov access to the network and worked with the FBI to apprehend Zezov and his counterpart in London, where they had agreed to "resolve" the issue.

Although to this day, the details of the software flaw and the computer systems surrounding the break-in remain unclear (at least in the public domain), it is clear that an accurate assessment had not been made regarding the threat posed to the various technological assets at Bloomberg L.P., especially when it came to the insider threat. Although Zezov was not an employee of Bloomberg, in some ways he can be considered an insider, given that his attacks against Bloomberg were made possible through authorized access he had to Bloomberg's database services as a customer. This case study is further examined in Chapter 7.

Cyber Terrorist: A Media Buzzword?

The term *cyber terrorist* falls under the same media buzzword umbrella as *black hat* and even the overused and abused *hacker*. The idea that a so-called cyber terrorist can compromise the security of a computer system and cause actual bodily harm as a direct result of the system compromise, even in today's world, is somewhat far-fetched, where many compromises have only resulted in defacements of sites or temporarily downed servers. But, even these defacements of government websites are more common than many people realize. Figure 1.2 displays the defacement of the official Whitehouse website, by the notorious group "Global Hell".

It has, however, become more probable that a terrorist group could seek the skills of a hacker to augment a more conventional act of terrorism. The following account is loosely based on such an event where a teenage male was approached by an individual, known to be associated with an eastern terrorist group.

Figure 1.2 Whitehouse Website Defacement by *Global Hell*

In June 1999, an Alaskan hacker named Ryola (aka "ne0h") was chatting on his favorite Internet Relay Chat channel as he did every other night, bragging about his latest hacked systems (see Figure 1.3) and comparing the speeds of their connection speeds with those of the other hackers in the channel. After deciding to call it a night, he went to check his e-mail one last time and noticed a message from an individual claiming to be from a group of eastern "freedom fighters" who had been given Ryola's contact details by an unidentified friend. In the e-mail, the individual, who identified himself as Kahn, detailed a "project" he was engaged in that required the schematics of three specific models of aircraft. The offer being put forward to Ryola consisted of a one-time payment of $5,000 in return for the schematics of the aircraft models listed in the e-mail message.

Figure 1.3 One of Many Web Defacements Carried Out by the Notorious ne0h

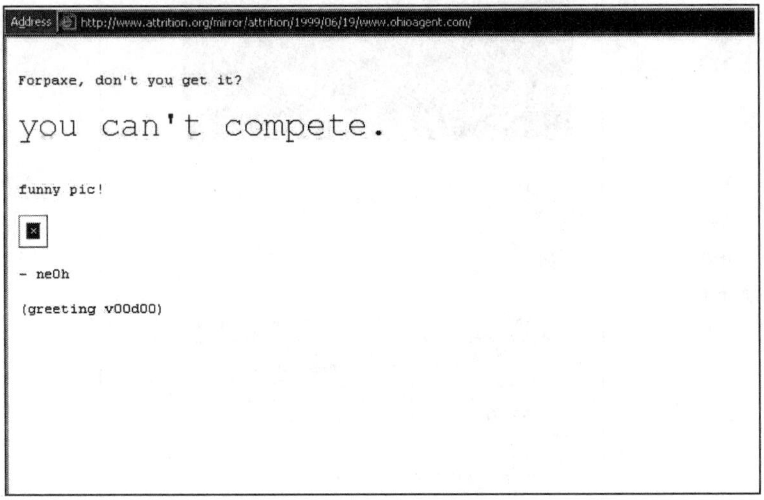

```
Address  http://www.attrition.org/mirror/attrition/1999/06/19/www.ohioagent.com/

Forpaxe, don't you get it?

you can't compete.

funny pic!

[x]

- ne0h

(greeting v00d00)
```

At the time, Ryola had a job at a local computer vendor, fixing and building home and business computer systems, but he needed the additional money to fund the trip to Las Vegas he had planned for the following month. After a short telephone call between Ryola and Kahn, made to a local call box that Ryola used to protect his identity, the details of the task at hand were confirmed. Several days later, after he had completed his initial network scans and determined the most likely place to find the schematics he had been asked for, Ryola made his move and compromised multiple systems on one of the aircraft designer's many networks. He then used this access to leverage further attacks against internal Windows networks, which the designer's engineers used to store schematics and other sensitive documents. Although it is arguable that Ryola "got lucky," he did complete the requested task and within days, the schematics of three of the requested aircraft types were in Kahn's hands. Months later, an aircraft matching the type documented by the schematics Ryola stole was hijacked over Saudi Arabia by the same group Kahn had identified himself as representing to Ryola.

A year went by and Ryola remained unpaid for the task he had undertaken for Kahn, who Ryola now knew was a terrorist. In spite of several failed attempts to contact Kahn and request the money he thought he had earned, he remained unpaid. It wasn't until February 2001 that Ryola heard once more from Kahn. In an e-mail from a new address, Kahn apologized for having failed to pay Ryola, claiming he had been in hiding as a result of investigations made to find the perpetrators of the previous year's hijackings. To make up for this, Kahn promised Ryola more than five times the sum previously promised to him, in return for the retrieval of schematics of four more aircraft types. By this time, Ryola had found a better job and was left with a bitter taste in his mouth from his previous dealings with Kahn, so he gracefully declined the offer.

No more e-mail communications occurred between the two, and for Ryola, his dealings with the individual were over. Several months later that same year, Ryola had been up until 5:00 in the morning chatting to some of his online friends about their plans to compromise the security of a South African-based ISP. The next day, he awoke at about 2:00 in the afternoon and turned on the television. The day was Tuesday, September 11, 2001, and before his eyes were reports of four planes being used for acts of terrorism, purportedly by a sister organization of the "freedom fighters" he had previously worked for, using planes matching the descriptions in the e-mail from Kahn some seven months previously.

NOTE

It should be noted that although real names, group names and other details have been removed from the this account; the story is based upon real life occurrences which are very real.

Although the connections between the portions of this fictional story that are based on real events and the tragic events of September 11 are somewhat unclear, the hijacking in 1999 was very real, as was the evidence linking the compromised airplane schematics and the group that carried out the hijacking. When we think about adversary characterization, it is important that we keep the bigger picture in view.

> The second that we become narrow-minded about the security of our organizations and the resolve of our enemy is the second that we become vulnerable.

In this case, the compromise of data on a poorly protected computer network didn't by itself create the hijacking situation—only the act of the hijacking's perpetrators stepping onto the aircraft and taking it into their control did that. However, the schematic data would have almost certainly aided them in planning the execution phase of the hijacking, increasing their chances of success and reducing their chances of their plot being foiled during execution.

When performing a characterization, especially when it involves characterizing the threats to assets within an organization and trying to establish which information would be of most value to an adversary, it is vital that we remember things like the system that holds airplane schematics. Sure, it isn't a database server holding thousands of credit card numbers or authentication credentials. But different assets have different values to different adversaries. The key lies in knowing which adversaries value which assets and how those adversaries are most likely to go about compromising those assets. The hijacking is an excellent example of data that was of high value to an adversary that at the end of the day compromised a very high-value asset, aided by compromising data that was clearly characterized as being of low value, at low risk, and therefore poorly protected.

Failures of Existing Models

Cyber adversary characterization as a whole is a rather large topic, and it would create an unworkable situation if we were to attempt to solve the characterization problem by creating one large metric designed to take all possible data into account. Past attempts at making sense of the vast amounts of adversary-related data have in one way or another failed. Perhaps the primary reason for this failure is that there is simply so much potentially meaningful data to take into account and so many perspectives that it is extremely easy to lose focus of the data that matters and, indeed, what you are actually trying to achieve. In past characterization workshops and research groups, attended by most contributing authors of this book, we have often asked the seemingly obvious question, What are we all doing here? What is the common goal that brings us together, and how can what one of us comes up with, which might on the surface apply to only his individual work practices, help another? The problem here is that this way of thinking is far too high level; a lower level of thought is required to answer these questions.

The answers to these questions should become apparent as you read this book, and they are fairly straightforward. At the end of the day, no matter what your use for characterization data—whether to achieve greater levels of security during the design of software, for more accurate network threat assessments, for improved incident analysis, or to detect an insider threat—the group we are trying to characterize remains the same, and the properties of this group remain the same, and therefore, so does the set of characterization metrics required to assess said adversarial/group properties. To summarize, a set of metrics to assess the individual properties of the adversary and a methodology to assess meaningful relationships between these metrics would aid the characterization in almost every circumstance.

Some of the problems encountered in attempting to deal with adversarial data in other manners are discussed in the following sections.

High Data Quantities

Vast amounts of adversary data need to be, or at least could be, considered when attempting to complete a characterization. Often much of this data in its raw form is of little use to an individual attempting to perform a characterization and does little more than present itself as "white noise" around the data that actually means something. Due to often large data volumes, data must be categorized and attributed to adversary properties for us to stand a chance of understanding it, and if we were to attempt any kind of detailed characterization, high data volumes would make this impossible without such a methodology.

Data Relevancy Issues

Certain types of characterization data are often only of relevance in certain cases. Indeed, the data that is available regarding a subject will also differ from case to case. For this reason, use of a single metric and lack of a methodology for breaking down an adversary's individual properties would probably result in a certain amount of the subject data being of no relevance to your circumstance, potentially skewing your final result.

For example, during the characterization of a theoretical adversary type for a threat assessment, no forensic data from an actual attack may be available since no incident has occurred. Since a single characterization metric would have to take forensic incident data into account, this would leave a black hole in the middle of your metric because a dependency of the metric has not been met. Furthermore, it would make it a tricky task to predict the kind of forensic data that may be available.

As we already stated, much of the data that needs to be considered for an accurate characterization is often of little use in its raw form—in other words, without any supporting research or data evaluation metric to give it some meaning. For the purposes of this book, we refer to this type of data as *analog data*. An example of such analog data is an attempt to profile an individual through the operating system she uses. Although this information can be of use, on its own, without the presence of a data evaluation or additional research data, it is of little use. Because we are dealing with the profiling of real people here and not artificial neural networks, all data associated with properties of an adversary tends to be analog. "Digital data" types are almost always encountered by processing analog data via a data evaluation metric of some kind.

For example, we hypothesize that through the evaluation of the tools an attacker uses in his or her attempt to compromise a system (an analog data type) via a characterization metric, we are left with an integer type "score" that may be representative of the threat that individual poses to a defined asset—and indeed, their skill level. Whether this assessment is true or not, the point here is that any two "digital" results should be directly comparable to one another; where s the analog data that we started with is not. This strengthens the case for the use of multiple metrics to assess the various properties of the cyber adversary rather than trying to address the problem as a whole, which we outline in greater detail in the following chapters.

Characterization Types

Typically, characterizations of cyber adversaries fall into one of two categories: theoretical and post-incident (actual or forensic) characterization types. The primary purpose for making this distinction is that parameters the metrics use to assess the adversarial properties will differ substantially, as will the uses for the final characterization. To qualify whether a characterization is going to use theoretical or characterization methodologies, we must assess the nature of the situation and the information that is available to us to conduct the characterization.

Although metrics used to assess no observable data and attribute to adversarial properties during a theoretical characterization and the observable data to attribute to adversarial properties during the characterization of an actual adversary will differ, many metrics used during an actual characterization are also commonplace during a theoretical assessment, but not vice versa.

This is due to almost all metrics that are used for theoretical characterization also being of use in the characterization of actual adversaries, but not the other way around, since the additional metrics used in forensic characterizations rely on data that will not always be available during a theoretical characterization, since no actual incident has occurred. Although past attack data is of use for building profiles of adversary types, during a theoretical characterization we can only speculate that the subject will tender similar behavior to that displayed in a past attack. To this end, past attack data is of most use for improving the metrics used during theoretical characterizations rather than for making sweeping assumptions that the behaviors of a past, purportedly similar adversary bearing similarity to a theoretical one. Remember, no two adversaries will behave exactly the same way.

Theoretical Characterization

Theoretical characterization theory is possibly of most use for performing and improving on the accuracy of asset threat characterizations, for improving the designs of network topologies and data systems, and for conceiving efficient methodologies to test said systems' resilience against the known and unknown.

Introduction to Theory

Many members of groups developing trusted computer systems have expressed that it would be an extremely useful thing to be in a position whereby a developer is able to assess the profiles of a handful of real hackers, identified as possibly posing a threat to whatever it may be that's being designed. This way they could assess how each adversary would go about attacking their platform, using characterization theory to explain how each adversary behaved in the test and why they behaved as they did.

Although such an approach may very well uncover several previously unseen problems in the design or implementation of the solution, it is a somewhat ad hoc methodology, since the hand-picked individuals would, without careful assessment prior to the exercise, possess several unknown properties. Furthermore, the process of using "real" hackers may itself taint any value gained due to the individuals who agree to take part in the tests sharing common properties. In this scenario, the preferential methodology would place a developer in a situation where he or she may "fuzz" adversaries by changing the properties (the variables) of said adversary and, using the same techniques used to enumerate each adversary, assessing how the resulting characterized adversary would behave in a given situation. This methodology has the advantages of being highly controlled and scalable, and in a testing environment, tests to test the accuracy of the methodology itself would be trivial to orchestrate with the use of adversary case studies. More information on this topic is presented in Chapters 2 and 3.

This is one of the many uses for theoretical characterization theory. This example is fairly specific to system design; the second most common use for theoretical characterization has been in the characterization a specific threat poses to a given asset. Although the theory used for asset threat characterization remains the same, the fact that you are now dealing with assets (computer systems or other) that have already been designed changes the process you must go through considerably.

Post-Incident Characterization

During the course of most days on today's increasingly hostile Internet, systems administrators, network administrators, and personnel working in the network operations centers of managed security service providers are faced with what would be, if printed out, hundreds of reams of reports detailing information pertaining to purported incidents on their or their clients' networks. Back in the bad old days of intrusion detection, having a system that would report events on host and network-based intrusion devices was considered sufficient. Of course, it wasn't long before most large organizations realized that the $20,000 IDS they just invested in was generating more event logs per second than there were employees in their organization to review each log entry. These organizations realized they could either action a measured response, turn a blind eye to the event, or (possibly most significantly) mark the event as a false positive. With this came the age of the managed security service (MSS) provider who bought IDS event correlation and false-positive detection technology into the commercial marketplace. For most organizations the introduction of an MSS provider solved the problem of having spent substantial amounts of their budgets on host and network-based intrusion detection devices that they couldn't afford to manage, but one perhaps unseen problem remained.

For a moment, place yourself in the shoes of a systems administrator for a large organization that has been through the process of purchasing network-based intrusion detection devices, coupled with the acquisition of managed services from an MSS provider. You log onto the MSS portal site and view the tickets that have been raised for your network segments as a result of multiple, correlated IDS events. The first ticket you spot informs you that someone coming from an IP address located in China has been scanning several specific port ranges on one of your development networks. A note on the ticket says the event has reoccurred several times over the last three days. Below the summary of information are several pages of technical spiel regarding the determined source operating system of the packets and the most likely tool that was used to perform the scan—but you ignore this, since the port ranges scanned are of no significance to you and you have 90 other IDS tickets to go through before your operations meeting in an hour.

Two days later, a new-hire systems administrator announces over the company intranet message board that a Web server on your production network has been compromised through stolen login credentials. It is now your job to lead the investigation into what happened. Aside from your suspicion that an insider was involved in the compromise of the host, which served the company's primary cooperate Web site, you really aren't sure in which direction you should take your investigation. Although the server hosts a Web site and it is currently receiving more than one 100,000 hits a day, the site content was not defaced in any way; there are no logs of what the individual did while on the system, and all you have is IDS data and a potential insider with no clue of what your adversary "looks like" or his motivations for the attack.

An Introduction to Characterization Theory

When we talk about post-incident or forensic adversary characterization, we are referring to a situation where an incident of undetermined type has occurred, presenting some form of data with which you will base the data you may have after an incident, similar to our short example. There are several primary objectives of this form of characterization. Each objective hopefully provides leverage to justify a measured reaction to an incident, whether that reaction is to leverage to action change in the design of a production network to a more secure model, to come up with an accurate profile of the adversary to aid in his or her capture, or most important, to glean a better understanding of the kinds of people who really want to break into your network, their motivations, and the kinds of attacks you are likely to see coming from said characterized subset of adversaries.

Because an actual event has occurred, the starting point at which the characterization begins changes from the typical starting point of a theoretical characterization to the data (IDS or other) pertaining to an incident. To this end, one of the applications of theoretical adversary characterization that has attracted substantial interest and raised many questions in the past is the possibility of a technology that can automate the characterization of adversaries from IDS data alone, providing a real time "score" of the adversary responsible for triggering an IDS. Although its important to remember that such an automated mechanism could never be as accurate as doing things by hand due to the limited data IDS has access to and limitations drawn from the IDS drawing its conclusions based on hard and fast rules, therefore allowing an attacker to either trick or bypass those rules, such a technology is very possible. Metrics such as those that examine the semantics of an attack could be used to draw conclusions about an adversary from data such as the operating system the attacker is using, the exploit they are using, the operating system of the target, and the difficulty of the hack.

The following chapters address some of the topics (and problems) introduced in this chapter. Chapter 2 examines much of the characterization theory alluded to in this chapter, including that which can be used for both theoretical (asset type) characterizations and that we can use in the unfortunate times when incidents occur, giving us a framework through which we can seek attribution.

Theoretical Characterization Metrics

Topics in this Chapter:

- **The Adversary Object Matrix**
- **Adversary Property Relationships**
- **The Adversary Model—"Adversary Environment Properties"**
- **The Adversary Model—"Attacker Properties"**

Introduction

As previously stated, cyber adversary characterizations can be divided up into two categories:

- Those that are of an entirely theoretical nature (such as characterizations of the risk that a specific, theoretical adversary subset may pose to a given asset)

- Post-incident or forensic characterizations, where the threat that a "real," characterized individual may pose to a given asset, using information available only after an incident has occurred (such as intrusion detection data)

Although this definition may seem fairly clear cut, the moment you begin to put either type of characterization into practice, the line between the two becomes somewhat blurred.

This is primarily due to capability characterizations of actual (living, breathing) cyber adversaries often being heavily reliant upon projected (assumed) data variables and therefore theoretical metrics. This is the case because more often than not, collating sufficient data to satisfy all characterization metrics and form a clear picture of what your adversary really "looks like" is just not practicable.

By a similar token, theoretical characterization metrics, which largely rely upon quantitative data, can never be accurate without first considering "real" case studies (of actual cyber adversaries), from which the quantitative data must be derived.

A large part of adversary characterization theory is therefore dependent upon the following:

- Making accurate projections regarding what the values of unobservable variables "might be," using vectors derived from available/observable data.

- Being able to corroborate the accuracy of the final characterization through the analysis of proven relationships between utilized metrics (more on this later).

In accepting these statements, we must therefore accept that there is a need for a set of theoretical characterization metrics (or measures) that can in some way be attributed to adversarial behaviors (or properties) and ultimately—an attack. After all, the properties of the adversary are what we're really interested in.

The characterization metrics we utilize are simply a means of processing often-qualitative data into a quantitative, meaningful form and are a function of the final characterization.

In the same way that we could never understand the composition of complex molecules without a basic understanding of the table of the elements, basic atomic science, and the formulas we use to explain how complex molecules are formed, we could never understand today's cyber adversary and his or her reactivity with a given element (the asset or target); without a basic understanding of the elements (an adversary's properties), which form the complex molecules that are cyber adversaries. To take this analogy one step further, just like the possible number of molecular constructs in our universe, the number of cyber adversaries and types of people in the world is infinite. By the same token that we cannot possibly hope to enumerate each molecule that will ever or has ever existed, we cannot hope to enumerate each cyber adversary that has ever and will ever exist. But is this really an issue? Consider that in the same way that we acquire an understanding regarding the periodic table of the elements (our adversarial properties) and the ways in which those elements interact with one another, we can predict the behaviors and state of any given configuration of adversarial properties. To this effect, we are able to project the most likely values of unknown adversarial variables in cases where not all necessary data is observable.

Analogies aside, let us start of by looking at the observable properties (or elements) of the cyber adversary and the ways in which they impact upon the final characterization.

The Adversary Object Matrix

Prior to examining any actual adversarial elements and the data associated with them, we require a model (See Figure 2.1) in order to establish a set of core adversarial "properties" and the "objects" associated within those properties. The secondary objective of such a model is to categorize the adversarial properties in a manner that represents the way in which different adversarial properties and objects interact with one another.

Figure 2.1 Adversarial Property Model Skeleton

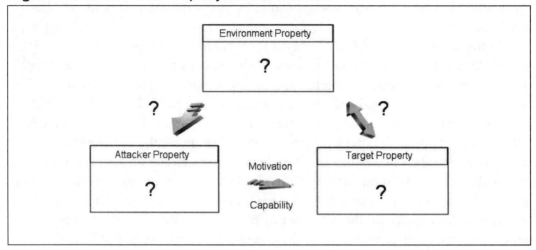

You will see various ways of representing adversarial data throughout this book, however, Figure 2.1 depicts the adversarial property model skeleton, from which all other characterization models in this book are in some way associated. The current model has been intentionally left incomplete so that we can address each property in this and following chapters. The three primary adversarial properties that are shown (environmental, attacker, and target properties) form the framework for their component "objects." We will see in this chapter, and following chapters how both theoretical and forensic characterization metrics can be applied in order to resolve the values of the objects and what they really mean to us.

Figure 2.2 attempts to demonstrate the hierarchical way in which data is processed through the adversary model. It moves from its initial form as "raw" adversarial data (qualitative or quantitative), becomes an "adversary element" as it is passed through an adversary data assessment metric, and takes its final place as a part of an adversarial "object." Note that an object may be populated by multiple elements (data from one or more characterization metrics or data sources).

Figure 2.2 Hierarchy of Information in Adversarial Model

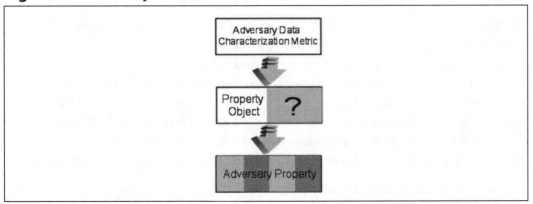

Figure 2.1 also outlines some of the more key relationships between populated adversary properties and the ways in which the value of their component objects cause an impact upon neighboring adversary properties. Although the semantics of these relationships will be covered in more detail later, first we'll take a brief look at the more key relationships depicted in Figure 2.1.

Adversary Property Relationships

The cyber adversary model is all about providing a framework that when populated, we are able to analyze and define relationships between all observable data. For this very reason, the cyber adversary model is divided into three properties, aiding us in our ultimate goal of being able to accurately observe the relationship between adversary and target. The following sections summarize some of the constant and conditional property relationships that can exist.

Environment Property to Attacker Property

To state the obvious, an attacker's environment impacts directly upon the "way the adversary is (or behaves)." Bearing in mind that the attacker property contains objects that attempt to describe an adversary's behaviors in a given attack situation (such as his or her preferences to risk), it is clear why this is such a vital relationship.

The relationship that exists between the environment and attacker property is constantly subject to change due to the ever-changing nature of the security industry and the volatile nature of the world we live in.

Attacker Property to Target Property

Possibly the most obvious relationships in Figure 2.1 is the one between the attacker and target.

When look at the specifics of a target and the attacker property, we can observe the ways that objects within the attacker property will impact an adversary's motivation toward a target, and more importantly his or her capability against a target. Ultimately, it is the elements held within an attacker's property that will determine their relationship with the target that will determine two vital factors contributing to both post-incident and theoretical characterizations:

- Will the attacker actually *initiate an attack* against *the target*?
- What is the adversary's *capability* and *motivation*?

Other (Conditional) Adversarial Property Relationships

There are many other, more subtle relationships that exist between the properties. However, these relationships are not always present; their existence is normally determined by the presence of additional adversarial variables within the three properties and their impact on the property relationships that we have just outlined.

An example of how such a conditional relationship may exist, Figure 2.1 alludes to a possible relationship between the attack target, the environment of the adversary, and the ability of the attacker's environment to impact the target.

To provide an example of how a property of a target could impact the environment of an adversary, suppose that an adversary has initiated an attack on a U.S. government–owned computer system, is detected, and is attributed. Although the attack may not have been successful, due to the nature of the target, the adversary is detained and imprisoned at a Guantanamo Bay detention camp awaiting trial—perhaps an extreme example, but nevertheless, a significant impact upon our adversary's environment, which would not have occurred had the target not been a government-owned system.

Over the following pages, we will examine the relevance of the objects that contribute to the cyber adversaries' three core properties, depicted in Figure 2.1.

The Adversary Model— "Adversary Environment Properties"

The adversaries' environment property is where most good characterizations of cyber adversaries should begin. When this property is populated with data, it often aids in understanding the root causes of adversarial acts. This will often include being able to explain *why* it is that an adversary is motivated into an attack, and the level and origins of the resource (and ultimately *capability*) that they possess. Perhaps a cyber adversary engages a target due to peer pressure from an online community to which he or she belongs—a property environment impact upon the adversary's driver (motivator). Or perhaps the adversary lives in a state with so little law enforcement awareness of cyber crime that he or she feels entirely comfortable attacking almost any system—a direct environment property impact upon the adversary's preference to risk. Over the following pages, we will examine some of the adversarial impacts, which given the correct conditions, the objects within the environment property can have.

Political and Cultural Impacts

In early April 2001 a U.S. Navy EP-3E class spy plane collided with a Chinese E-8 type fighter jet over the South China Sea, damaging the tail of the E-8 and purportedly killing its pilot, "Wang Wei," who, according to eyewitness reports, had attempted to eject from his stricken craft. Quick to pick up on the story, the world media reported the differing reports from U.S. and Chinese authorities. The U.S. claimed that "Wei" was well known for his past attempts to buzz U.S. aircraft in his fighter jet, while a Chinese eyewitness to the event argued that "Wei" was the victim of a negligent American crew. Back in the United States, politicians negotiated with the Chinese government to secure the safe return of the EP-3E's crew, but events elsewhere took an interesting turn for the worse. Approximately one month after the midair collision, a group of Chinese hackers waged what media groups dubbed as "cyber war" on a series of American Web sites, purportedly in retaliation for the death of Wang Wei. A number of the Web sites defaced during this time were operated by U.S. government bodies, including systems run by the U.S. Geological Survey, the hurricane liaison team of the Federal Emergency Management Agency, and the headquarters of the commander of the Naval Surface Force of the U.S. Atlantic Fleet—an obscure list by all accounts. Defacements donned anti-American, pro-Chinese slogans, many of which protested the death of Wei.

Other than their American connections, there were no obvious patterns regarding the Web sites being hacked, indicating that the selection process used by the Chinese hackers to select hosts for compromise was based upon factors other than whether the hosts were high profile or not. Within hours of the first Chinese defacements, a number of hackers either based in, or supporting America, began their defacement onslaught of a slew of Chinese-operated Web sites. They similarly targeted a fairly random series of systems, clearly chosen for factors other than the perceived value of any individual target. It is interesting to note that both groups of adversaries placed value in the sheer number of compromised hosts, rather than the value of any single target. It is of equal interest that the hosts chosen for compromise were those that our adversaries were able to compromise, possibly due to a lack of vulnerability intelligence. The events in the online world that followed the U.S./Chinese mid-air collision exemplifies our first adversarial character property: the environment.

When we talk about the environment in this context, we refer to such things as the *political environment* in the state from which our adversary originates, the *wealth of the state*, and indeed, the *wealth of the individual*, which may or may not be impacted directly by the wealth of his or her state of residence. We are not referring to the groups or individuals with which the adversary associates.

The Chinese/American incident in May of 2001 was an example of how the political environment within a state can motivate individuals who almost certainly had no direct involvement with a political incident into performing an adversarial act. By the same token, patriotism was the primary motivational factor, which led to the eventual retaliation by American hackers and those sympathetic to America, who equally, didn't have direct links to the events over the South China Sea earlier that year. So we have established that the motivational factor that drove the initial assault by Chinese adversaries was that of patriotism for their nation, but was it really? Were the Chinese adversaries really driven by their political environment, and if so, why did it not drive them to compromise higher profile United States government systems? Or did the political environment simply provide justification for their actions in the minds of those involved—an excuse to hack? Unfortunately, the answers to these questions will have to wait; at this stage we have neither enough adversarial data or enough theory to enable us to figure out what really motivated these attacks.

Before most of us ever became aware of underground online groups, in the computer security industry and online cultures we were very aware of the semantics of the physical environment we lived in, and moreover, the social and moral values that were seen as acceptable in that environment. Such an awareness (or indeed a lack of) of what is acceptable in the adversary's physical environment plays an important role in the impact the environmental property has upon the property of our attacker and ultimately, the relationships that may or may not exist between attacker and target properties. Many of today's "physical-world" cultures see certain adversarial activities, particularly against other nation states. Justifications differ for finding these activities acceptable. The horrific events that unfolded in New York, Washington D.C., and Pennsylvania on September 11th, 2001 were justified in the minds of many as being an act of Jihad—or "holy war" (the equivalent of a Crusade or "war of the cross" in the Western world). Many other cultures considered the actions as a blatant act of terror and/or war. In the same way that the 9/11 attackers' cultures and environments impacted the individuals' perceptions of what was acceptable, a growing number of world cultures are accepting adversarial acts in the cyber world as being justified. Although China and the United States have laws prohibiting certain adversarial activities in cyber space, the initial Chinese attacks and the eventual American retaliation demonstrated that at least for some, a political event such as the U.S. spy plane row provided sufficient justification in the minds of Chinese adversaries that what they were doing was "right." It was also apparent that the high levels of patriotism within the United States provided sufficient justification for the counter attacks.

Comparing the mind states of those who believed the events of 9/11 were justified with those of the individuals involved in the relatively harmless U.S.–Chinese cyber attacks would be a gross mistake. But there are a growing number of nations whose regimes and societies are not only beginning to deem cyber attacks against the assets of foreign states acceptable, but they are condoning the attacks and in some cases aiding their execution. Although the semantics of state-run programs in nations condoning these activities are outside of the remit of "the environment" in this particular context, the knowledge of their existence within the countries and nation states running them can only result in a growing acceptance that such activities are OK.

Another factor that can act as a catalyst for adversarial activities in cyberspace are the laws, or lack thereof, to prohibit such activities. Many countries in both the Eastern and Western worlds have failed to pass laws that provide a sufficient deterrent to would-be cyber adversaries. The United States was one of the first countries to recognize this fact, adding a clause to the U.S. Patriot act (2001) amongst other laws, ruling that under the correct circumstances, certain adversarial acts against U.S. government–owned computer systems can constitute "an act of terrorism." Several other countries, including England, have followed America's lead. But several countries with regimes that have encouraged adversarial acts in cyber space in the past or currently operate initiatives to verse their military in the art of "cyber-war" have neglected to take steps to harden their aging computer crime laws or indeed create them.

The wealth of the state where a potential adversary lives is also an important factor for numerous reasons. The U.S.-led 2003 invasion of Iraq sparked media speculation of whether Iraq would resort to technological attacks—seeking to offset its inferior military power—against the critical infrastructures of nation states cooperating with the United States. At the time, at least to anyone within the defense or information security communities, it was clear that Iraq had insufficient infrastructure and resources to pose a technological threat to the United States or its allies. Iraq aside, a number of highly wealthy nation states have invested considerable resources toward telecommunications infrastructures and research initiatives aimed at versing their nation in the art of cyber warfare. The wealth of a state can become extremely relevant if it indirectly endorses adversarial activities to support political objectives abroad. Although there are no documented instances of this, suppose that a well-funded state were to financially support an adversary through the course of his or her actions. This would increase the time (T) the adversary has to conduct his or her act, it would increase the wealth (W) of the individual, and may very well impact the intelligence (I) to which the individual has access.

From the perspective of the individual adversary, (groups will be dealt with later in this book), the wealth of a state hosting a potential adversary is primarily a function of the wealth of the individual. Although the financial wealth of an adversary obviously impacts the resources at his or her disposal, the presence of wealth (or more importantly, a lack thereof) is a clear motivational factor. Since the turn of the millennium, adversarial activity directed against the high-value assets of financial institutions, private companies, and individuals has shot up at a disproportional rate and shows no sign of declining. One of the more memorable adversarial activities during this era has perhaps been the increase in e-mail borne "scams" or email "phishing." Although certain activities have been linked to organized crime rings, many of the scam emails we see arrive in our mail box are the work of one or two individuals, primarily residing in countries that, although they have considerable telecommunications infrastructures, are financially suffering in one way or another.

Nothing to Lose— Motivational Impacts on Attack Variables

A wise man once said that a thief without hope is a hacker without fear.

Whether you're talking about stealing bread from a store or stealing shadow files, this statement always seems to ring true. Financial desperation is perhaps one of the most powerful motivators and is the function of a set of adversarial behaviors that is perhaps one of the most predictable. From the types of assets that the adversary will pursue to the risks he or she will take to ensure success, an attack by an adversary of this type will tend to stick out like a sore thumb. In general, a lack of funds will act as a modifier on the technological resource an adversary possesses; relative to the asset being compromised, reducing the chances of success. However, the chances of success are increased when the subject feels that he or she has nothing to lose. This state of mind results in a degree of complacency, which results in the neglect of several factors that may otherwise be considered by an adversary, which are displayed in Tables 2.1 and 2.2.

Table 2.1 State of Mind Results (Change in Variables)

Impacted Attack Variables	Variable Impact Given Motivation	Weight
The likelihood of success given a fixed asset	The likelihood that our adversary will succeed in his or her attack is not taken into as much consideration as perhaps it otherwise would have been. As far as our adversary is concerned, they must succeed.	Increase
The likelihood of detection	The likelihood of detection during the attack is also not taken into as much consideration as it perhaps otherwise would have been. Although the adversary is probably aware to some degree of the likelihood of detection, its weight is greatly reduced.	Decrease
The consequences of detection	As with the likelihood of detection, the adversary is probably aware of the consequences of being detected. The consequence of detection is a function of the asset itself.	Decrease
The nature of the asset	Considerations regarding the asset itself. The value of the asset is a fixed variable at this point, but factors such as initial access required and efforts required in acquiring such access may be neglected more than it would perhaps otherwise be.	Decrease

Continued

Table 2.1 State of Mind Results (Change in Variables)

Impacted Attack Variables	Variable Impact Given Motivation	Weight
Resources required	The adversary is less likely to consider the resources required in order to ensure success. This is due in part to the lack of ability to acquire additional resources, even if required.	Decrease

Table 2.1 displays a reduction in the weight behind most risk-oriented variables and an increase in the perception that he or she will succeed. This also increases the chances of the adversary going through with the attack. Although the "reckless factor" may contribute toward the attack being a success, our focus for now is on the environmental/financial variable upon motivation. Further more, this isn't something that we can easily factor without further information regarding a real or theoretical asset (see Chapter 5, Asset Threat Characterization).

Table 2.2 State of Mind Results (No Change in Variables)

Impacted Attack Variables	Variable Impact Given Motivation	Weight
The likelihood of success given fixed asset	The likelihood of success is reduced; it is far less likely that adversary will go through with an attack against the same asset without the right motivator.	Decrease
The likelihood of detection	Due to the lack of the environmental property and therefore the motivator, the importance/weight our adversary puts in this attack property remains unchanged.	Equal
The consequences of detection	Due to the lack of the environmental property and therefore the motivator, the importance/weight our adversary puts in this attack property remains unchanged.	Equal
The nature of the asset	In the eyes of the adversary, without the financial (environment property) motivator, the value of the asset is greatly reduced.	Equal

Continued

Table 2.2 State of Mind Results (No Change in Variables)

Impacted Attack Variables	Variable Impact Given Motivation	Weight
Resources required	The adversary is more likely to take heed of the resources he requires in order to ensure the attack is a success.	Equal

All weights invested in risk-oriented variables remain unchanged. No motivation properties due to financial environment have been defined and are therefore equal to their previous values. The weight of the "likelihood of success given fixed asset" is decreased because without the correct motivation, which there is none, the attack would never have occurred.

Associations and Intelligence Sources

In physical-world theatres of war, knowing whom an adversary is loyal to, whom an adversary is associated with, and who is aiding that adversary is a vital. Such highly useful information can lead us to making several determinations with a greater degree of certainty that our determinations are accurate. Such determinations can include the arsenal that may or may not be at the disposal of the adversary. Determining what resources various adversary types have access to enables us to make fairly informed determinations regarding the kind of attacks we can expect from the adversary, or from a post-incident perspective, the kind of adversary that initiated an attack. Although the resource and capability of our adversary is not an object of the environment adversary property, the associations and intelligence source object is, and is possibly the primary contributing object impacting the adversary's resource object (covered later).

The way in which an adversary's associations and other sources of intelligence will impact an attack against a given target will differ substantially, according to the semantics of the attack construct. For example, was there a need to seek out additional information at the reconnaissance phase of the attack? And does the adversary really need to use a valuable intelligence resource, when he or she can still be a success without retaining the resource? This will also be dependent upon the nature of the resource. Does the resource run out? Does the adversary have to "give something back" to that resource for it to remain available to him or her, or is it something that is freely available and without risk of exhaustion? The associations and intelligence object is primarily populated by data pertaining to the knowledge the adversary possesses. Such information can include vulnerability and exploitation data learned through associations, data regarding the schematics of possible target networks, and any other additional information that the adversary may use to:

- Increase his or her chances of success
- Provide initial access to the adversary

One of the less obvious but growingly more common sources of such information are in fact, not online associations or software vulnerability discussion mailing lists, but *insiders*. Insiders within organizations are increasingly being used to provide external adversaries with both the information they need, whether it be system passwords or network schematics of proprietary source code. They also provide the initial access that the adversary may require to execute their attack. It is important to remember, that although an insider may have achieved his status as the result of a previous social engineering attack, the adversary model deals with the adversary on a regular basis. The insider at the point of reaching insider status is already within the "environment" of the adversary, and therefore a part of the associations and intelligence object.

Although cyber and real-world adversaries are alike in many ways, they differ in the ease of access to key resources. By definition, a cyber-adversary must have some form of access to "cyberspace" and the recourses it yields. In the physical world, adversaries do not have such immediate access to targets. Distance is an issue, and most aren't born into the world surrounded by an arsenal of weapons. To the cyber adversary, the Internet represents a huge, relatively unrestricted and unmoderated resource of tools and information that is available on a fairly on-demand basis. However, much like in the real world, the Internet is home to a myriad of information that isn't so freely available. In the right situation, this type of information can be invaluable to the adversary in both the physical world and cyberspace. An adversary's ability to access such illicit information is almost always a function of his or her ability to establish and maintain the right associations.

Without a doubt, the richest source of intelligence for the modern cyber adversary is the Internet itself. There exists a vast number of online communities whose soul purpose is to facilitate the discovery and further research of vulnerabilities—many of which impact some of the most sensitive information systems in existence today. Using mediums such as Internet relay chat and private mailing lists, such groups often engage in the sharing of tools to take advantage of unpublished vulnerabilities in operating systems and proprietary source code for closed source operating systems such as Microsoft Windows, SGI IRIX, Cisco's IOS, and many others. Other commonly traded artifacts include confidential hardware documentation for commercially available products and even network schematics of some of the world's most sensitive computer networks. An adversary's ability to tap this information, however, will vary substantially and depend heavily on his or her associations. For more information on this topic, please see Chapter 3.

Environment Property/ Attacker Property Observable Impacts

The following are often observable changes in the way that the environment property can impact upon the attacker property:

- **Attack objective** The objective of the adversary may involve those he or she associates with, but without the presence of the group object (covered later), the objective will normally be that of the individual adversary rather than the objective of a group or association.

- **Knowledge/skills** The skills and knowledge resources available to the adversary will be the same resources available and/or attached to the associations and intelligence object. Due to the attack objective being that of the individual and not of a group or those attached to the associations and intelligence object, the degree of information shared by said parties will vary substantially.

- **Attitude to AA risks of attack** The individual attitudes towards the attack will be that of the adversary alone, and not necessarily shared by a group or associations in the adversary's environment property. The individual attitudes of the attack are far more likely to be impacted by the objective than they would otherwise be in a group situation.

- **Group affiliations** One of the many challenges that today's defensive player faces is how one goes about defending from organized groups of adversaries, determining how their attacks may differ from those of an adversary acting alone, and how the risk from such attacks can be mitigated. The group object is the final and only conditional object within the environment property.

Adversarial Group, not "Hacker Group"!

It is important at this stage to be clear about the difference between groups and associations. So-called information sharing "hacker groups," who are normally associated with the "associations and intelligence" object (just covered) are not considered to be of an adversarial nature and are therefore not associated with the adversarial group object. Unless a peer associated to an adversary is knowingly aiding an adversarial act, he or she is considered to be associated. Table 2.3 outlines the conditions, which a group may meet, in order to be associated with this object.

Table 2.3 Conditions for a Group

Condition	Description
1	The group must in some way partake in the adversarial activity (must contribute to at least one part of the attack).
2	The group or a group member is partaking in the adversarial act, and the group or individual must be aware that his actions are indeed of an adversarial nature ("dumb agents" do not count).
3	The group is considered to be a part of the object if the group or one of its members is motivating an individual into an adversarial act.

Many "groups" of cyber adversaries, such as the now non-existent globalHell and Keebler elves would in most cases, be classified as members of the associations object rather than as an adversarial group. The reason for this is that most adversarial activities against computer systems carried out by such groups are executed by individuals acting alone, most of the time without the knowledge of other members of their "group." Although most "hacker groups" fail to meet the prerequisites to be considered an adversarial group, there are several exceptions (defined by condition 3 in Table 2.3) that can result in their classification as part of the group object. Other than in the rare cases when such groups do engage in adversarial activities in a coordinated manner, they can be considered to be a part of the group object if the group, or a member of the group motivates another group member into an adversarial act. An example of this would be if a group decision were made to compromise a specific target or group of targets, tasking a group member to carry out the attack.

NOTE

The group "globalHell" (or "gH") was founded in February 1998 by Patrick W. Gregory (otherwise known as "MostHateD"), and Chad Davis (otherwise known as "Mindphasr"). Between 1998 and 2000, the group (whose membership was estimated between 15 to 20) globalHell compromised the computer systems and defaced the Web sites of multiple government agencies and private companies—most notably the official Web site of the White House. On April 12th, 2000, the 19 year old globalHell cofounder Patrick Gregory pled guilty to one count charging him with conspiracy to commit telecommunications fraud and computer hacking, a violation of Title 18, United States Code, Sections 371, 1029 (a)(2) and 1030 (a)(5).

The kinds of adversary that will more often possess the group object usually belong to groups of highly organized and sometimes very well funded cyber adversaries who will carry out multistage attacks, utilizing all available skills held by group members. Because they are acting as a group, there are elements of endangerment by peers within such groups that more than often causes a greater amount of time to be spent planning an attack to increase the chances of success and decrease the chances of detection. They are also almost always directed at very specific targets hosts, as opposed to the random-targeting methodology, typical to so-called "hacker groups." It's worth noting again that the random-targeting methodologies used by such hacker groups is indicative of the fact that the attacks are executed by individuals (as opposed to a group effort), scanning massive numbers of potential targets in the search for a host they are able to compromise, something that would be next to impossible to orchestrate as a group. Table 2.4 measures can be used to characterize what may be an attack from an adversary whose group object is populated.

Table 2.4 Measures used to Characterize

Condition	Description
1	The attack will be focused on a specific target or group of targets.
2	The reconnaissance and planning phase of the attack is likely to be considerably more detailed.

Continued

Table 2.4 Measures used to Characterize

Condition	Description
3	The scope of the attack will be much broader than if it were from a single adversary. Even if an individual is involved in the execution of the attack, the techniques used are likely to be more thorough.

The following are often observable changes in the way that the environment property impacts the attacker properties due to the presence of the group object:

- **Attack objective** If the attack occurs as part of an adversarial group, the objective will almost always be an objective that in some way benefits the group, whether it be financially or other. The group will have discussed the objective, that is the remit of the attack.

- **Knowledge/skills** The knowledge/skills used during the attack will more than often be those of multiple members rather than any one individual. As previously mentioned, an attack from an adversary with the group object present within his or her environmental properties will probably be part of a multistage attack, so the information used during "his or her" phase of the attack could well have been retrieved by other group members during preparatory attacks.

- **Finance** If finance is required for execution of the attack, finance is often more readily available to adversaries who have a group present in their environment, than if not.

- **Time** The time available to invest in the attack and its preparation is greatly increased by an adversary possessing the group object within their environment property. Time is an element of the resource object within the attacker property.

- **Initial access** An adversary possessing the group object within their environment property may be able to gain an elevated level of initial access through other group members. This being the case, there will be a knock on effect on many other objects within the attacker property.

- **Attitude to attributes of attack (given an attempt)** The attitude to the attributes of the attack will probably be that of the group attached to the group object within the adversary's environment property, rather than that of just the adversary. For example, a group decision may be made if the attack is likely to be a success or not and therefore if it should be taken to execution.

Figure 2.3 Adversary Property Matrix

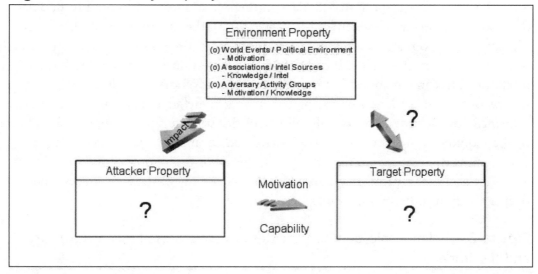

Figure 2.3 displays the adversary property matrix with completed environment property objects. The impact arrow is representative of the impact that artifacts attached to the environmental property object have upon the objects within the attacker properties. Note that the impact's listed objects in Figure 2.3 are not a complete list, but represent the primary impacts of the respective objects. See the respective object descriptions for a more complete listing of attacker property impacts.

The Adversary Model—"Attacker Properties"

The objects and respective elements held within the attacker properties are a function of the data passed to the attacker property from the environment properties. None of the objects or respective elements within the attacker property are static—they are all impacted upon by the values of objects contained within the environment property.

Resources Object

The elements within the resources object are primarily impacted by the associations and intelligence and group objects within the adversary's environment properties. It's important to note that all data and resource information used to populate the resource object and its elements is derived from the environmental objects and is relative to a given attack attempt (A) or moment in time. The primary function of the resources in this object is to offset the variable values contained within the inhibitor object in a manner that is in favor of the adversary and ultimately, the success of the attack. When preparing for an attack, the adversary will make various informed (and at times, not so well informed) decisions regarding the resources he or she requires in order for their attack (given an attempt) to be a success. Figure 2.4 attempts to demonstrate the relationship between the resources possessed by an adversary and the tradeoffs made in order to increase the chances of success and decrease various other risks, such as being caught.

Figure 2.4 Relationship between the Resources Possessed by an Adversary and the Tradeoffs

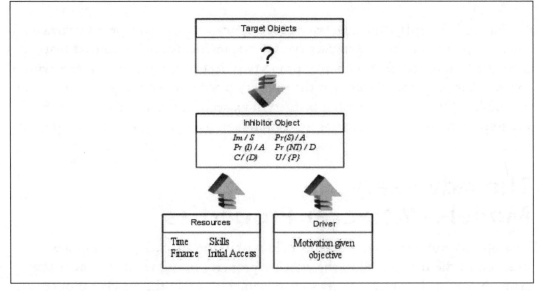

The Time Element

- Group object (More bodies, more time!)
- Political/personal object (Acting as part of funded project/lack of other time-consuming obligations, and so on)

The time element is a measure of the time that an adversary takes to execute his attack against a target. This is not necessarily a measure of the time that the adversary *has* to execute the attack. The time used to execute the attack will also be varied by the skill and experience of the adversary. A low-end, sloppy adversary will more than likely rush into the execution phase of his or her attack. To this end, *time (or lack thereof) is far more likely to be an issue for high-end adversaries.* Another secondary consideration to make is that time can also be a measure of the time the adversary has to compromise the target, for example, in a case where an adversary knew that the firewall on a network would be updated every Sunday night at 11pm, giving him or her an hour of opportunity.

Skills/Knowledge Element

- Group object (A group often represents a large knowledge base.)
- Associations object (Offers variable amounts of knowledge—see Chapter 3)

The skills and knowledge possessed by an adversary are perhaps the most significant part of the resource object, in terms of offsetting the properties of the target host. They both account for exploitation of vulnerabilities held by the target (which are a property) and repress various elements within the inhibitor object in favor of the attack being success. There are two subcategories in which the skills and knowledge element can be divided. These are the skills that the adversary possesses, and in the context of a given attack, the skills and knowledge that the adversary makes use of. The degree that the adversary will make use of their skills and knowledge will vary greatly and primarily be based upon the values of elements within the inhibitor object (which are dependent upon the target properties).

"You Use It—You Lose It"

To most cyber adversaries, and for that matter, security professional's vulnerabilities and their exploit codes, have variable values, whether those values are financial or other. Most cyber adversaries with access to unreleased exploit code or information pertaining to nonpublic vulnerabilities understands that they run the risk of the vulnerability being discovered by a network or host-based intrusion detection mechanism. Due to the presence of this risk, adversaries possessing such artifacts will often make calculated decisions based upon the values of the inhibitor object. For example, does the payoff for the adversary offset the value of the exploit code, given success on attack? In the case that the adversary developed his or her own exploit code, he or she will know information that may otherwise not be so obvious, such as how reliable the exploit code is and how much "noise" the attack generates, which impacts other inhibitor objects such as the chances of detection given an attempt. This issue is exemplified in the inhibitor object description.

Finance Element

- Group object (Distributed burden on any financial requirement)
- Political/personal environment (Possible involvement with state-funded program and/or financial health of the adversary)

The finance element provides a measure of the liquid finance to which the adversary has access for the purposes of their attack. As the Internet's short history of computer security incidents has shown, finance is by no means a prerequisite for the cyber adversary to execute a successful attack, but it can certainly act against elements of the inhibitor object to the advantage of the adversary by opening up new attack opportunities to the adversary. Finance could (for example) enable the adversary to acquire an elevated level of initial access through the bribery of an insider, increasing chances of success given an attempt. This is not to say that the same level of access would be available to the unfounded adversary—however in the case of the latter, the inhibitor elements would probably not be as favorable for the adversary.

Initial Access Element

- Group object (Group resource may yield higher level of initial access.)
- Association object (Certain associations may yield or provide the means to yield an elevated level of initial access.)

Because the initial access element provides somewhat of a stepping-stone, the starting point of the adversaries' attack, an elevated level of initial access, with the exception of the payoff given success, changes all inhibition elements to a variable degree.

Inhibitor Object

The inhibitor object and its elements are representative of the adversaries' attitude(s) to the adverse attributes of an attack against a known target, given an attempt. As we have already established, the primary objects that impact the elements of the inhibitor object are

- The objects within the properties of the target

- The resource object within the attacker property

- The driver object or "motivator" object within the attacker property

Table 2.5 summarizes the abbreviations and operators used in the rest of this section. An example of their use would be: (I/S) = Impact Given Success.

Table 2.5 Summary of Abbreviations and Operators

Type	Object	Meaning
Operator	/	Given
Operator	:	Relative to
Abbreviation	I	Impact
Abbreviation	S	Success
Abbreviation	p	Probability
Abbreviation	d	Detection
Abbreviation	A	Attempt
Abbreviation	P	Attack Parameters
Abbreviation	U	Uncertainty
Abbreviation	C	Consequence(s)

Payoff/Impact Given Success (I/S)

Conditions The result of the impact given success calculation is only considered to act as an attack inhibitor where the payoff given success is less than the resources required to ensure success.

Description Impact given success is a measure of the impact on the target and resultant return on investment (ROI) in resources for the adversary. The impact/result given success may vary in nature, from a denial of service (or loss of service/availability) to loss of data (resulting in data theft). Although it may be the aim of the attacker to use the system to leverage an attack against a secondary information system, the attack property matrix is always in the context of a single attack with a given target (or objective), therefore the secondary attack may be within the remit of the original objective and taken into account within the inhibitor object.

Perceived Probability of Success Given an Attempt (p(S)/A)

Conditions The result of the probability of success given an attempt calculation is only an inhibitor under two conditions:

- In cases where an adversary does not believe that they are capable of achieving an objective.

- In the case that strong motivator is present, therefore the determination of probability of success given an attempt is most likely going to be grossly miscalculated or even neglected by the adversary in the face of a strong motivator (see driver object).

Description The probability of success given an attempt is the likelihood of completion of an objective in the eye of an adversary. The perceived probability of success given an attempt is primarily impacted upon by the adversaries' perceived self-capability, which is a function of the adversary environment property.

Perceived Probability of Detection Given an Attempt (p(d)/A)

Conditions None

Description The accuracy of the (p(d)/A) calculation by the adversary will be dependent on the observable properties of the target and the data attached to the driver (or motivation) attacker property object. As with the probability of success given an attempt, it is possible for an adversary to neglect the probability of detection given an attempt. Such neglect could occur for several reasons:

- The attacker is unaware of sufficient target properties to determine a high or low probability of detection.

- The attacker is unaware of whether his or her resource is sufficient for success given an attempt.

- The attacker is unaware of the consequences of detection and attribution.

The adversary may offset the probability of detection given an attempt with the use of additional resources. He or she may augment the attack with the use of lesser-known or nonpublic target vulnerability exploitation techniques, which may not be so easily detected. He or she may also use further resources (such as money) to escalate the levels of initial access, as in our example where we postulated that an adversary could use a financial resource to bribe an insider to gain access.

Perceived Probability of Attribution (of Adversary) Given Detection (p(A)/d)

Conditions None

Description The following objects impact the perceived probability of attribution given detection:

- The resource object (attacker property)

- Target property objects (TP)

- The environment property

In the eye of the adversary, the most significant of these points are the properties held by the target. This is due to many adversaries asking the question of their probability of attribution given detection in a rather simplified form.

"What Effort (If Any) Will Be Made to Identify Me, Given Detection?"

Of course, attribution of the adversary does require effort to be applied, but is not the determining factor of whether a successful attribution occurs. Many adversaries will simplify this calculation because of a lack of information regarding the *target property objects*—which even to high-end adversaries, are not always available to the extent required to make an accurate calculation of $(p(NT)/d)$. Because of the potential for this calculation to be inaccurate, adversaries may use additional resources to ensure that their activities are not detected in the first place. On top of this, additional measures may also be taken to ensure the integrity of the attackers identity given detection. An example of this may be the use of secondary attacks against infrastructures responsible for intrusion detection; such secondary attacks obviously consume a lot of resources.

Perceived Consequences to Adversary Given Detection and Attribution (C/(d))

Conditions None

Description The following objects impact the consequences to an adversary given detection and identification (attribution):

- Political/personal object (environmental property [EP])
- Target property objects (TP)

The consequences to an adversary given detection are primarily in proportion to the environmental properties, in relation to the target properties due to the law and politics of the country where the adversary lives playing such a large part of determining the plight of such individuals and groups. Many countries will choose to not punish individuals caught performing adversarial acts against computer systems, especially those residing in foreign nations. This was the case when Oleg Zezev, a Russian hacker was detected and identified as being responsible for both computer crimes and attempts to extort money from Michael Bloomberg. of Bloomberg Cooperation. Because of the political environment where he resided at the time the crimes were committed, it wasn't until Zezev was enticed into visiting the United Kingdom (and therefore a change of environment) to take collection of the funds he had attempted to blackmail from Michael Bloomberg that authorities were able to capture and charge Zezev with the crimes he had committed.

The perpetrators of computer crimes committed in the United States, against U.S. government systems that cost the sponsor of the systems over $5,000 in damages can expect to be charged under the Patriot Act of 2001 and face as much as 20 years in jail (and more). However, the same adversaries, with the same targets, residing in North Korea will more than likely not even be contacted, given the lack of laws prohibiting such activities in North Korea and the lack of leverage the United States would have to extradite the perpetrators.

Adversary Uncertainty Given the Attack Parameters (U/{P})

Conditions None

Description U/{P} is a fairly ambiguous measure of any uncertainty that may exist in the mind of an adversary, given a lack of information regarding any of the elements within the inhibitor object and therefore a lack of ability to make informed decisions regarding a cause of action. The most likely result of high levels of uncertainty on the part of the adversary is that the attack will be aborted. This determination will be impacted upon by the driver/motivation object and the objective of the attack (an element of the driver object).

Driver/Motivator Object

The driver object is primarily impacted by the events/political environment object within the environmental adversary property and is responsible for describing the adversaries' objective and ultimately, their motivations. The data held within the motivator object will often impact the attitude toward the attributes of the attack represented by the inhibitor object. For an example of this, refer to the case mentioned earlier in this chapter where an individual has "nothing to lose." In an instance where money is involved, and an adversary really has nothing to lose, the strong motivators (drivers) attributed to the attack will outweigh many of the adverse attributes associated with said attack (the attack inhibitors).

The primary objects impacting the elements of the driver object are:

- The objects within the properties of the target
- The resource object within the attacker property

Payoff/Impact Given Success (I/S)

Conditions The result of the payoff/impact given success calculation is considered to be an attack driver (or motivator) if the payoff is considered by the adversary to be of *greater value than the resources consumed in an attack's execution.*

Description The following objects impact the payoff/impact given success:

- All environmental property objects (EP)
- All target property objects (TP)

Impact given success is a measure of the impact on the target and resultant return on investment in resources (ROI) for the adversary. The impact/result given success may vary in nature, from a denial of service (or loss of service/availability) to loss of data (resulting in data theft). Although it may be the aim of the attacker to use the system to leverage an attack against a secondary information system, the attack property matrix is always in the context of a single attack with a given target (or objective). Therefore the secondary attack may be within the remit of the original objective and taken into account within the inhibitor object.

The payoff/impact given success motivator is perhaps the most dominant amongst a majority of cyber adversaries.

Perceived Probability of Success Given an Attempt (p(S)/A)

Conditions The result of the probability of success given an attempt calculation is considered to be an attack driver (or motivator) under the following conditions:

- If the perceived probability of success given an attempt is preferential!

■ If the presence of a dominant attack inhibitor such as the probability of detection given an attempt does contradict an attack objective, which includes not being detected or indeed, attributed to the attack.

Description The following objects impact the perceived probability of success given an attempt:

■ Inhibitor object (attacker property)

■ Resources object (attacker property)

■ Target property objects (TP)

The probability of success given an attempt is the likelihood of completion of an objective in the eye of an adversary. The perceived probability of success given an attempt is primarily impacted by the adversaries' perceived self-capability, which is a function of the adversary environment property.

Summary

The cyber adversary characterization model forms the basis for much of the theory that is presented in the remainder of this publication. In the next two chapters, we zero in on specific areas of the model, examining some of the issues surrounding the technical capabilities of the cyber adversary—from how the capability is acquired through the presence of certain variables in an adversary's environment (Chapter 3) to what we can lean about an adversary from the tools they use, and the ways in which they are used. It is advised that before moving forward, the reader has a clear understanding of the adversary model and the object held within it.

Figure 2.5 displays the adversary property matrix, complete with attacker property objects and relationships between attacker properties, target properties, and vice-versa. Note that target property objects are discussed in greater depth in Chapter 5, in the context of asset threat characterization.

Figure 2.5 Adversary Property Matrix, Complete with Attacker Property Objects

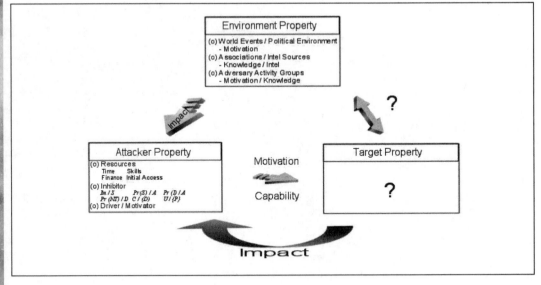

## Chapter 3

Disclosure and the Cyber Food Chain

Topics in this Chapter:

- **Vulnerability Disclosure and the Cyber Adversary**

- **Disclosure Attack Capability and Considerations**

- **The Vulnerability Disclosure Pyramid Metric**

- **The Disclosure Food Chain**

Introduction

In Chapter 2, we discussed the various properties of the cyber adversary and the elements that contribute to those properties. The primary objective of this was to enable us to make determinations relating to a theoretical cyber adversaries' capabilities and motivation. As previously discussed, the key relationship that we must be able to observe is that which exists between the cyber adversary and the target in a given attack scenario. We allude to the way in which the cyber adversary makes calculated (and uncalculated) judgments regarding the risks attached to an attack and how he or she can utilize available resources to offset any attack inhibitors. One of the most important judgments we allude to is the perceived likelihood of success on the part of the adversary. This observation will be based upon the adversaries' perceived capability to compromise the target, given an attempt, making use of the resources available to the adversary and therefore the adversary's perceived self-capability. Although under certain motivation-related circumstances where an adversary will go through with an attack in spite of a lack of sufficient resources (an inadequacy which they may not be not aware of), a result of the capability–target observation by an adversary will often determine if the cyber adversary will go through with an attack or not.

In the kinetic world, an adversary that is intent on destroying a target with an explosive device will probably be aware if his or her tool (the device) is fit for the task in hand, that is, destroying their target. By the same token, in the cyber world, the cyber adversary is perhaps most aware of his or her cyber skills, that is, their technical capability to achieve an objective. This technical ability may involve their knowledge of an operating system, a vulnerability, or the possession (or not) of an exploit code for a specific vulnerability affecting a target host. Because of the prerequisite nature of such an capability in order for an attack to take place, we will examine the cyber adversaries' abilities to acquire what some describe as the ballistic missiles of cyberspace (the vulnerability exploit code) and the vulnerabilities or infrastructure weaknesses that pertain to them.

Vulnerability Disclosure and the Cyber Adversary

Unlike ballistic missiles and physical infrastructure weaknesses, hundreds of new vulnerabilities are discovered and published every month, often complete with exploit codes—each offering cyber adversaries new tools to add to their arsenal and therefore augmenting their adversarial capability. The marked increase in the discovery of software vulnerabilities can be partly attributed to the marked increase in software development by private companies and individuals, developing new technologies and improving on aging protocol implementations such as FTP (file transfer protocol) servers. Although the evidence to support this argument is plentiful, there has also been a marked increase in the exploration of software vulnerabilities and development of techniques to take advantage of such issues, knowledge that through the end of the 20th century remained somewhat of a black art. Although many of those publishing information pertaining to software vulnerabilities do so with good intentions, the same well-intentioned information can be, and has been many times over, used for adversarial purposes. For this reason, many, often highly heated discussions have been commonplace at security conferences and within online groups, regarding individuals' views on what they see as being the "right" way to do things. Whereas one school of thought deems that it is wrong to publish detailed vulnerability information to the public domain, preferring to inform software vendors of the issue, causing it to be fixed "silently" in the preceding software version, there also exists a school of thought that believes that all vulnerability information should be "free"—being published to the public at the same time the information is passed to its vendor. Although there is no real justification for the view, this full-disclosure type approach is described by some as the "black hat" approach. To gain an understanding of some of the more common disclosure procedures, the next few pages will examine the semantics of these procedures and the benefits and drawbacks of each, from the perspective of both the adversary (offender) and defender. Through doing this, we ultimately hope to glean an insight into the ways in which variable vulnerability disclosure procedures benefit the cyber adversaries abilities and to gain an improved understanding of the problems that organizations such as the CERT® Coordination Center and software vendors face when addressing vulnerabilities.

"Free For All": Full Disclosure

Figure 3.1 depicts what some view as the more reckless of the vulnerability disclosure processes. The ethic that tends to drive this form of disclosure is usually that of free speech, that is, that all information pertaining to a vulnerability should be available to all via a noncensored medium.

Figure 3.1 "Free For All": Full Disclosure Model

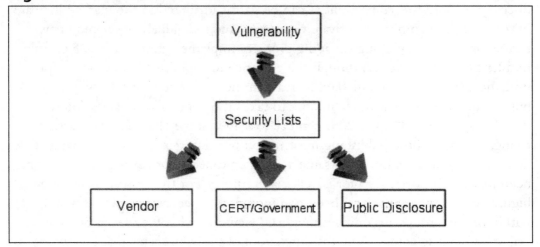

The distribution medium for this form of information is more often than not the growing number of noncensored security mailing lists such as "Full Disclosure," and in cases where the list moderator has deemed that information contained within a post is suitable, the Bugtraq mailing list operated by Symantec Corp. As vulnerabilities are being released to a single point (such as a mailing list), the time it often takes for the information to be picked up by organizations such as CERT and the respective vendor is left to the frequency that the mailing list is checked by the relevant bodies. In spite of the great efforts made by CERT and other advisory councils, it can be days or even weeks before information posted to less mainstream security lists will be noticed.

Due to the nature of organizations such as CERT, it is often the case that a vendor's first notification of a vulnerability for one of their products has been announced via one of these lists will be from CERT itself, as it is within the remit of CERT (and organizations like it) to ensure that the respective vendor is aware of an issue and ultimately that the issue is remedied, allowing a CERT advisory to be released, complete with information about the fix that the vendor has come up with. The way in which advisory councils will respond to emerging threats and feed information back into the computer security community is depicted in Figure 3.2.

Figure 3.2 Method of Response to Emerging Threats

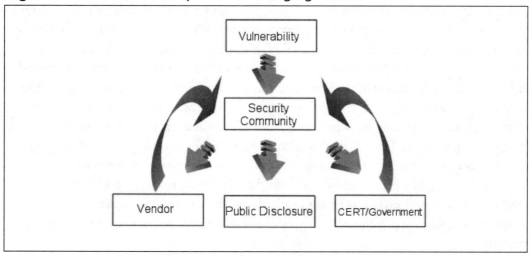

"This Process Takes Time"

In some cases, weeks may pass before a vendor will respond to an issue. The reasons can range from issues related to the complexity of the vulnerability, resulting in extended time being required to remedy the problem, to the quality assurance process, which the now-fixed software component may go through prior to it being released into the public domain. The less security-savvy vendor can take prolonged periods of time to even acknowledge the presence of an exploitable condition.

Disclosure Attack Capability and Considerations

The event, or a combination of the previously mentioned events, leaves the skilled cyber adversary with a window of time, which in many cases will result in a greatly increased capability against their target. This window of opportunity will remain open until changes are made to the target to inhibit the attack. Such changes may include, but are not limited to the vulnerability being fixed by the vendor. Other attack inhibitors (or risk mitigators), which may be introduced at this point, include "workarounds." Workarounds attempt to mitigate the risk of a vulnerability being exploited in cases where vendor fixes are not yet available or cannot be installed for operational reasons. An example of a workaround for a network software daemon may be to deny access to the vulnerable network daemon from untrusted networks such as the Internet. Although this and many other such workarounds may not prevent an attack from occurring, it does creates a situation where the adversary must consume additional resources. For example, the adversary may need to gain access to networks that remain trusted by the vulnerable network daemon for this particular attack. Depending on the adversary's motivation and capability, such a shift in required resources to succeed may force the adversary into pursuing alternate attack options that are more likely to succeed, or force a decision that the target is no longer worth engaging.

Although attack inhibitors may be used as an effective countermeasure, during the period of time between a vendor fix being released and information pertaining to a vulnerability being available to the masses, we make three assumptions when considering an inhibitor's capability of preventing a successful attack:

- That we (the defender) have actually been informed about the vulnerability.

- That the information provided is sufficient to implement the discussed attack inhibitor.

- That the adversary we are trying to stop knew about the vulnerability and gained the capability to take advantage (exploit) of it (a) at the same time as the implementation of the inhibitor *or* (b) after implementation of the inhibitor.

NOTE

The relationship between adversarial type and capability is examined later in this chapter in the "The Disclosure Food Chain" section.

In spite of a defender's ability to throw attack inhibitors into the attack equation, in almost all cases that vulnerability information is disclosed, and the adversary has the upper hand, if only for a certain period of time.

We hypothesize that an adversary may have the capability to exploit a recently announced vulnerability and that there is currently no vendor fix to remedy it. We also hypothesize that the adversary has the motivation to engage a target affected by this vulnerability. Although there are multiple variables, there are several observation, we can make regarding the adversarial risks associated with the attack. (These risks relate to the inhibitor object within the attacker properties.) Before we outline the impact of the risks as a result of this situation, let's review the known adversarial resources (see Table 3.1).

Table 3.1 Known Adversarial Resources

Resource	Value
Time	Potentially limited due to vulnerability information being in the public domain
Technologies	Sufficient to take advantage of disclosed flaw
Finance	Unknown
Initial access	Sufficient to take advantage of disclosed flaw as long as the target state does not change

NOTE

The matrices associated with an attack (also mentioned in Chapter 2) such as likelihood of success and likelihood of detection are representative of the attributes associated with an attack *through the eyes of the adversary, with the information available to them.* They do not necessarily reflect the attributes associated with the attack in reality. For example, the likelihood of detection (as perceived by the adversary) may be substantially higher than it really is because the target may not have intrusion detection capabilities, but the adversary is not necessarily aware of this.

Probability of Success Given an Attempt

The adversary's probability of success is high, given his or her elevated capability against the target. Probability of success will be impacted by the amount of time between the vulnerability's disclosure and time of attack. The more time that has passed, the more likely it is that the target's state will have changed, requiring the adversary to use additional resources to offset any inhibitors that may have been introduced.

Probability of Detection Given an Attempt

Probability of detection will be low to begin with. But as time goes by, the chances of the detection given an attempt will increase because it's more likely that the type of attack will be recognized.

Figure 3.3 depicts a typical shift in probability of success, given the attempt versus probability of detection over a four-day period. Note that day 0 is considered to be the day that the vulnerability is released into the public domain and not the more traditional interpretation of the "0 day." As you can see, the probability of success decreases over time as the probability of detection increases. We postulate that day 3 may represent the day on which a vendor fix is released (perhaps with accompanying CERT advisory), resulting in the decrease in the probability of success given an attempt [P(S/A)] and an increase in the probability of detection given an attempt [P(D/A)]. Note that unless the adversary can observe a change in state of the target (that it is no longer vulnerable to his attack), the P(S/A) calculation will never reach zero.

Figure 3.3 Typical Shift in Probability of Success

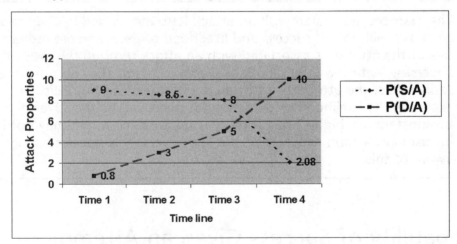

"Symmetric" Full Disclosure

A "symmetric" full disclosure describes the disclosure procedures that attempt to ensure a symmetric, full disclosure of a vulnerability (and often an exploit) to all reachable information security communities, without first notifying any specific group of individuals.

This kind of disclosure procedure is perhaps commonly committed by those who lack an understanding of responsible disclosure procedures, often due to a lack of experience coordinating vulnerability releases with the software firms or those capable of providing an official remedy for the issue. In the past, it has also been commonplace for this form of disclosure to be employed by those wanting to publicly discredit software vendors, or those responsible for maintaining the software concerned. It's noteworthy that when this occurs, exploit code is often published with the information pertaining to the vulnerability, in order to increase the impact of the vulnerability on the information technology community, in an attempt to discredit the software vendor further.

Figure 3.4 attempts to demonstrate the symmetric information flow, which occurs when a vulnerability is released into the public domain using an "equal-opportunity," full-disclosure type procedure (or lack of procedure as is often the case). It's important to note that public disclosure is defined (at least in this context) as the point at which information pertaining to a vulnerability enters the public domain on a nonsubscription basis—the point at which the vulnerability information appears on security or news Web sites, for example. Although most security mailing lists such as Bugtraq and Vuln-Dev are available to the general public, they operate on a subscription and therefore not fully public basis. Although the procedure depicted in Figure 3.1 does not constitute responsible disclosure in the minds of most responsible disclosure advocates and software vendors, the vulnerability is being disclosed to the vendor, government, and the rest of the security community at the same point in time.

Figure 3.4 Symmetric Information Flow

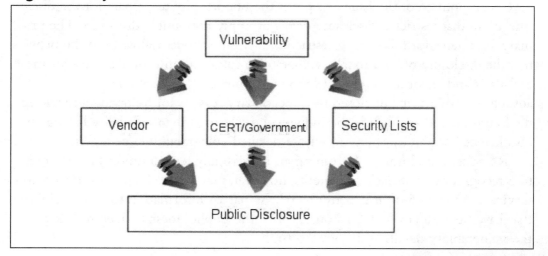

The result of this type of disclosure is that the software vendor and government vulnerability advisory authorities such as CERT stand a fighting chance of conducting their own vulnerability assessment, working on a *fix* or *workaround* for the issue, and ultimately releasing their own advisory in a reasonable time scale, before the issue draws the attention of the general public and perhaps more importantly these days, the media.

Although this form of disclosure procedure leaves those responsible for finding a remedy for the disclosed issues a certain amount of time to ensure that critical assets are protected from the new threat, the ball (at least for a short time) is in the court of the cyber adversary. Depending on the skill of the individual and quality of information disclosed, it can take a highly skilled and motivated adversary as little as an hour to acquire the capability to exploit the disclosed vulnerability.

Responsible Restricted "Need to Know" Disclosure

When we talk about restricted disclosure, we are not necessarily referring to restrictions that are placed on the distribution of information pertaining to vulnerabilities, but rather the restrictive nature of the information provided in an advisory or vulnerability alert release. For the purposes of characterizing disclosure types, we define responsible, restricted disclosure as the procedure used when partial information is released, while ensuring that the software or service vendor have been given a reasonable opportunity to remedy the issue and save face - prior to disclosure. It will usually also imply that organizations such as CERT/CC and MITRE have been notified of the issue and given the opportunity to prepare for the disclosure. Note that restricted disclosure does not imply responsible disclosure. The primary arguments for following a restricted disclosure model follow from the belief that the disclosure of "too much" vulnerability information is unnecessary for most end-users and encourages the development of proof of concept code to take advantage (exploit) the disclosed issue. Secondary reasons for following a restricted disclosure model can include the individual disclosing the vulnerability having an insufficient research capability to release detailed vulnerability information.

Restricted disclosure is becoming an increasingly less common practice due to a recognition of its lack of benefits; however, many closed-source software and service vendors believe it is better to release partial information for vulnerabilities that have been discovered "in-house," since the public doesn't "need to know" the vulnerability details—just how to fix it.

Responsible, Partial Disclosure and Attack Inhibition Considerations

Unless additional resources are invested toward an attack, the capabilities (given an attempt) of a cyber adversary aiming at exploiting a flaw based upon the retrieval of partial vulnerability information from a forum such as Bugtraq or Vuln-Dev, which has been disclosed in a responsible manner will be severally impacted upon, compared to our first two full disclosure–oriented procedures. The two obvious reasons for this are (1) that due to the nature of the disclosure, by the time the adversary intercepts the information, a vendor fix is already available for the issue and (2) that only partial information regarding the vulnerability has been released—excluding the possibility that proof of concept code was also released by the original vulnerability source. Even in the eventuality of a proof of concept code (to take advantage of the issue on a vulnerable target) being developed by the adversary, this takes time (a resource), which has been seriously impacted upon by the vulnerability being "known." Therefore, a high likelihood exists that the state of a potentially vulnerable target will change sooner rather than later. Also, because the vulnerability is "known" and possible attack vectors are also known, the likelihood of detection is also greatly heightened.

Figure 3.5 plots comparative values of probability of success given an attempt versus probability of detection given an attempt. Note that because of the previously discussed facts, driven by the nature of the vulnerability disclosure, the initial probability of success is greatly reduced, and the probability of detection is heightened.

Figure 3.5 Comparative Value of Probability Given an Attempt

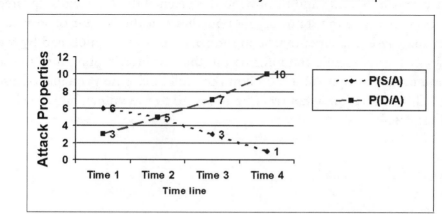

"Responsible" Full Disclosure

A common misconception amongst many involved in the information technology industry is that providing "full" disclosure implies recklessness or a lack of responsibility.

Full, responsible disclosure is the term we use to refer to disclosure procedures that provide the security communities with all ("full") information held by the discloser pertaining to a disclosed vulnerability and also make provisions to ensure that considerable effort is made to inform the product or service vendor/provider (respectively) of the issues affecting them.

So-called full-disclosure policies adopted by many independent security enthusiasts and large security firms alike often specify a multistage approach for contacting the parties responsible for maintaining the product or service, up to a point that the vulnerability has been remedied or (in less frequent cases) the vendor/provider is deemed to have no interest in fixing the problem. Responsible, full-disclosure policies tend to differ on their approach to contacting organizations such as CERT/CC and MITRE, however, it is more common than not that such organizations will be contacted prior to the (full) disclosure of information to the security community (and ultimately the public).

Figure 3.6 depicts the timeline of a typical full, responsible vulnerability disclosure. As previously discussed, the vendor and more often than not CERT, MITRE, and other such organizations will be contacted prior to public disclosure. Typically, during the time period between vendor/CERT/MITRE notification, a substantial amount of coordination will occur between the respective party and the source of the vulnerability information. The purpose of these communications is usually twofold: to clarify details of the vulnerability, which at this stage may remain unclear, and to provide the original discloser with updated information regarding the status of any remedies that the vendor or service provider may have implemented. Such information is often published by the original discloser alongside the information they eventually publish to the security communities and public. This follows the full disclosure principal of disclosing "all" information, whether it be in regard to the vulnerability itself or vendor fix details.

Figure 3.6 Timeline of a Typical Full, Responsible Vulnerability Disclosure

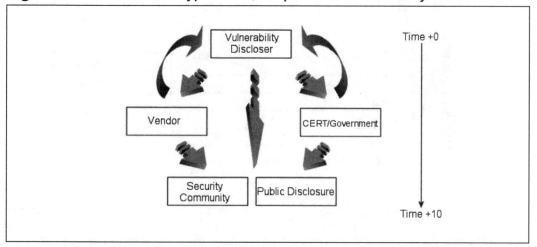

Although in many cases the vulnerability discloser will contact the vendor, organizations such as CERT and MITRE ensure that the vendor has been contacted with appropriate information to provision for the less-common cases where an individual has contacted such an organization and not the vendor or service provider.

Responsible, Full Disclosure Capability and Attack Inhibition Considerations

The adversaries' *perceived* capability would take a significant blow if an increased level of technical data pertaining to a vulnerability was also offered and available through the full disclosure of unfixed vulnerabilities. This would increase the likelihood that that state of the target has changed, and would thus modify the perceived likelihood of a successful attack. However, the likelihood of detection also increases, due to the high probability that the security community would detect attack vectors at an early stage (See Figure 3.7).

In spite of adverse changes in the discussed two attack inhibitors, the initial probability of success given an attempt remains high, due to the likelihood that the information disclosed either included a proof of concept code or alluded to ways in which the issue could be exploited in a robust manner. This makes the exploit-writing adversaries' task much easier than if only few, abstract details regarding exploitation were disclosed.

Figure 3.7 Adversaries' Perceived Capability

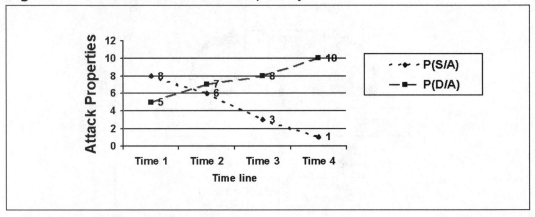

Although the perceived probability of success given an attempt is high at first, it tapers off at a greater rate than the hypothetical data used to represent P(S/A) for the restricted responsible disclosure model.

While many systems may remain theoretically vulnerable for days—even weeks post-disclosure—the detail of the disclosure may have allowed effective workarounds (or threat mitigators) to be introduced to protect the target from this specific threat. In the case of a large production environment, this is a likely scenario, because certain mission-critical systems cannot always be taken out of service at the instant a new vulnerability is disclosed.

Although the use of responsible disclosure model—the full disclosure of vulnerability information and possible attack vectors—results in an initial high-perceived probability of success given an attempt, the eventual perceived probability of success given an attempt over a relative period of time is reduced at a far greater rate. Over time, the value of P(S/A) coupled with P(D/A) may very well result in the attack being aborted due to the adverse conditions introduced by the disclosure procedures.

Security Firm "Value Added" Disclosure Model

A growing number of information security firms, already well known for their disclosure advisories into the public domain, have begun to offer a "value" added vulnerability alert and advisory service. Typically, such services will involve a vulnerability being found in-house, or paid for by a provider of such services, and the disclosure of the vulnerability is made in the form of an alert or full advisory to a closed group of private and/or public "customers" who pay a subscription-driven fee for the service.

The time at which the affected vendor or service provider will be notified of the issue will vary, depending on the policy of the advisory service provider. However, it is often after an initial alert has been sent out to paying customers. Certain security firms will also use such alert services to leverage the sale of professional services for clients who are concerned about a disclosed vulnerability and want to mitigate the risk of the vulnerability being exploited. After disclosure to paying customers—and conditionally, the vendor—it is the norm that the vulnerability will be then disclosed to the remainder of the security community and ultimately the general public. Again, the nature of disclosures to paying clients and the security community will vary, based upon the policies of the security firm providing the servers; however, most appear to be adopting the full-disclosure model.

Although we will deal with the semantics of prepublic disclosure issues further on in this chapter, the value-added disclosure model creates the possibility for several scenarios—unique to this disclosure model—to arise. As detailed in Chapter 7, the risk of adversarial insiders within large organizations is a very real one. One of the possible scenarios caused by the value-add disclosure model is in the lack of control the provider of the value-add service has over a disclosed advisory (and often exploit code) once a vulnerability has been disclosed to its paying customer base.

Value-Add Disclosure Model Capability and Attack Inhibition Considerations

Often, value-add advisories and alerts will be circulated throughout the systems administration and operations groups within the organizational structures of firms paying for the service. It goes without saying that the providers of value-add vulnerability alerting services will go to great lengths to ensure legally tight nondisclosure contracts are in place between themselves and their customers, it is seldom sufficient to prevent disclosed information from entering the (strategically) "wrong" hands.

Although there are only a few publicly documented instances where a value-add vulnerability advisory provider has published an advisory to a paying client, resulting in an insider within the paying client using the information for or to augment an adversarial act, let's hypothesize toward how the previously discussed attack inhibitors may be impacted in such a scenario.

NOTE

Although the adversary in this scenario is termed as an insider, they are only an insider from the perspective of their technical capability, and the scenario does not presume any elevated levels of initial access.

The values displayed in Figure 3.8 are rather arbitrary because the conclusions we assume the adversary will draw (such as the adversaries' ability to enumerate the target's capability to detect the attack given an attempt) will depend upon other data to which we do not necessarily have access, such as available skill-related resources.

Figure 3.8 Hypothesized Scenario with Attack Inhibitors

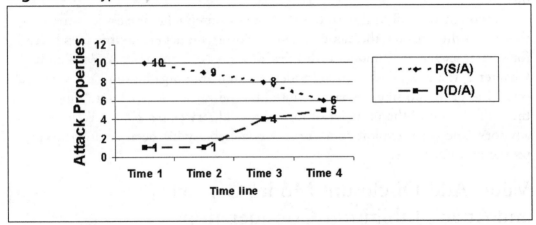

This said, it does represent the kind of perceived probability of success (given an attempt) and perceived probability of detection (given an attempt) that would be typical of an adversary who has insider access to vulnerability data provided by a value-add vulnerability information provider.

Regardless of other resources available to the adversary, we are able to observe a greatly elevated initial perceived probability of success given an attempt due the low probability that the target's properties consist of sufficient countermeasures to mitigate the attack, and a low initial perceived probability of detection given an attempt due to the low likelihood that the targets properties consist of the capability to detect the attack. Of course, even in the most extreme cases, the perceived probability of detection given an attempt will never be zero, and likewise, the probability of success never is finite due to the existence of the *uncertainty* inhibitor. The adversary may very well be uncertain regarding issues such as the possibility of the attack being detected through intrusion-detection heuristics or even if the maintainers of the target also subscribe to the very same value-add vulnerability notification service.

Non-Disclosure

In many cases, it wouldn't be exaggerating to state that "For every vulnerability that is found and disclosed to the computer security community, five are found and silently fixed by the respective software or service vendor."

As the software vendor and Internet service providing industries become more aware of the damage that could occur through the disclosure of problems inherent to their products, they are forced into taking a hard line regarding how they, as a business will handle newly discovered problems in their products. For the handful of software and service vendors who choose to remain relatively open regarding the disclosure of information pertaining to vulnerabilities, discovered "in-house," a vast amount remain who will fix such vulnerabilities, without informing the security community, the public, or their customers of said issues with their product or service.

Common reasons for employing this type of policy include a fear that disclosing the issue will cause irreparable damage to the company's profile and the fear that the disclosure of any vulnerability details, as few and abstract as they may be, may lead to the compromise of vulnerable customer sites and ultimately an adverse impact on the reputation of the software vendor or service provider.

In contrast to the nondisclosing vendor phenomena, a vast community of computer security enthusiasts equally choose not disclose information pertaining to vulnerabilities they have discovered to anyone other than those closest to them. More often than not, they keep the vulnerability secret because the longer it is kept "private," the longer potential target systems will remain vulnerable, hence heightening the perceived probability of success given an attempt.

The Vulnerability Disclosure Pyramid Metric

When we talk about vulnerability disclosure, one of the first models we tend look to is the "pyramid metric." A pyramid is used because its increasing breadth from top to bottom (the X axis) is said to be representative of the increased distribution of information pertaining to a vulnerability, in relation to time—time therefore being represented by the Y axis. In simple terms, the wider the pyramid gets, the more people that know about any given vulnerability. Figure 3.9 depicts the disclosure pyramid metric in the light of a vulnerability being disclosed via a practice such as the full responsible disclosure.

Figure 3.9 Disclose Pyramid Metric

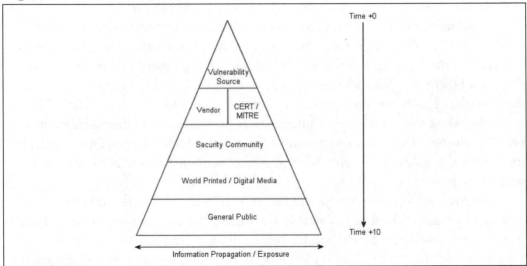

The pyramid metric clearly works well as a visual aid; however, up until now, we have dealt with vulnerability disclosure and the consequences of vulnerability disclosure in the light of an individual placed at a lower point in the pyramid than the "source" of the vulnerability (those who make the original disclosure). In doing this, we make a fatal error—the discloser of a vulnerability is hardly ever the actual source of the vulnerability (he or she who discovered its existence).

To remedy this error, let us consider the following improved version of the disclosure pyramid (see Figure 3.10).

Figure 3.10 Improved Version of Disclosure Pyramid

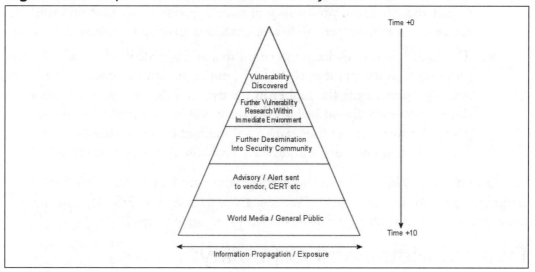

Figure 3.10 depicts the new and improved version of the disclosure pyramid, which includes two additional primary information dissemination points:

- The vulnerability's actual discovery

- The research that takes place on the discovery of a vulnerability, along with further investigations into details such as possible ways in which the vulnerability could be exploited (attack vectors) and more often than not, the development of a program (known as an exploit) to prove the original concept that the issue can indeed be exploited, therefore constituting a software floor rather than "just a software bug"

Pyramid Metric Capability and Attack Inhibition

We hypothesize that for any given vulnerability, the higher the level at which an individual resides within the pyramid metric, the higher the individual's perceived (and more often than not, *actual*) capability will be. The theory behind this is based around two points, both of which pertain to an individual's position within the pyramid:

- The higher an individual is in the pyramid, the more time they have to perform an adversarial act against a target prior to the availability of a fix or workaround (attack *inhibitors*). And, as we discussed earlier in this chapter, the earlier in the disclosure timeline the adversary resides, the higher the perceived probability of success given an attempt and the lower the perceived probability of detection given an attempt will be.

■   The higher in the disclosure pyramid that an individual resides is in direct proportion to the number of "other" people that know about a given issue. In other words, the higher in the pyramid that an adversary resides, the lesser the likelihood is that the attack will be detected (due to less people knowing about the attack) and the higher the likelihood is of success given that countermeasures have probably not been introduced.

To summarize The higher in the disclosure pyramid an adversary is, the higher the perceived probability of success given an attempt [$P(S/A)$] and the lower the perceived probability of detection given an attempt [$P(D/A)$].

Pyramid Metric and Capability: A Composite Picture Pyramid

Due to the nature of vulnerability disclosure, it would be somewhat naive to presume that a given adversary falls at the same point in the disclosure pyramid for any given vulnerability. We must however remind ourselves that when we perform a characterization of an adversary, it is on a per-attack basis. In other words, what we are really trying to assess is the "average" or composite placing of the adversary within the disclosure pyramid in order to measure typical inhibitor levels such as the perceived probability of success given an attempt. To demonstrate this point more clearly, Figures 3.11 and 3.12 depict the composite placing for two entirely different adversary types.

Figure 3.11 Composite Placing for Adversary Types, Example 1

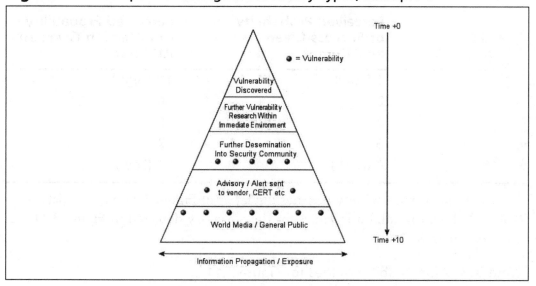

Figure 3.11 depicts a disclosure pyramid complete with the points at which a single adversary was placed for multiple vulnerabilities. This kind of result is typical of adversaries who have a degree of interaction with the security community but not to the extent that they are discovering their own vulnerabilities. Although not implied, they are more than likely not developing their own proof of concept (exploit) code to take advantage of the depicted vulnerabilities. We postulate that through the ability to determine the "mean" placing, we are also able to determine the "mean" values for inhibitors, which are impacted upon by technical capability. (See Chapter 2 for a full description of inhibitor/resource relationships.) For purposes of demonstrating this theory, score values have been attributed to the respective sections into which the pyramid diagram has been divided. In addition to this, some example values of the previous discussed inhibitors have been attributed to the values displayed within the pyramid for the respective categories. (Note that a high number represents a high, perceived probability.)

Table 3.2 Vulnerability Placings

Pyramid Category Value	Perceived Probability of Success Given an Attempt	Perceived Probability of Detection Given an Attempt
1	1 (Low)	10 (High)
2	2	6
3	4	5
4	6	2
5	9 (High)	1 (Low)

Given the 14 vulnerability placings displayed in Figure 3.11 and the data in Table 3.2, the mean inhibitor values for the adversary depicted in Figure 3.11 are illustrated in Table 3.3.

Table 3.3 Mean Inhibitor Values for Figure 3.11

Inhibitor Object Element	Mean Value
Perceived P(S/A)	$((1*7) + (2*2) + (4*5))/14 =\sim 2.214$
Perceived P(D/A)	$((10*7) + (2*6) + (4*5))/14 =\sim 7.288$

Admittedly, these numbers are rather arbitrary until we put them into context through a comparison with a second example of an adversary whose placings within the disclosure pyramid are more typical of an individual who is deeply embedded within the information security community and is far more likely to be involved in the development of proof of concept codes to take advantage of newly discovered vulnerabilities. Note that in spite of the adversary's involvement in the security community, a number of vulnerability placings remain toward the bottom of the disclosure pyramid. This is because it's nearly impossible for a single adversary to be involved in the discovery or research of each and every vulnerability—a prerequisite if every placing were to be toward to the top of the pyramid metric. The mean inhibitor values for Figure 3.12 are shown in Table 3.4.

Figure 3.12 Composite Placing for Adversary Types, Example 2

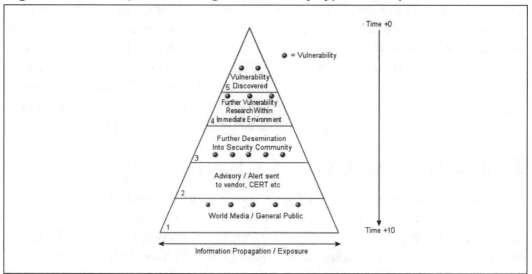

Table 3.4 Mean Inhibitor Values for Figure 3.12

Inhibitor Object Element	Mean Value
Perceived P(S/A)	((6*1) + (5*3) + (3*6) + (2*9))/14 =~ 4.071
Perceived P(D/A)	((6*10) + (5*5) + (3*2) + (2*1))/14 =~ 6.642

Comparison of Mean Inhibitor Object Element Values

The higher an adversary's composite placing within the vulnerability disclosure pyramid, the *lower* the *mean* perceived probability of detection given an attempt, and the *higher* the *mean* perceived probability of success given an attempt, as demonstrated in Table 3.5.

Table 3.5 Example of Adversary's Composite Placing within Vulnerability Disclosure Pyramid

Example #	One (Figure 3.11)	Two (Figure 3.12)
Mean perceived P(S/A)	2.214	4.071
Mean perceived P(D/A)	7.288	6.642

Do not be mistaken into the assumption that the disclosure pyramid metric is also an indicator of the threat that an individual who is often placed at a high location within the disclosure pyramid may pose. Threat is measured as a result of observing both the motivations and capabilities of an adversary against a defined asset—the pyramid metric not being any kind of measure of adversarial motivation. It does however play an important role in outlining one of the key relationships between an adversary's technical resources and perceived attack preference observations, such as perceived probability of success given an attempt.

The Disclosure Food Chain

As we allude to the existence of multiple possible procedures and eventualities, which may play a part in the life cycle of data pertaining to system vulnerabilities, the disclosure pyramid becomes increasingly more complex, eventually outliving its usefulness. This resulted in the birth of what is now known as the "disclosure food chain," a pyramid-like Web chart. Similar to the disclosure pyramid, it depicts the dissemination of vulnerability data to the public domain over time, but it also attempts to demonstrate the multiple directions in which vulnerability data can flow, depending on the way in which the vulnerability data was disclosed. Although not in its entirety, a partial disclosure food chain is depicted in Figure 3.13, outlining some of the more common routes that vulnerability information takes post-discovery.

Figure 3.13 Partial Disclosure Food Chain

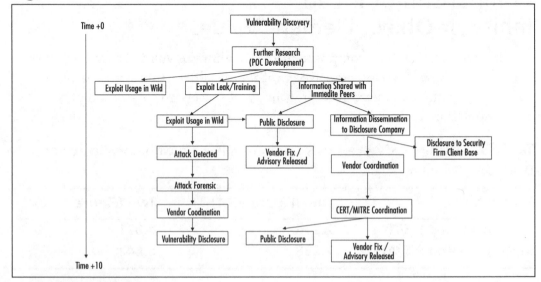

Security Advisories and Misinformation

Amongst the plethora of invaluable pearls of security wisdom available on forums such as the full-disclosure and even Bugtraq mailing lists, the more informed reader may find a few advisories and purported security alerts that for some reason just don't seem to make sense. Although there's a chance the information you've been reading was in fact been written by a 14-year-old, more interested in sending out "shoutz" to his hacker friends than conveying any kind of useful information, there's an equal chance that the information you've read has been part of a plot to misinform the computer security community in some shape or form.

As corporate security became higher on the agendas of IT managers around the globe and more frequently discussed within the world media, peoples' perceptions about secure communications also changed.

Peoples' fear of what they have heard about on TV but fail to understand is the very artifact played upon by an increasing number of groups and individuals publishing misleading or otherwise entirely false information to forums such as the full-disclosure mailing list. Past examples have included false advisories concerning non-existent vulnerabilities in the popular server software OpenSSH, causing panic among the ill-advised systems administration communities, and perhaps the more significant GOBBLES RIAA/mpg-123 advisory. In January 2003, the infamous group GOBBLES posted an advisory detailing a specific vulnerability in the relatively unknown media player called mpg-123 to Bugtraq.

In the advisory, the author made claims that the group had been hired by the Recording Industry Association of America (RIAA) to author a software worm to take advantage of vulnerabilities in more popular media players (such as the Microsoft Windows Media Player). The aim of this alleged worm was to infect all users of file-sharing platforms such as KaZaa and WinMX, ultimately taking down all those who share copyrighted music (the copyright holders being clients of the RIAA). Of course, all but the information pertaining to the mpg-123 vulnerability within the advisory was totally fabricated. At the time, however, the RIAA was well known for its grudge against the growing number of users of file sharing software, and the mpg-123 vulnerability was indeed real. This resulted in a huge number of individuals believing every word of the advisory. It wasn't long before multiple large media networks caught on to the story, reciting the information contained within the original GOBBLES advisory as gospel, reaching an audience an order of magnitude larger than the entire security community put together. Naturally, the RIAA was quick to rebut the story as being entirely false.

In turn, news stories were published to retract the previously posted (mis) information, but it proved a point that at the time the public was extremely vulnerable to a form of social engineering that played on fear of the unknown and the fear of insecurity.

The following are extracts from original GOBBLES advisory. Please note that certain statements have been removed due to lack of relevance and that GOBBLES is not in fact working for the RIAA.

"Several months ago, GOBBLES Security was recruited by the RIAA (riaa.org) to invent, create, and finally deploy the future of antipiracy tools. We focused on creating virii/worm hybrids to infect and spread over p2p nets. Until we became RIAA contracters, the best they could do was to passively monitor traffic. Our contributions to the RIAA have given them the power to actively control the majority of hosts using these networks. We focused our research on vulnerabilities in audio and video players. The idea was to come up with holes in various programs, so that we could spread malicious media through the p2p networks, and gain access to the host when the media was viewed.

During our research, we auditted and developed our hydra for the following media tools:

1. mplayer (www.mplayerhq.org)
2. WinAMP (www.winamp.com)
3. Windows Media Player (www.microsoft.com)
4. xine (xine.sourceforge.net)
5. mpg123 (www.mpg123.de)
6. xmms (www.xmms.org)

After developing robust exploits for each, we presented this first part of our research to the RIAA. They were pleased, and approved us to continue to phase two of the project — development of the mechanism by which the infection will spread.

It took us about a month to develop the complex hydra, and another month to bring it up to the standards of excellence that the RIAA demanded of us. In the end, we submitted them what is perhaps the most sophisticated tool for compromising millions of computers in moments.

Our system works by first infecting a single host. It then finger-prints a connecting host on the p2p network via passive traffic analysis, and determines what the best possible method of infection for that host would be. Then, the proper search results are sent back to the "victim" (not the hard-working artists who p2p technology rapes, and the RIAA protects). The user will then (hopefully) download the infected media file off the RIAA server, and later play it on their own machine.

When the player is exploited, a few things happen. First, all p2p-serving software on the machine is infected, which will allow it to infect other hosts on the p2p network. Next, all media on the machine is cataloged, and the full list is sent back to the RIAA headquarters (through specially crafted requests over the p2p networks), where it is added to their records and stored until a later time, when it can be used as evidence in criminal proceedings against those criminals who think it's OK to break the law.

Our software worked better than even we hoped, and current reports indicate that nearly 95% of all p2p-participating hosts are now infected with the software that we developed for the RIAA.

Things to keep in mind:

1. If you participate in illegal file-sharing networks, your computer now belongs to the RIAA.
2. Your BlackIce Defender(tm) firewall will not help you.
3. Snort, RealSecure, Dragon, NFR, and all that other crap cannot detect this attack, or this type of attack.
4. Don't fuck with the RIAA again, scriptkids.
5. We have our own private version of this hydra actively infecting p2p users, and building one giant ddosnet.

However, as a demonstration of how this system works, we're providing the academic security community with a single example exploit, for a mpg123 bug that was found independently of our work for the RIAA, and is not covered under our agreement with the establishment."

Summary

In this chapter, we have covered various real-world semantics of the vulnerability disclosure process, and in turn, how those semantics affect the adversarial capability. But what relevance does it have in the context of theoretical characterization?

Just as it is of great value to have the ability to gain an understanding for the ways in which adversaries in the kinetic world acquire weapons (and their ability to make acquisitions), it is also of huge value to have the capability to characterize the lengths at which a cyber adversary must go to in order to acquire technical capabilities. The vulnerability disclosure process and structure of the vulnerability research communities play a vital role in determining the ease (or not) with which technical capabilities are acquired. As we have also seen, an ability to assess the ease at which adversary may acquire technical capabilities through their placement in the disclosure food chain also entails the ability to glean an insight into the adversaries' attitude to attack inhibitors such as the adversaries' perceived probability of success given an attempt and perceived probability of detection given an attempt. In the following chapters, we will see how an understanding of the disclosure food chain can also be of great help when performing asset threat characterizations and post–incident adversary characterizations.

## Chapter 4

Rating the Attack: Post-Incident Characterization Metrics

Topics in this Chapter:

- Are Attack Source Addresses Enough?
- Attack Tool Differentiators
- Types of Attack Tools
- Attack Technique Differentiators
- Types of Attack Techniques
- Caveats: Attack Behavior Masquerading

Introduction: Theoretical Crossover and the Attack Point Scoring Systems

Whether we are characterizing an adversary from a theoretical standpoint or with the power of hindsight (after an incident has occurred), the types of adversary with which we are dealing remain the same, and therefore so do many of the adversary characterization metrics we use.

A basis for many of the post-incident characterization metrics is that one is able to "score" an attack to determine the values of a number of variables pertaining to the adversary's level of skill, preference to risks associated with the attack, and even (in some cases) the adversary's motivation.

We hypothesize that qualitative data associated with variables such as those relating to an adversary's skill can be enumerated by analyzing quantitative, observable attack data such as that pertaining to the complexity of a given attack. Through consideration of the theories we established in earlier chapters (such as those governing the adversary's risk exposure versus resources the adversary used), we are able to glean invaluable insight into adversarial variables such as preference to risk, the adversary's motivators, and in laymen's terms, how badly the adversary wanted to compromise the attacked target host or network.

The Source of the Problem

Anyone who has ever dabbled with intrusion detection technologies and/or run their own host-based (HIDS) or network-based (NIDS) intrusion detection device on an Internet-connected host or network will acknowledge the fact that more often than not, a large majority of attack activity appears to originate from a specific set of network IP ranges. As with Internet domain names, IP addresses can be associated with an individual or group to which the address is registered. Due to the contact in the IP registration record often being the group responsible for maintaining the systems that reside on an allocated IP address, such data is often useful for providing a "first point of call" in tracing the origins of an attack. Information regarding to whom an Internet address is assigned can be retrieved from the Web sites of the authorities whose job it is to allocate IP addresses, such as the American Registry for Internet Numbers (ARIN; www.arin.net) and Reseaux IP Europeens (RIPE; www.ripe.net).

Figure 4.1 displays the output of a typical *whois* query—in this case, of an IP address that is registered to an organization in Beijing, China.

Figure 4.1 Typical Output* of a *whois* Query

```
%  [whois.apnic.net node-2]
%  Whois data copyright terms    http://www.apnic.net/db/dbcopyright.html

inetnum:       202.108.0.0 - 202.108.255.255
netname:       CNCGROUP-BJ
descr:         CNCGROUP Beijing province network
descr:         China Network Communications Group Corporation
descr:         No.156,Fu-Xing-Men-Nei Street,
descr:         Beijing 100031
country:       CN
admin-c:       CH455-AP
tech-c:        SY21-AP
mnt-by:        APNIC-HM
mnt-lower:     MAINT-CNCGROUP-BJ
changed:       hm-changed@apnic.net 20031017
status:        ALLOCATED PORTABLE
source:        APNIC

role:          CNCGroup Hostmaster
e-mail:        abuse@cnc-noc.net
address:       No.156,Fu-Xing-Men-Nei Street,
address:       Beijing,100031,P.R.China
nic-hdl:       CH455-AP
phone:         +86-10-68019956
fax-no:        +86-10-68019958
country:       CN
admin-c:       CH444-AP
tech-c:        CH444-AP
changed:       abuse@cnc-noc.net 20031016
mnt-by:        MAINT-CNCGROUP
source:        APNIC

person:        sun ying
address:       Beijing Telecommunication Administration
address:       TaiPingHu DongLi 18, Xicheng District
address:       Beijing 100031
country:       CN
phone:         +86-10-66198941
fax-no:        +86-10-68511003
e-mail:        suny@publicf.bta.net.cn
nic-hdl:       SY21-AP
mnt-by:        MAINT-CHINANET-BJ
changed:       suny@publicf.bta.net.cn 19980824
source:        APNIC
```

* The mention of the IP range in Figure 4.1 in no way implicates its association with an attack.

Although many of today's observed Internet-based attacks appear to originate in Asian countries, the question of the true origins of the people instigating those attacks is often into question. Are the individuals responsible for these attacks really located in Asia? Or are the attacks launched by individuals in other countries who are using their access to compromised systems in Asia to leverage an attack?

With IP data alone, it's next to impossible to answer the question of an attacker's origins, at least with any degree of certainly—something to consider the next time you or someone from your organization thinks that you are being attacked by the Chinese.

A large body of data, derived from IDS and other attack data sources, suggests that during the Internet boom, the hundreds of Asian-based computer networks were some of the most insecure on the Internet. Taking this into consideration, suggesting that an attacker's origins are Asian or other based solely on the IP address from which an attack originates would be somewhat fatuous.

There are two categories of *observable* data we are able to analyze in performing an attack characterization. Both categories pertain to the "Technology" element within the resource object, a member of the attacker property (see Chapter 2). These are:

- The tools used during a single attack or attack attempt
- The techniques used during a single attack or attack attempt

Variables of Attack Tools to Consider

There are a vast quantity of attack tools in existence today, some of which are available within the public domain, many of which or not. When we sit and gaze at intrusion detection logs after an incident has occurred, the question of how to differentiate between attack tools used by one attacker and not another often dwindles. Does the use of a certain attack tool by one attacker make him or her "better" than the next? Is the tool used in the attack available within the public domain? If not, what do I make of the adversary who used it successfully? The next section of this chapter attempts to introduce some ways we can differentiate between attack tools and what we can learn about our adversaries from these differentiators.

Tool-Scoring Metrics

Although it is true that many attack tools are endemic of a specific attack technique and it could therefore be argued that they and technique-scoring metrics are one and the same set of measures, there is a fundamental reason that this is not the case. Although an attack tool may employ a specific attack technique (which, under the correct circumstances, could yield a high-capability level to an adversary), many technique metrics do not take into account factors such as the availability of an attack tool or its ease of use and, most important, do not define the *capability differentiators* between different attack tools employing a similar or identical attack technique. For example, two attack tools exploiting a remote stack overflow, although using identical attack techniques, may yield variant capability levels to an attacker due to differences in the way the attack technique has been *implemented*.

Attack Tool-Scoring Metrics Alone Are *Not* an Accurate Measure of Capability

An attack trait that has been well emphasized by the world media is the ease with which would-be adversaries can search for and download attack tools, allowing them to leverage attacks against sometimes highly sensitive Internet-connected target systems. This simple trait emphasizes the fact that it would be a gross mistake to characterize an adversary through the tool the adversary most recently acquired from his or her favorite computer security Web site. For this very reason, we are required to find additional sets of metrics to score not just the attack tools to which our adversary has access but the semantics surrounding the ways the tools are used.

In short, the cyber adversary attack tool variables we would like to consider are:

- The ease with which the attack tool is used
- The availability of the attack tool
- Nontechnical skill prerequisites

Note that "success" is always 1 (true) in the context of the these variables. In other words, we are only interested in the properties of an attack tool when it is used in a successful attack—not in attacks that failed due to the value of an attack tool variable, such as its misuse. Misuse of attack tools is considered a technique, or lack thereof, and is covered in the attack technique section of this chapter.

The Ease With Which an Attack Tool Is Used

This variable relates to the skill (technical knowledge) required to use an attack tool in order for the attack to be a success.

Many of the publicly available exploits (an *exploit* being a type of attack tool) on the Internet today require a moderate to advanced level of technical understanding for the vulnerability that an exploit is leveraging in order for the exploit to be run and the attack succeed. To truly understand why this is the case, we must first understand some of the intentions held by the authors of attack tools such as exploits themselves.

What can we measure from an attack tool's ease of use?

Types of Technical Ability or Skill

Typically, different technical skill types are required in order to use different types of attack tools. We believe that through analyzing the attack tool in use, we are able to make determinations regarding the types of technical skills an adversary possesses. Table 4.1 exemplifies some of the skill-type deductions that can be made by examining tool types and the skill sets that are endemic of individuals capable of utilizing them. In the context of the table, the tool "semantic" is the "thing" that determines the attack tool's ease of use.

Note that the tool semantics noted in Table 4.1 are for demonstration purposes only and are not necessarily endemic of their respective tool type.

Table 4.1 Skill-Type Deductions

Tool	Semantic	Programming	Networking	OS Specific
Remote, kernel exploit	Target memory layout information required	Yes	No	Yes
SSL man-in-the-middle attack tool	Target media access control (MAC) address required	No	Yes	No
Mass rooter: remote stack overflow exploit	Target network IP range required	No	No	No

Programming

The adversary possesses the ability to both create and modify code in the language in which the attack tool is authored and an ability to understand the details of the flaw being exploited, such as the semantics of buffer overflow vulnerabilities.

Networking

The adversary has the ability to understand basic networking concepts such as the seven-layer OSI network model and the ability to understand the topology of the network on which the target host resides.

OS Specific

The adversary possesses an ability to understand details of the operating system the target host is running. Such details may include the location of configuration files to the inner workings of the kernel, specific to the operating system.

> **NOTE: PREREQUISITE TO TECHNICAL ABILITY/SKILL-TYPE DETERMINATION**
>
> It is important to note that without access to the attack tool itself, your ability to determine both the types of and levels of technical abilities an adversary possesses is greatly reduced. In cases such as these, determinations must be made on the basis of the tool's availability and the principles presented in the attack technique portion of this chapter.

Technical Ability/Skill Levels

Since the use of known attack tools (for which ease of use is determinable) enables us to determine the types of skill an adversary possesses, it would be a logical assumption that with the same data we would be able to measure the levels of said skills in a greater granularity than a 1 (that they possess the skill) or a 0 (that they do not).

The Availability of an Attack Tool

In the context of attack tool scoring, the availability of an attack tool is either a 1 or a 0; or in other words, the tool is either available in the public domain or not.

In this context, we are only interested in the availability of the tool because we want to analyze the tool to determine other attack tool properties, such as the tool's ease of use. In the case that an attack tool is not available within the public domain, we must turn to attack technique scoring metrics to score the attack through the technique used rather than the tool itself.

Nontechnical Skill-Related Prerequisites

This variable refers to any noncapability-related prerequisites an adversary must possess to be able to use a specific attack tool. Such prerequisites may include local area network access to a local account or even physical access to the target system.

Common Types of Attack Tools

The following pages describe and summarize what we can learn from the adversarial use of some common types of attack tools.

Note that the aim of the following list of common attack tools and their semantics is to exemplify some of the determinations we are able to make through the analysis of utilized attack tools. This list by no means provides a conclusive inventory of all available attack tools and respective adversary traits associated with those attack tools.

Mass Rooters

Mass rooters (not routers) are attack tools that, when executed correctly, are able to scan through large numbers of computer systems in the search for hosts with a specific vulnerability or set of vulnerabilities.

Once a vulnerable host is detected, the mass rooter will attempt to automatically exploit the vulnerability, then notify the adversary as to whether the attack has proven successful or not. Mass rooters employ a varied level of logic to determine whether a host is vulnerable (or not) to a specific software flaw. In some cases, mass rooters apply no such logic whatsoever, attacking hosts irrespective of their vulnerability to a specific flaw. In either case, the general use of mass rooters makes for an extremely noisy attack, given their highly unsubtle nature. Figure 4.2 depicts a widely used mass rooter, designed to take advantage of a vulnerability in OpenSSL, Common Vulnerabilities and Exposures ID: CAN-2002-0656.

Figure 4.2 Example of a Mass Rooter

```
SSL mass scanner - Project started by Phill & mafiaboy
Greetingz to Solar Eclipse, teso team...

USAGE: ./sslmass [OPTIONS] <ip-mask>
The <ip-mask> is the class to scan (eg: 192.168.1.* 192.168.*.* 192.*.*.*)

The options are:
  -p --port=<#> - the port to check (default: 443)
  -s --sockets=<#> - # of sockets to use (default: 100)
  -t --timeout=<#> - connect timeout in seconds (default: 10)
  -l --log=<file> - log file (default: sslscan.log)
  -c --clean-log - log only the ips.
  -h --help - display this help and exit

Examples:
  ./sslmass 192.168.0.1
  ./sslmass 192.168.10.* --sockets=100
  ./sslmass 192.168.*.* -s 200 -p 80
  ./sslmass 192.*.*.* -s 800
```

Typical Skill Level Required

Although it is conceivable that a mass rooter that requires a high level of technical skill for its operation could exist, mass rooters are generally designed for the less skilled adversary who is set on compromising nonspecific hosts on public networks for the sake of compromising something—"hacking for the sake of hacking." Operation of a typical mass rooter involves the adversary simply inputting the target network to be attacked (such as 123.0.0.0/8) and sending the tool on its merry way.

The Availability of the Attack Tool

Many of the mass rooters in existence today are available within the public domain, since many of them are written to enable adversaries with little technical background knowledge to compromise computer systems, attempting to use vulnerabilities (which are often relatively old news) through scanning large numbers of computer systems in the hope that at least one will prove vulnerable. It is therefore the tool authors' nature and intention to make their tools highly available on public security Web sites for their intended target audience to download.

Nontechnical Skill Prerequisites

There are no prerequisites of significance in the context of this tool type.

Adversary Profile

As previously discussed, the typical types of cyber adversary who engage in the use of mass rooters are those who are not concerned with compromising a specific target but rather compromising *any* vulnerable target that happens to fall into their path. Due to the levels of noise generated by mass rooters, their general use is considered in many circles to be rather reckless. Thanks to the previously noted semantics endemic of mass rooters, we are able to make deductions regarding the risk preferences (the adversary's attitude to risk inhibitors detailed in Chapter 2) of adversaries utilizing such tools.

Port-Scanning Tools

To state the obvious, port scanners are tools written with the primary purpose of performing port scans. An adversary will engage in a port scan to enumerate the network services that are available on a target host. Network services installed on a host are often left wide open, with no form of access control to protect them—often lending themselves well to an attacker gaining access to a target host. For this reason, a port scanner is one of the first tools many adversaries use to prepare for an attack. Figure 4.3 depicts the results of a port scan using the popular tool Nmap—as used by Trinity in *Matrix Reloaded* to compromise the control systems of a power plant!

Figure 4.3 Port Scan Using Nmap

```
Starting nmap 3.40PVT17 ( http://www.insecure.org/nmap/ ) at 2001-03-02 11:20 PST
Interesting ports on TARGET (10.158.4.52):
(The 1647 ports scanned but not shown below are in state: closed)
PORT       STATE SERVICE          VERSION
135/tcp    open  msrpc            Microsoft Windows msrpc
139/tcp    open  netbios-ssn
445/tcp    open  microsoft-ds     Microsoft Windows XP microsoft-ds

Device type: general purpose
Running: Microsoft Windows 2003/.NET
OS details: Microsoft Windows .NET Enterprise Server (build 3604-3790)

Nmap run completed -- 1 IP address (1 host up) scanned in 87.588 seconds
```

Although the scanning techniques implemented by port scanners (covered in the techniques section of this chapter) often differ, many publicly available port scanners share common sets of properties relating to the quality of the implementation itself, rather than the actual techniques implemented.

Typical Skill Level Required

Although the typical skill level required to simply execute many publicly available port scanners is extremely low, it is often the case that to attain the intended result from such a tool, a more in-depth knowledge of networking technologies is required (detailed in the attack techniques section of this chapter).

The Availability of the Attack Tool

Port-scanning tools are widely available on many information security-related sites around the Internet. Perhaps the most popular of all port scan tools is Nmap by Fyodor, available at www.insecure.org. Nmap (which originally found fame through an article titled "The Art of Scanning" in *Phrack* magazine, www.phrack.org, in 1997) now dons several features over and above that of a basic port scanner. These include a remote operating system enumeration capability and the ability to attempt to enumerate the versions of network services available on a target. In addition to Nmap, a multitude of other port-scanning tools are available in the public domain. These include Strobe and SuperScan.

Adversary Profile

Even though port-scanning tools are a part of almost every cyber adversary's tool box, it is not possible to profile an individual based on his or her possession of such a tool alone. Instead, we must look to the ways in which such tools are used, a topic examined in depth in the attack technique portion of this chapter.

Operating System Enumeration Tools

Operating system enumeration tools are used by cyber adversaries to determine the operating system a target host is running. Such tools are often highly automated and come complete with a set of OS "definitions"—allowing the tool to cross-reference detection scan results with the OS definition library to provide an immediate determination of the most probable OS installed on the target computer.

Typical Skill Level Required

As with port-scanning tools, OS enumeration tools can often be used with great ease but could require higher skill levels to attain the intended results. Many of the techniques used by OS enumeration tools to determine which operating system a target computer is running can be performed manually. To do this, a high level of technical ability and knowledge of several slightly more complex tools is required. To this end, adversaries often use OS enumeration tools such as Sprint (see Figure 4.4) to save the time required to perform a similar task by hand.

Figure 4.4 Example of an OS Enumeration Tool: Sprint

```
* --- -- -- Sprint 0.4.1

Using interface        : eth0
Loading fingerprints
Starting to fingerprint
Using localport 1315
Kernel filter, protocol ALL, raw packet socket
Current PID: 2336
Received packet from   : 10.35.2.1
Received TTL           : 54
IP ID                  : 20335
Dont Frag bit          : 1
Initial Window size    : 57344
Time taken             : 3.-441780 seconds
Remote system guess    : FreeBSD >= 4.6 (10.35.2.1:80)
```

The Availability of the Attack Tool

As with port-scanning tools, remote OS enumeration tools are widely available on various Internet sites. In addition to Nmap's built-in OS detection capabilities, several other popular tools exist within the public domain. These include Sprint by zillion and p0f by Michal Zalewski and William Stearns.

Adversary Profile

Although OS enumeration tools, like port-scanning tools, form a part of almost every cyber adversary's tool kit, it would be a reasonable to assume that an adversary who utilizes an OS enumeration tool is interested in his or her target's OS version and that, once that information is found, they have some use for it. As basic as this concept might be, adversaries who feel that they need to know a detail such as a target's operating system tend to be a cut above those who will blindly attempt to compromise a target, irrespective of OS type or version. For more information on the use of OS enumeration techniques, see the attack techniques section later in this chapter.

Software Exploits

Software exploits are the large family of attack tools that adversaries use to take advantage of various classes' programmatic flaws in computer software. Such flaws include some of the more well-known issues, such as stack and heap overflow vulnerabilities or format string vulnerabilities, and several less widely understood issues, such as program signal and other forms of race conditions. Figure 4.5 depicts the screen of an adversary utilizing a software exploit to leverage a vulnerability in Microsoft Windows, described in Microsoft advisory ID: MS03-026.

Figure 4.5 Adversary Using Software Exploit

```
(hacker@host) [/dev/.../]# ./dcom 0 10.24.1.19
-----------------------------------------------------------
- Remote DCOM RPC Buffer Overflow Exploit
- Original code by FlashSky and Benjurry
- Rewritten by HDM <hdm [at] metasploit.com>
- Using universal return address of 0x77838eef
- Dropping to System Shell...

Microsoft Windows 2000 [Version 5.00.2195]
(C) Copyright 1985-1999 Microsoft Corp.

C:\WINNT\system32>net user
net user

User accounts for \\

-----------------------------------------------------------
Administrator                Guest
The command completed with one or more errors.

C:\WINNT\system32>
```

Software exploits (public or not) account for a significant part of a cyber adversary's arsenal; in fact, it is estimated that such software exploits accounted for approximately 85 percent of compromises of Internet–connected hosts between 2000 and 2003.

The Ease With Which the Attack Tool Is Used

Software exploits account for a broad spectrum of attack tools; one can therefore gain a greater understanding of an adversary's skill levels through the ways he or she uses a software exploit rather than via the semantics of the attack tool itself. There are several properties of software exploits that (in cases where the exploit code is available for assessment) we may consider in an attempt to characterize the adversary's skill level. Such considerations include:

- Does the exploit require detailed knowledge of the respective vulnerability?
- Does the public version of the exploit require any modification to function?

The Availability of the Attack Tool

A large number of software exploits are available in the public domain, with many new such exploits published every day to Web sites and forums such as the Bugtraq and "Full Disclosure" mailing lists. The use of and disclosure of previously nonpublic exploits (and vulnerabilities) is discussed in detail in Chapter 3 of this book.

Adversary Profile

Due to the broad nature of software exploits, we cannot expect to be able to profile an adversary just from the fact that he or she has used a software exploit.

Commercial Attack Tools

Several commercially available attack tools have become available in recent years, designed to allow nonsecurity-savvy IT workers to detect and demonstrate vulnerabilities in the infrastructures for which they are responsible. Unlike many attack tools in the public domain, commercially available attack tools often come with an easy-to-use graphical user interface. Also unlike many publicly available attack tools, these tools function on desktop operating systems such as Windows XP without the need for software compilers or any other third-party software.

Typical Skill Levels Required

Due to the skill level possessed by the users such tools are authored for, commercially available attack tools are almost always focused on providing an easy-to-use interface requiring few technical skills. Typical users of commercially available attack tools include systems and network administrators.

The Availability of the Attack Tool

Commercially available attack tools are far less available than many other forms of attack tools on the Internet. Due to their high costs, many commercially available attack tools are not accessible by adversaries who lack sufficient resources to acquire them through legitimate means. However, like most software, illegal ("pirated") copies of commercially available attack tools are available; illegal copies of commercial attack tools tend not to be as readily available as mainstream pirated software due to their specialist nature and are therefore only available to adversaries sufficiently well connected to acquire the tools.

Adversary Profile

If you think that your systems have been accessed by an unauthorized party by leveraging a vulnerability exploited by a commercial attack tool, chances are that the attack tool was stolen. Due to their nature, commercial attack tools are tightly licensed and are often watermarked (digitally fingerprinted) to the purchasing user or organization. In other words, an adversary attacking a target with his or her own copy of a commercial attack tool would be performing the digital equivalent of committing a robbery with a gun licensed to someone other than him- or herself.

Caveats of Attack Tool Metrics

When the correct attack data is available to us, assessing the tools used by an adversary in an attack can aid us in understanding an adversary a lot better. Unfortunately, many of the metrics alluded to up to this point are often of no use given their over reliance on one having access to the attack tool itself for analysis. It is often the case that simply not enough attack data is available in order to identify the tool, which was used by an adversary, therefore making the acquisition and tool analysis process next to impossible. To counter this caveat, we look to metrics which do not fall foul of these issues, assessing not the attack tool but the attack methodology itself. These metrics are introduced through out the remainder of this chapter.

Attack Technique Variables

When we refer to an *attack technique*, we are referencing the specific technologies and attack methodologies leveraged to perform a given attack. Although (unlike the attack tool metrics) attack technique metrics are nonspecific to the tool used to leverage an attack technique, the tool used is often endemic of the technique. To provide a basic example of why this is of value, many Web application (Web site) vulnerabilities (or weaknesses) can be exploited (taken advantage of) with a Web browser such as Microsoft Internet Explorer or Mozilla alone.

This creates a situation in which, if one were to characterize an adversary's technological resource through the scoring of just the tool used (in this case, a Web browser), the observed capability would be greatly diminished (and inaccurate), given that although the technique used may require a high level of skill, a Web browser is a resource that is hardly difficult to come by and by no means constitutes a "zero day" exploit. Attack technique scoring metrics attempt to solve this lack of information through assessing the specific ways the Web browser (the tool in this case) is used to leverage a Web application's weakness.

There are several variables we might want to consider when assessing an attack technique; those that are applicable will vary on a case-by-case basis.

Nontechnological Resources Required

Additional resources required to leverage an attack technique could include any of the resource elements held within the attacker resource object (see Chapter 2), such as the level of initial access. All attack techniques require at least some additional resources. An initial level of access, for example, is always required. Whether the initial level of access is access to a Web server over the Internet or physical access to a device in a data center, it remains a resource that is always a factor.

The Distribution Level of the Attack Technique

The distribution level of an attack technique is an indicator of how well known an attack technique is. Assessing the distribution levels of an attack technique is often paramount to answering other capability-related questions such as an adversary's placement within the "disclosure pyramid" or "adversary food chain" (see Chapter 3). In many attacks in which a known technique is used, gauging said attack technique's distribution level is often no harder than performing an Internet search, but measuring distribution levels of many other attack techniques is often not quite as simple.

This increased complexity is often due to these attack techniques being something of a black art—the information pertaining to them existing only in the minds of members of nonpublic (or "underground") communities. In cases like these, simply knowing that a utilized attack technique is not publicly known is enough to enable you to allude to an adversary's placement within the disclosure pyramid and projected capability (see Chapter 3).

Any Attack Inhibitors Reduced Through the Use of the Attack Technique

An adversary might use certain attack techniques with the specific intention of reducing certain adverse parameters that are often associated with an attack. Such adverse parameters often include the likelihood of detection, attribution, and the more obvious—the likelihood that the adversary may fail to achieve an objective.

An example of how an attack technique can be used to reduce the probability of attribution is if an adversary were to use what is known as a "bounce" scan when attempting to enumerate vulnerable services on a host. In short, a bounce scan will "use" a misconfigured system on the Internet to perform a port scan "through"—hence masking the real IP address of the adversary from any systems administrators who might have observed the adversarial activity.

An example of a technique that adversaries can use to reduce the probability of detection given attempt ($P(d) / A$) is through the use of an "encoded" attack payload, or shell code. The attack payload is normally referenced when providing a description of what an exploit does after it has successfully gained control of a piece of software through the exploitation of vulnerability. Due to the variant nature of software exploits in general, detecting an attack through a semantic of the vulnerability alone is often nontrivial; it is therefore often the exploit payload (or shell code) itself on which an IDS will rely for detecting such an attack. Through encoding the shell code through a technique such as XOR (bitwise exclusive or) encoding, an attacker is able to reduce the probability that at least the payload (and therefore the attack) has caused the attack to be detected by an IDS or other network security artifact, hence reducing the perceived probability of detection given attempt.

The Ease With Which the Attack Technique Is Implemented

The ease with which an attack technique is implemented is only to be considered in cases in which the distribution level of an attack technique does not include the public domain. This is not a measure of how easily an attack tool is used; rather we are attempting to measure of how easy it was for an attacker to implement a specific technique—whether in the form of a self-authored tool or through the use of conventional attack tools in creative ways. A situation in which this would be a consideration would be if an adversary had attacked a software component, using a known flaw in that component but using a previously unknown technique to bypass a firewall protecting said vulnerable software component. Although it is clear that expecting to be able to determine the exact way in which an adversary implemented an attack technique is not practical, through the careful analysis of all available attack data we can postulate the ways the attack might have been achieved.

Technique-Scoring Metrics

The problems associated with scoring attack tools are twofold:

- One must be able to determine the tool that is being used in the first place.

- One must be able to acquire said tool to satisfy most tool-scoring metrics.

In many post-incident cases, filling the two conditions is often not an easy task. To this end, we must look to the information that we do have, such as IDS logs, packet dumps of an attack, and forensics data from compromised systems.

We hypothesize that with this and other attack data, we are able to create a generic attack-scoring interface, scoring not the attack tools used to generate the attack data in our possession but the very technologies and methodologies implemented by the attack tools. Because of dependence on available attack data only, we are neither required to have any knowledge of nor have access to the attack tools used in the attack.

Before we look at the metrics themselves, let's consider some differentiators between attack methodologies that permit us to create said metrics in the first place.

Common Types of Attack Techniques

To further understand some of the ways that technique differentiators can be identified, let's examine some of the more common attack techniques, identifying the common attack differentiators that exist for each. It should be noted that the purpose of the attack technique summary is not to provide a conclusive inventory of attack techniques used by adversaries but instead to exemplify the differentiators that can exist between the ways the respective techniques are utilized.

Network Service and Vulnerability Enumeration Techniques

Network service and vulnerability enumeration techniques are employed by cyber adversaries during the early phases of an attack to allow them to identify weaknesses in a system that they can go on to exploit in the later phases of their attack. The port-scan tools discussed earlier in this chapter implement several attack techniques, some of which form a part of this attack technique category. Due to the fact that many network service enumeration tools implement multiple techniques, some of which are more effective than others, we are able to draw differentiators between said techniques. Some of the more common network service and vulnerability enumeration techniques are detailed in the following discussion.

Common Technique Differentiators

When performed in a reckless manner, the network service and vulnerability enumeration phase of an attack can be an extremely noisy event—something that a technically astute adversary will want to avoid at all costs, given that it could mean his or her attack being detected at a very early stage. In other cases, if implemented incorrectly, network service and vulnerability enumeration techniques can prove totally ineffective—throwing multiple false positives and leading the unseasoned adversary's eye to believe something that simply is not true. Some of the semantics attached to an adversary performing network service enumeration of a target host or multiple hosts are summarized here.

Knock, Knock

Many network service enumeration techniques begin with sending an "Are you there?" message, known as a *ping request*, to the target host to determine whether a system is available on a specific address. Although such messages are often ignored by firewalls protecting targets or the targets themselves and are easily detected by IDSs, many less astute adversaries fail to acknowledge these facts and fail to take any measures to prevent said ping requests to be sent to targets. Figures 4.6–4.8 exemplify a simple port scan. In Figure 4.6, the bespoke "Are you there?" packet is sent, triggering an IDS running Snort (see Figure 4.7) and failing to retrieve the data the adversary expected. The second example, shown in Figure 4.8, demonstrates the exact same port scan, using the exact same tool (Nmap), this time succeeding in retrieving the expected data and failing to trigger the IDS.

Figure 4.6 A Network Service Enumeration Attempt Fails

```
(adversary@host) [~]# nmap -P0 10.4.1.1 -p 22,110,111,143

Starting nmap 3.40PVT17 ( http://www.insecure.org/nmap/ ) at 2004-06-06 10:54 BST
Interesting ports on target (10.4.1.1):
PORT     STATE     SERVICE
22/tcp   open      ssh
110/tcp  open      pop-3
111/tcp  filtered  rpcbind
143/tcp  filtered  imap

Nmap run completed -- 1 IP address (1 host up) scanned in 1.977 seconds
(adversary@host) [~]#
```

Figure 4.7 An Intrusion Detection System Generates an Alert

```
IDS LOG:

snort: [1:469:1]  ICMP PING NMAP: {ICMP} 10.29.3.7 -> 10.4.1.1
snort: [1:469:1]  ICMP PING NMAP: {ICMP} 10.49.3.7 -> 10.4.1.1
```

Figure 4.8 A Network Service Enumeration Attempt Succeeds and Is Undetected by the IDS

```
(adversary@host) [~]# nmap 10.4.1.1 -p 22,110,111,143

Starting nmap 3.40PVT17 ( http://www.insecure.org/nmap/ ) at 2004-06-06 10:51 BST
Note: Host seems down. If it is really up, but blocking our ping probes, try -P0
Nmap run completed -- 1 IP address (0 hosts up) scanned in 12.039 seconds

(adversary@host) [~]#
```

As simple as this example might be, it suffices to demonstrate that information as subtle as an adversary failing to employ techniques as simple as not sending "Are you there?" ping requests to their target host can be used to gauge the following:

- Whether the adversary understands that many target hosts ignore ping requests and that the adversary's tool of choice will not even attempt to enumerate the network services of those targets that do not respond to ping requests.

- Whether the adversary understands that by sending an "Are you there?" ping request he or she is increasing the noise generated by the attack and therefore probability of detection given attempt.

Pick a Port, Any Port

The "noise" generated by network service enumeration techniques often results from the process of attempting multiple connections to a target host in a very short period of time—something that in general is not expected during the everyday operation of a server and is endemic of a network service enumeration attempt, making the event easy to identify by an intrusion detection device.

An adversary who is familiar with this principle can reduce the "noise" created by a network service enumeration attempt in two ways:

- By ensuring that the connection attempts are made over a drawn-out period of time

- By attempting service enumeration on host ports that the adversary is "interested in"

Operating System Enumeration Techniques

Earlier in this chapter we examined some of the properties of OS enumeration tools. As with network service enumeration tools such as port scanners, OS enumeration tools can implement differing techniques for getting a similar job done. Many such techniques have advantages over others, pertaining to the accuracy of the technique and its respective level of covertness. We outline two broad categories of OS enumeration technique as detailed in the following sections.

Natural-Cover OS Enumeration

Natural-cover OS enumeration techniques take a passive, nonintrusive approach to detecting the OS of a target system. They operate on the basis that there is no need to request the data required for the OS enumeration attempt from a target host, rather simply "waiting" for enough such data to be sent the way of the attacker, from the target host. In many situations, this is not wholly possible because, under normal circumstances, target hosts simply have no reason to communicate with the attacker's computer system. Therefore, the adversary must find ways of giving the target system a reason to send data back to his or her system.

It is the way that the attacker chooses to retrieve the required data that we may be able to detect and rate. An example of a way that an adversary could cause the required data to be sent back to his or her system is if the target host were a public Web server, hosting a large commercial Web site. A simple Web request with a normal browser such as Internet Explorer or Netscape would cause more than a sufficient quantity of data to be sent back to the adversary's system, allowing the adversary to determine the OS of his or her target.

Nonpassive OS Enumeration

A less covert way of retrieving the same data is through the adversary establishing an unauthorized connection to a File Transfer Protocol (FTP) service on the target system. Although this would indeed cause the required data to be sent back to the adversary's system, because there is no reason for the adversary to be connecting to the FTP service on the target, it is far more likely that the attempt will be detected.

Technique Differentiators

The key to scoring detected OS enumeration attempts is to examine the ways that the adversary retrieved the data required to perform the enumeration.

In cases where a noisy attempt was made—such as multiple connections to network services on the target host—we can make one of two deductions:

- The adversary was negligent of the techniques implemented by the OS tool that he or she was utilizing. This may be indicative of an adversary with little technical knowledge.

- Although he or she understood that the attempt would raise their probability of detection, the adversary's preference to perceived probability of detection is such that the adversary does not believe that the attempt will result in any kind of attribution.

Automated and Mass-Exploitation Techniques

The aim of automated, mass-exploitation techniques is literally to compromise as many systems as possible, with as little effort as possible on behalf of the cyber adversary.

Technique Differentiators

Several attack differentiators exist between the techniques utilized by conventional attack tools such as software exploits and those implemented by automated, mass exploitation tools. These are:

- **The levels of attack noise created** Due to the techniques implemented by automated attack agents such as mass rooters, a significant amount of attack noise is generated.

  The first reason for this is that an attack tool utilizing a mass-exploitation technique will attack multiple hosts, often sequentially, in a very short space of time—an attack trait that is easily spotted by an intrusion detection device. The second is that automated exploitation agents will often attempt to attack a target irrespective of its vulnerability to the issue that the attack tool has been written to leverage. Neither of these attack traits is necessarily endemic of a nonautomated attack agent and, when seen together, are almost always indicative of a mass rooter-style tool utilizing mass-target exploitation techniques.

■ **Reduced numbers of attack phases** Typically, an attack tool utilizing mass-target exploitation techniques will fail to perform the initial reconnaissance phases of an attack that will normally be performed by an adversary when targeting a host using nonautomated attack techniques. This is the case because there is often no need for an attack tool utilizing a mass-exploitation technique to engage in any form of target reconnaissance, because doing so would both add noise to an already very noisy attack and extend the period of time required by the tool to attack each host.

Automated Agent Attitude to Attack Inhibitor Deductions

We postulate that through considering the discussed attack traits associated with the use of mass rooter attack tools, we are able to make deductions regarding the values of several elements held within the inhibitor object (see Chapter 2 on the attacker property).

Perceived Probability of Detection Given Attempt

An adversary's attitude to the probability of detection given attempt is determinable through the liberal use of mass rooter-type tools due to the amount of attack noise endemic to these tools. Unfortunately, two possible deductions can be drawn:

■ **The adversary is unaware of the increased probability of detection caused as a result of the use of a mass rooter-type tool.** This deduction is also indicative of an adversary who lacks a technical understanding of both what it is that the attack tool does and network security artefacts such as IDS.

■ **Although the adversary is fully aware of an increased probability of detection caused as a result of the use of a mass rooter, he or she is negligent of said increased probability.** This attitude is typical of an adversary who feels that although attack detection may occur, attack attribution is highly unlikely.

Perceived Probability of Attribution Given Detection

An adversary's attitude to the probability of attribution detection is determinable as a result of previous observations made regarding an adversary's attitude to the probability of detection given attempt. The following observations therefore come hand in hand with the previously noted observations regarding the adversary's attitude to the perceived probability of detection:

- **In cases where the adversary is unaware of the increased probability of detection caused as a result of the use of a mass rooter-type tool, the perceived probability of attribution given detection is likely to be unaffected.** It is worth noting that in cases like these, the *actual* probability of attribution given detection is likely to be increased, given that the adversary will have taken no additional measures to prevent attribution.

- **In cases where an adversary is fully aware of the increased probability of detection and therefore increased probability of attribution, the attacker will have almost certainly taken additional measures to prevent attribution in case detection occurs.** As we read in Chapter 2, taking such measures to offset attack inhibitors such as the probability of attribution almost always means the consumption of additional resources. A real-world example of a resource that could be used to reduce the probability of attribution could be a secondary, compromised system to launch mass-rooter attacks from, hence further protecting the attacker's identity and reducing the probability of attribution.

Web Application Exploitation Techniques

Just as security-related programmatic flaws exist within software such as Microsoft Windows and Linux, the applications written to drive Web pages (known as Web applications) can suffer from a wide range of vulnerabilities, from those that allow remote attackers to modify data such as the prices of products sold on e-business Web sites to those that, when exploited correctly, allow remote attackers to gain full access to the servers hosting the vulnerable Web sites. Because of the wide range of technologies utilized to create Web applications, a large number of differentiators exist between the techniques in which an adversary may use similar flaws in different Web applications utilizing different technologies.

Technique Differentiators

A number of differentiators exist between the ways in which Web application flaws are leveraged and the difficulty level associated with the respective attack technique.

The difficulty levels associated with Web application exploitation techniques relate to various semantics of the language in which the application is authored and any other technologies, such as database servers, that the Web application uses.

An example of how such a differentiator could exist is a case where a Structured Query Language (SQL) injection-type flaw exists within a Web application. SQL injection flaws allow an attacker to execute arbitrary database queries on the database servers on which many Web applications (such as electronic shopping cart applications) rely to operate. For the purposes of this example, let's consider two cases.

In the first, the database connected to the vulnerable Web application is operated by Microsoft's SQL Server 2000. The server has had all the available security updates from Microsoft applied to it. In the second instance, the very same Web application is connected to a MySQL database server that has also had all the most recent security fixes applied to it. In the first instance, our adversary is able to exploit the SQL injection flaw, executing commands on the host running the MS SQL server and eventually acquiring a Telnet (remote administration) like shell on the system through the use of a feature built into Microsoft SQL server that allows the execution of system commands.

In the second case, our adversary cannot find any equivalent feature on the MySQL server and is forced to consume additional resources to find a vulnerability in MySQL server that allows the execution of system commands. Because the adversary does not possess the skill required to find and exploit a new vulnerability in the MySQL database server in total, this costs the adversary five days of a friend's time (to whom he now owes a favor) and potentially, the loss of the information pertaining to a previously unpublished vulnerability in MySQL in case his attack is detected.

This example demonstrates the variant skill level required to leverage the same flaw in a Web applicator with differing techniques—required because of the variant technologies utilized by the Web applications.

Table 4.2 further exemplifies how we can score the skill levels required to reach an objective through leveraging flaws in Web applications that utilize differing technologies.

Table 4.2 Web Application Flaws

Web Application Flaws	Public	Private
Proprietary Application Penetration: *SQL Injection*	3	5
Open Source Application Penetration: *SQL Injection*	3	5
Proprietary Application Penetration: *Arbitrary Code Injection*	2	4
Open Source Application Penetration: *Arbitrary Code Injection*	2	4
Proprietary Application Penetration: *OS command execution using SQL Injection (MS SQL)*	3	5
Proprietary Application Penetration: *OS command execution using SQL Injection (Sybase)*	3	5
Proprietary Application Penetration: *SQL Injection only (MS SQL)*	4	6
Proprietary Application Penetration: *SQL Injection only (IBM DB2)*	6	8
Proprietary Application Penetration: *SQL Injection only (Oracle)*	6	8

Additional Attack Scoring Examples

Tables 4.3 and 4.4 further demonstrate the ways we can score an attack based on the skill level required to exploit (and in the case of the Private column, find) flaws, depending on the technology in use and nature of the flaw. Note that for the score to apply, success is always true!

Table 4.3 Linux 2.4 User Space Software Flaw Exploits

User Land Software Exploits	Public	Private
Local Privilege Escalation (Linux 2.4)	3	6
Remote Daemon Exploitation (Linux 2.4)	4	8
Exploitation Via Mass Rooter (Linux 2.4)	1	3

Table 4.4 Linux 2.4 Kernel Exploits

Kernel Software Exploits	Public	Private
Remote Kernel Space Overflow Mass (Linux 2.4)	1	3
Remote Kernel Space Overflow (Linux 2.4)	5	9
Local Kernel Space Overflow (Linux 2.4)	3	6

Caveats: Attack Behavior Masquerading

One of the caveats of rating an adversary through the techniques and tools utilized in an attack is that a more advanced adversary could purposefully masquerade as an unskilled adversary in the hope that he or she will lure those responsible for defending their target into a false sense of security, exploiting a well-known fact that there is a tendency among many systems administrators to pass judgment on their cyber adversaries as being incapable of breaking into their systems.

A secondary reason for an adversary to masquerade as a less skilled attacker is to camouflage the real attack within a high volume of attacks, supposedly from a highly unskilled adversary. The good news is that in either case, even if an attack is masked by a large quantity of "dummy" attacks from supposedly unskilled adversaries, the use of several well-placed IDSs should ensure that the real attack stands a good chance of being logged. In the case that an adversary has attempted to camouflage an attack in other activity, it is almost always the case that they have done so because they believe that without these measures, the attack would have been noticed immediately. To this end, the only purpose that such activity serves is to slow the detection process—after all, 10,000 lines of intrusion detection log files take a whole lot more time to process than 10 lines.

Summary

In this chapter, we introduced some of the key principles regarding scoring an attack based on data which is commonly available after an incident has occurred. It is important to note that the attack tools and techniques detailed in this chapter are only a tip of the iceberg. Those tasked with characterizing cyber adversaries at an incident analysis phase are encouraged to be creative with the attack data available to them, while referring back to the characterization principals introduced in this chapter. In the next chapter, we will examine how we can use the theory presented thus far to characterize those who pose a threat to our most valuable assets -- moving one step closer to truly "knowing thy enemy."

## Chapter 5

Asset Threat Characterization

Topics in this Chapter:

- **Target Property Influences on Attack Drivers and Inhibitors**

- **The Asset Threat Characterization**

- **Fictional Asset Threat Characterization Case Study**

Introduction

In the first four chapters of this book, we have theorized, postulated, and hypothesized about the behaviors of cyber adversaries. We have established a framework for helping us understand the cyber adversary (Chapter 2) and examined some of the key components of the model, including an adversary's preference to risk, the adversary's associations and motivations, and some tools and techniques adversaries use. Now that we have established some of the key principles, we are almost ready to apply these principals to one of the most important information security problems: characterizing the specific threats to specific key assets. Before we can start answering this question in depth, in this chapter we first resolve the final part of the cyber adversary puzzle: the target (or asset) property.

Just to refresh our minds, Figure 5.1 displays the adversary model we left off with in Chapter 2. In it, the two adversary-related properties (environment and attacker) are complete, including the key relationships between an adversary's environment and attacker property and the relationship between the attacker properties and the target.

Figure 5.1 Adversary Model with Environment and Attacker Properties Complete

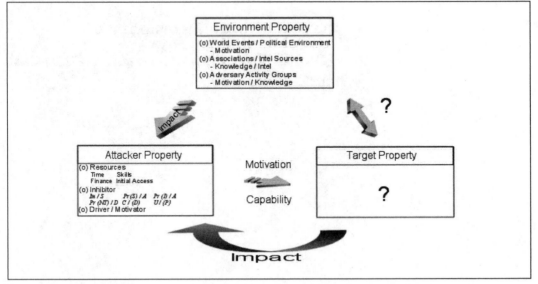

As we also alluded to in Chapter 2, to truly understand and anticipate the cyber adversary to perform tasks such as asset threat characterization, we must

fully understand the relationship between the attacker and target properties. To do this, we must first examine the properties of the target and how those properties influence the adversary/target relationship.

Figure 5.2 displays the adversary model, complete with the target property and the objects contained within it, which are detailed in the next section.

Figure 5.2 Adversary Model with Target Property

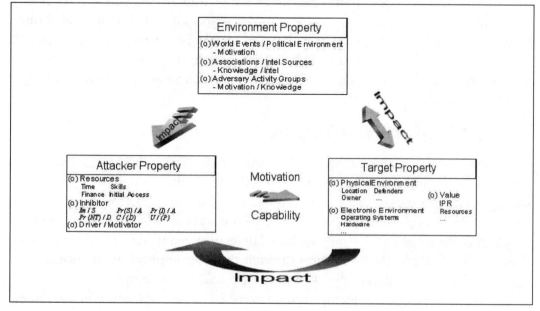

The Target Property

The target property is divided into three fairly broad categories that represent the target as the cyber adversary sees it. The first of the three categories is the physical environment object, covering aspects of the target such as its physical location, its owner, and any defenders that exist within the target's physical environment. Second is the electronic environment object, which consists of everything from the computer hardware attributed to the target to the target's operating systems, network operating systems, and any other technologies associated with the target. Finally, the value object consists of the elements of the target that may be considered of value to the cyber adversary; these could include intellectual property, Internet bandwidth, and any other returnable that could add to any of the elements located within the attacker's resource object (such as finance or initial access to future targets).

Who Cares About Your Systems Today?

Something that almost all systems administrators are guilty of at some point in their careers is the integration of security artifacts (such as firewalls, intrusion detection devices, and application proxies) without any real degree of fore-thought regarding the specific threats they are mitigating by integrating the respective technology—and indeed, considering whether any new threats have been introduced through the integration of the technology. As you will learn in this chapter, through a careful consideration of who exactly it is that cares about your systems and therefore who it is that you should be caring about, we begin to form a way of establishing not only a course of threat mitigation but a stead-fast methodology to allow you to explain why a certain course of threat mitigation is appropriate.

Attack Preference Tables

In Chapter 2 we examined some of the variables that can influence the way a cyber adversary addresses a given attack profile. As we discovered, some of the most prominent variables were those associated with the risk of an attack—the attack inhibitors. Furthermore, we alluded to the ways an adversary may offset attack inhibitors, such as the probability of detection given attempt and the probability of attribution given detection through the consumption of additional resources from the resource object (within the attacker property).

When addressing an objective, almost every adversary will consider a number of options from which he or she must pick. These options may pertain to anything from the individual systems to be targeted during an attack (in cases where the attack target is a network of information, or computer, systems) to the way the attack itself is carried out against the target host. Through our ability to acknowledge the existence of an adversary's choices when considering attacking a target, we can begin to consider the reasons an adversary chooses one option over another—more over, the reasons the adversary *prefers* one attack option over another.

As we concluded in a previous chapter, many of the factors that contribute to an adversary's likelihood of actually going through with an attack are attributed to the adversary's inhibitor object (a member of the attacker property). Therefore, to make an attempt at fully understanding an adversary's attack options and the reasons a given adversary chooses one option over another, it is logical to assume that we must first understand which attack variables contribute to an adversary's preference to the inhibitors attached to an attack (values of an adversary's inhibitor object). This knowledge leads to an understanding of which attack variables ultimately influence an adversary's choice of attack option.

Unfortunately, we must cover a final part of the theory before we can move on: what determines the ways the properties of the attack target influence the values of the inhibitor object elements, or in laymen's terms, the ways an attack target influences an adversary's attitude toward risk.

Target Property Influences on Attack Drivers and Inhibitors

Let's look at each of the member objects of the target property, examining how each in turn is able to negatively or positively influence the cyber adversary's preference for risk and ultimately how each can influence the adversary's attack preferences.

Target Environment Property Influences

The target property has almost as many influences upon an attacker's behaviors (and therefore the attacker property) as the attacker's environment. The following pages will explore some of the ways in which the target property and its values can influence the behaviors of the cyber adversary.

Geographical and Physical Location

The geographical location variable of the target property can have as much importance as the adversary's physical location.

Target Property: Location Object
Influence on Perceived Consequences of Attribution

The geographical location of a target often has a significant impact on cyber adversaries' perception of what will happen to them if attribution (identification) occurs. The reasons that geographical location is an influence are summarized in the following list:

- **Physical separation** The first reason for this phenomenon lies in many adversaries' perception that the greater the physical separation between themselves and their target, the lesser the consequences of attribution at times when their attacks are detected. In the past, such a belief among many large groups of cyber adversaries resulted in increased numbers of cyber attacks against countries such as Korea and China. The result: an increased geographical distance between target and adversary. The belief that the distance is significant often results in a reduced perceived consequence of attribution given detection, making the attack *more attractive!* Of course, the exact opposite is also often the case, because many adversaries will find themselves highly reluctant to engage in attacks against targets located within their geographical proximity— the attack in such cases being far less attractive given the increased perceived consequences of attribution given detection.

- **"It's your law, not mine"** Another reason for the geographical location influencing cyber adversaries' attitude toward the consequences of attribution/identification is the lack of knowledge cyber adversaries hold (or don't hold) in regard to the laws that govern how cyber attacks are handled in both their country of residence and foreign states. This misunderstanding commonly leads to a perception that because the adversary is not a resident of the country in which the attack is occurring, he or she is in no way liable for any repercussions of the attack. This belief often leads to an incorrect perception of the consequences of attribution, as was the case when a Kazakhstan adversary named Oleg Zezov was arrested in London for attacks against targets located in the United States. Shortly after his arrest, Zezov was extradited to the United States for questioning and trail.

Target Property: Location Object Influences on Drivers and Motivators

As with attack inhibitors, attack drivers (or motivators) are also frequently affected by the geographical location of an attack target. In fact, as we will see, a target's location alone can provide a sufficient reason for it to be engaged by some adversaries.

As we saw in the case of the so-called Chinese/American "cyber war," the locations of multiple targets were the sole reason for attacks initiated against them. Although during the conflict adversaries appeared to prefer systems owned by the government of the foreign state, hundreds of nongovernmental systems were attacked on the basis that their physical location was either China or the United States.

The Target's Owners and Defenders

As we previously discussed in this chapter, the location of a target can play a large part in a cyber adversary's attitude toward an attack. But is it really the target's location that makes the difference? Rather, is it the individual or organization that owns the attack target that causes the observed changes in adversarial attitude toward a target.

Adversaries often consider the owner of an attack target prior to an adversarial act. Just as during forensic examinations of incidents, public databases can be queried to determine the owner of an IP address range or domain from which an attack came, attackers can and do frequently query the domain and/or IP ranges of their targets to determine information such as the owner of the IP range or domain and/or any information pertaining to those responsible for administering or defending the target. But what does this information tell adversaries, and how does it influence their attitude toward attacking their target?

Target Property: Owner Object Influence on Perceived Consequences of Attribution

The owner of a target system can play a significant role in determining the perceived consequences of attribution of a cyber adversary for a number of reasons. Some of the more common reasons are an adversarial perception that the owners of an attack target may seek compensation more aggressively and, perhaps more commonly, that the owner of a target has a mechanism to increase the consequences if attribution occurs:

- **"Just don't go there" syndrome** Among the rafts of information that passes between the many underground communities of potential adversaries that exist today is a long string of stories that in the context of this chapter serve as the cyber version of old wives' tales.

  Many of the stories tell of the experiences of cyber adversaries, past and present, who have been unfortunate enough to have been detected, attributed, and suffered the consequences of all of the above. Now; in many cyber adversaries' minds, attribution is the very worst thing that can happen, and so the resulting effect among many of the small communities sharing such stories has been that attack deterrents have been inadvertently created, ultimately based on the owners of the attack targets. To this end, it is commonplace for individual and groups of cyber adversaries to hold mental lists of organizations that are in simple terms too "dangerous" to target, given their purported hostility to cyber adversaries and therefore increased *perceived consequences of attribution given detection.*

■ **Target owner consequence multiplier ability** The owner of a target can also influence an adversary's perceived consequence of attribution (given detection) through a perceived or actual ability to increase the consequences of attribution. A typical example is when a target is owned by a government-funded agency, such as the U.S. Department of Defense (DoD) or the British Ministry of Defence (MOD). A cyber adversary targeting the systems of either department can be (in theory) tried as a terrorist under either the United Kingdom's antiterrorism act or the U.S. Patriot Act of October 2001. In either case, the penalty for attribution given attack detection is greatly elevated what it would be had the owner of the target not been a government-funded body.

Although many adversaries consider the ability for a target's owner to influence the consequences of attribution, this factor is often neglected, as was the case when Oleg Zezov targeted and attacked Bloomberg's computer systems. Although the owner of the target (in this case, Bloomberg) is by no means a government agency and could not try Zezov under such laws as the Patriot Act, Zezov clearly underestimated the possible consequences of attribution given detection—a reality with which he forcibly came face to face when he was extradited to the United States for questioning and trial.

Target Property: Owner Object
Influence upon Perceived Probability of Detection

As with the influence a target owner can cast on the perceived consequences of attribution given detection, the perceived probability of detection (the condition for attribution) can also be influenced. The reasons for this are similar to one of those given for the former inhibitor: this is what the target owner has a reputation for.

Target Property: Owner Object
Influence upon Attack Drivers/Motivators

The target owner property often has a strong influence over the adversary's attack drivers (or motivators). Reasons for an adversary choosing a target based upon its owner can include a grudge against the owners of a target , to the target holding a specific resource (such as intellectual property – source code, blue prints etc) which only exist on the systems of a specific organization. Targets are often chosen on the basis of their owners in disgruntled employee adversary cases.

Target Technical Property Influences

The technical property of the target includes all technological aspects of a target – whether the target be a single, one system ISP in a random town or a Fortune 100 company in New York. The technical property lends itself well to aiding us in measuring the kinds of technical resources required by the adversary in order to present a real threat – something we will demonstrate later on in the chapter.

Information System
Software and Operating System(s)

Operating Systems (OS), whether they be a Network Operating System (NOS) on a core router, the OS of a simple work station, or the operating system on your cable TV set top box, form the most critical part of any technology driven organizations infrastructure – second only to the hardware itself.

To begin our examination of the target's technical property, we will examine the ways in which the operating system and the software which runs on it, can influence the adversary's attitude toward an attack.

Target Property: Technical Object
Influences on Perceived Probability of Success

Other than in cases where an adversary attempts an entirely "blind" attack against a target (such as with mass rooters, described in Chapter 4), an adversary will always view the technical properties of a target in terms of whether the technical resources they possess are sufficient to ensure the success of an attack. The cyber adversary's perceived probability of success will therefore be heavily influenced by a target's technical property values, such as the operating system(s) and any other software attributed to the target. As we discussed in Chapter 4, the perceived probability of success can also act as a motivator if the adversary believes that the probability of success is in his or her favor. This accounts for instances where cyber adversaries are motivated to attack targets with no other attack drivers than that they believe they are likely to succeed—hacking because they can. Many cyber adversaries will go so far as to utilize tools such as Nmap (see Chapter 4) to scan for systems to target on the single target search criterion of a favorable perceived probability of success.

The Asset Threat Characterization

Asset threat characterization forms one of the primary applications of theoretical characterization theory. In short, the asset threat characterization serves two purposes. First, it allows us to determine whether a certain adversary type really poses a threat to a given target. Perhaps an organization is concerned that they are at risk from the threat of "script kiddies" attacking their proprietary web application; the asset threat characterization process allows us to test the legitimacy of such a belief and if it is found to be false, the same theory allows us to determine where the real threats come from. The second purpose of the asset threat characterization process is to, characterize the capabilities and motivations of the adversaries who we believe to pose a real threat to a target. Before this can happen, we must prepare for the characterization by examining "who" it is that we are trying to characterize.

Preparing for the Characterization

An analogy quoted in a previous chapter likened the issues surrounding attempts to characterize each and every cyber adversary type and their behaviors when attacking a given target to a nuclear physicist attempting to enumerate each and every molecular structure, characterizing their behaviors against one another.

The solution we presented for this comparison was not to attempt to enumerate all possible adversarial behaviors but instead to develop a theory as to why certain behaviors occur—much the way nuclear physicists theorize as to why certain molecular structures come about. Even now that we have established some key principles to guide us through the characterization of capability an adversary poses against a given target, we again find ourselves with the very same problem. Are we to use the principles we have established and painstakingly enumerate each and every possible adversary profile to determine the capability each poses against a given target? In the context of asset threat characterization, the key to the practical application of principles presented thus far lies in the identification of what is relevant to you.

There are two broad ways of looking at the theoretical characterizations of threats to assets:

- "This is where our threat may come from: I now want to understand the adversaries' capabilities and motivations in order to introduce attack deterrents" (see Figure 5.3).

Figure 5.3 Need to Understand Attacker Property

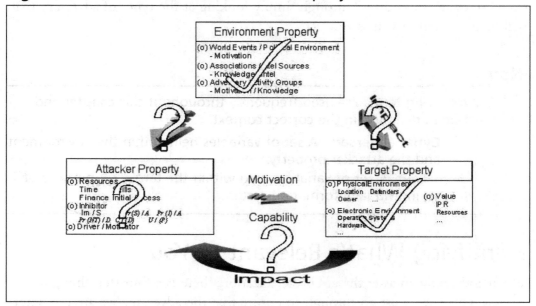

- "These are my target properties. What types of adversaries will I attract? What are their capabilities and motivation?" (see Figure 5.4).

Figure 5.4 Need to Understand Environment and Attacker Properties

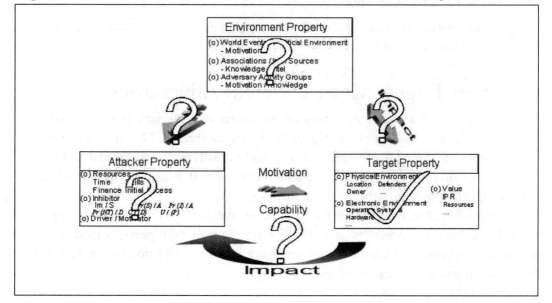

In either case, the scope of the characterization can be significantly narrowed from "all cyber adversaries" through simply looking at the types of adversary that will be interested in you as a target.

NOTE

The following terms are used frequently throughout this chapter and must be understood in the correct context:

- **Cyber adversary** A set of variables held within the environment and the attacker property.
- **Target** A set of variables held within the target property—*not* an individual information system.

Identifying What's Relevant to *You*

When addressing an asset threat characterization; there is a four step thought process which we must go through to ensure that the adversary we are characterizing poses a real threat and is not just a false alarm.

1. For which cyber adversaries do my assets become *attractive* targets?
2. What is the cyber adversaries' motivation?
3. What is their capability?
4. How can we make the inhibitors associated with an attack *unacceptable* to the adversary?

Different Targets Mean Different Adversaries

When performing a characterization of the threat an adversary poses to a specific asset, consider the realism of the threat being characterized. Not in the sense of asking whether the characterized threat could actually exist in the real world, but in the sense of asking whether the characterized threat would be interested in attacking the target in scope in the first place.

Remember that when we refer to a target, we are not referring to an individual information system but are referencing the target property, consisting of a group of elements that could consist of many hundreds of information systems, but more important, consists of *you* (the owner).

So, who are you? Are you a bank? Are you a government agency? Or perhaps you are an Internet service provider (ISP). We are not here to tell you who you are or to help you understand what your own business model looks like; you should know that better than anyone else. Furthermore, if yours is a large organization, you may already be aware of who you believe your adversary is. What we *are* here to tell you is how you can corroborate your suspicions as to who your cyber adversaries really are, *what motivates them*, and *what their capability is* to attack *you*.

Different Targets Mean Different Motivations

As we established when analyzing the influence the target property can have on an adversary's attack motivators (or drivers), target property variables such as the owner of a target can provide sufficient motivation to an adversary to initiate an attack. It is clear that different cyber adversaries have differing levels of motivation to engage in attacks against differing targets, and so identification of the motivators required to cause an adversary to engage a target is an important step in narrowing down the adversaries that need to be characterized.

Different Assets Mean Different Skill Sets

As obvious as it might be, although many cyber adversaries possess a broad range of technical skills, due to the steep learning curves involved almost all adversaries have a technical bent toward one technology or another. For that reason, adversaries often prefer attack targets they feel more able to compromise through an increased perceived probability of success. From the perspective of the defender, this simply serves as a reminder that we should be further restricting our adversary search to those who possess sufficient capabilities to constitute a threat to the targeted asset in the first place.

Consider a large (fictional) online auctioneer whose management would like to attempt to characterize the adversaries who pose the greatest threat to the company's online presence.

Because of the company's arrangement with its insurers, from a business perspective there is no real concern regarding isolated incidents of fraudulent purchases made through the site or, for that matter, the theft of individual user credentials resulting in fraudulent purchases. However, the business is concerned that an adversary might be able to harvest or modify customer data stored on company systems by leveraging vulnerabilities that could exist within the auction Web site application. Furthermore, the business is concerned that through similar means, an adversary could cause significant downtime of the Web site, resulting in a loss of customer confidence in the firm.

Although the firm in this scenario is attacked on a daily basis, what they are really looking for is to characterize not the adversaries who fail in their daily attacks but those who possess the correct technical bent to achieve success when attacking their target. By analyzing which technical resources (a part of the attacker resource object) must be present for the adversary to become a real threat to the organization, we are able to further eliminate from the characterization adversaries who are of no real concern.

Such an analysis of the technical resources required for an adversary to become of real concern (given the business's risk acceptance parameters) would be based on the target's technical properties, such as any operating systems and proprietary or third-party software it uses. Once the target's technical properties have been identified, the attack technique metric introduced in Chapter 4 can come into play. For the purposes of this example, let's assume that the target technical property currently being considered is the organization's public-facing Web application, written in Microsoft Active Server Pages (ASP) and driven by a Microsoft SQL Server 2000 database.

> **NOTE**
>
> The following is a summary of the steps involved in asset threat characterization objective (so far!):
>
> 1. Ascertain a common set of variables held by cyber adversaries who find a given target attractive.
>
> 2. Identify the variables (over and above that the target is attractive) that could motivate the adversary into attacking.
>
> 3. Further refine possible adversaries through the identification of attack variables that could result in an adversary capable of succeeding in an attack against the target.

In accordance with the Web application flaw attack score table shown in Table 5.1 and introduced in Chapter 4, the projected attack score for an adversary who successfully compromised the target through the current target property (the ASP application) would be six, in contrast to a four one that had knowledge of the flaw within the public domain. The point of this exercise was not to score a theoretical attack but to demonstrate that as far as the business in our example scenario is concerned, for an adversary to be a real threat he or she would require a quite specific technical resource—in this case, Microsoft ASP and Microsoft SQL Server 2000.

Table 5.1 Web Application Flaw Attack Scores

Web Application Flaws	Public	Private
Proprietary Application Penetration: *SQL Injection*	3	5
Open Source Application Penetration: *SQL Injection*	3	5
Proprietary Application Penetration: *Arbitrary Code Injection*	2	4
Open Source Application Penetration: *Arbitrary Code Injection*	2	4
Proprietary Application Penetration: *OS command execution using SQL Injection (MS SQL)*	3	5
Proprietary Application Penetration: *OS command execution using SQL Injection (Sybase)*	3	5
Proprietary Application Penetration: *SQL Injection only (MS SQL)*	4	6
Proprietary Application Penetration: *SQL Injection only (IBM DB2)*	6	8
Proprietary Application Penetration: *SQL Injection only (Oracle)*	6	8

This exemplifies that by considering the skill sets required to compromise a target, we are able to further eliminate certain adversary variables, aiding us in narrowing down the list of cyber adversaries to those that matter the most.

Waiter, There's a Fly in My Attack Soup!

The aim of refining our adversary down to a number of fixed characteristics (such as an ability to compromise a specific target) is so that we are left with a manageable set of adversaries, all of whom pose a significant threat to the defined target and that we can now begin to characterize in more detail.

One of the objectives of an asset threat characterization is to give us the ability to identify the reasons that a characterized adversary will find certain attack conditions preferable over others. This understanding allows us to modify the variables associated with an attack target to make the variables associated with an attack unacceptable to the adversary—at best causing the adversary to abort the attack attempt, and at worst causing the adversary to consume additional resources to counter the adverse conditions to which they are now subject.

Attacking Positive Attack Inhibitors

In the context of making an attack table less attractive to an adversary, attack inhibitors act as attack *deterrents*. Attack deterrents can be used as attack preference *countermeasures* if we understand why an adversary has a preference for one attack option over another.

Fictional Asset Threat Characterization Case Study

The following pages contain an entirely fictional scenario to demonstrate the process which one should go through to corroborate how real a perceived threat is and once identified, to characterize the adversary in a far greater granularity than simply stating that "we think we're secure from script kiddies / blackhats / insert media buzzword here" A government body of the United Kingdom was charged with developing and deploying a Web application to allow British citizens to cast their votes at the U.K. general elections the following summer. This move came as the United States moved toward an online/electronic voting model for their elections in two weeks' time. A certain amount of concern developed over a number of hacktavist groups who announced in public defacements that in their opinion, technology "is not ready" to be used for a purpose as sensitive as a nation's elections—encouraging other groups of hacktavists (adversaries) to engage in attacks against targets related to online voting systems. Furthermore, many of the groups have announced that if the online voting systems remain operational throughout the course of the vote, they would ensure that the results of the election would be fixed through the exploitation of vulnerabilities known only to them, impacting the Web site technology in use on the Internet voting systems site.

Back in the United Kingdom, there is a high level of concern that the same or similarly motivated adversary groups and individuals will target the Web site for the U.K. Internet vote in one year's time. In addition to the concerns regarding hacktivist groups, there is an even higher level of paranoia among members of the current British government that activities surrounding the U.S. Internet voting system could attract the attention of well-funded groups who may seek the skills of cyber adversaries to fix the British general election next year. Due to these risks, the British government would like to engage in a characterization exercise to determine the following facts:

- **Whether a real threat exists** The British government is fully aware that there are many groups of cyber adversaries that would like to break into the information (computer) systems of Her Majesty's (the British) government but is curious to which of those groups would actually go through with such an attack if it were directed against the British "U.K. e-vote" infrastructure, given the risks involved. Many argue that the risks involved would be so high that no cyber adversary would actually go through with the execution of such an attack.

- **If a real threat exists, what will it look like?** In addition, the British government would like to know, if there is indeed a threat of execution of an attack directed against the "U.K. E-vote" system, what would it look like? In other words, what is the likely motivation and capability of the cyber adversary creating the threat, and for what reasons are the variables associated with the attack acceptable to the adversary?

Does a Real Threat Exist?

To answer the question of whether a real threat exists, the first task involves the layout of available data into the target property of the cyber adversary framework (refer back to Figure 5.4).

Table 5.2 displays the basic set of data held within the adversary model's target property. Now that this data is in place, we can begin to examine the other properties of the adversary to deduce whether a real threat does in fact exist against the U.K. E-vote system.

Table 5.2 Basic Set of Data in Adversary Model's Target Property

Factor	Description
Target location	London, England
Significant world events	U.K. general election in one year
Target owner	U.K. government
Value	IPR, resources
Software	IBM AIX-based Web server
Software	MySQL-driven Web application

The first property we will examine is that of the cyber adversary's environment. As we learned earlier, enumeration of the environment property alone can be very telling as to an adversary's capability and motivation to strike against a given target. The first threat the government would like corroboration of is the hacktavist groups threats against the security of the U.S. voting system.

Examination of the language used in several Web site defacements carried out by the bespoke hacktavist groups suggests that English is the native language of those authoring the Web page defacements—further narrowing down the adversary search (at least for these adversaries).

Table 5.3 displays the first set of environment property variables for the adversaries within the hacktavist groups threatening the U.S. Internet voting system. Given the projected variables, we can assume the detections shown in Table 5.3 in regard to adversary attitudes toward an attack against the U.K. E-vote system—hence assessing whether the threat is indeed a real one.

Table 5.3 Environment Profile #1

Profile Question	Answer
Attacker location	United States
Significant world events	U.S. general election in two weeks
Significant associations	Embedded within hacker community
Significant action group associations	Several online hacktivism groups
Additional resource from environment	None

Influences on Attack Inhibitors Through Variables in Environment Profile #1

Utilizing the theory presented thus far, we can make the following deductions in regard to the adversaries' attack inhibitors, given the variables presented in Tables 5.2 and 5.3.

Perceived Probability of Detection Given Attempt—P (D/A)

The adversaries' perceived probability of detection given attempt is likely to be elevated given the owner variable of the attack target property (the British government). The perceived probability of detection is raised further given the objective of many hacktivism groups, which often involves publicly announcing the fact that they have successfully attacked a target such as the U.K. E-vote system. Such an announcement would obviously be endemic of the attack's detection.

Perceived Consequences of Attribution Given Detection—C (A/D)

Although the perceived consequences of attribution given detection will be elevated by the owner variable of the attack target property, if located in the United States, the adversaries' level of awareness of the laws in the United Kingdom that govern the consequences of attribution if the adversaries attack, will be detected.

Perceived Consequences of Failure—C/F

Cyber adversaries who are members of hacktivism groups often fear failure more than detection. This is often the case because of the adversarial perception that failing to achieve an attack objective means failing the action group to which they belong. To this end, an adversary who is a member of such an action group will infrequently engage in an attack objective in which they fear they could fail. This relates to the adversary's perceived probability of success.

Influences on Attack Drivers Through Variables in Environment Profile #1

The following observations can be made in regard to our third adversaries attack drivers (motivators).

Target Property: Owner-Influenced Drivers

The attack target, an online voting system operated and developed by the U.K. government, serves as an attack driver because of its high-profile nature. If defaced, the Web site operating such an Internet voting system would be viewed by potentially hundreds of thousands of visitors—something that would appeal to many hacktavist groups, who seek as much public exposure as possible—hence acting as an attack driver or motivator.

Environment Property: Significant Events-Influenced Drivers

For a hacktivist group whose aim is to persuade the public that we are not ready to engage in Internet voting due to security concerns, the occurrence of a general election utilizing an Internet voting system in their own country of residence (the United States) is likely to motivate the group because it will provide further justification that "something needs to be done" regarding the use of Internet voting systems for such critical events. It is noteworthy that such a hacktavist group located in the United States is unlikely to be motivated further by the Internet voting system pertaining to the British general election, since their motivation is drawn from a belief that *all* Internet election voting systems are bad.

Environment Property: Group Association Drivers

The action (hacktivist) group to which the adversary belongs is likely to be the source of the adversary's primary motivator (driver). This is likely to be true for a number of reasons:

1. Cyber adversary action groups such as hacktivist groups often consist of many members, all of whom see one another as peers. Because of the often highly political causes such groups support, there is often a great deal of pressure on individual group members to succeed and to impress their peers within the action group (true peer pressure!).

2. Many action groups often feed their members propaganda in support of the action group's cause. Such propaganda often justifies adversarial acts in the minds of group members, motivating them even further.

Table 5.4 displays a projected set of environment property variables of a typical group of British hacktivists who may be motivated to target the "UK E-Vote" system.

Table 5.4 Environment Profile #2

Profile Question	Answer
Attacker location	Great Britain
Significant world events	U.K. general elections in one year
Significant associations	Embedded within hacker community
Significant action group associations	Several online hacktivist groups
Additional resource from environment	None

Perceived Probability of Detection Given Attempt—P (D/A)

As with the previous environment property set, the adversary's perceived probability of detection is likely to be elevated given the owner variable of the attack target property (the British government). Again, as in the previous environment set, the perceived probability of detection is raised further given the objective of many hacktivist groups, which often involves publicly announcing their activities—for instance, that they have successfully attacked a target such as the U.K.

E-vote system. Such an announcement would obviously be endemic of the attack's detection.

Perceived Consequences of Attribution Given Detection—C (A/D)

In Chapter 2 we discussed the influences an adversary's environment can have on the adversary's perceived consequences of attribution given detection due to the legal variables associated with the adversary's location. Due to the location of the adversary in environment property profile #2 (shown in Table 5.4), there is a strong chance that the adversary will be aware of at least some of the laws that govern the consequences of attribution given detection when engaging a target owned by the government of the country in which he or she resides. To this end, the perceived consequences of attribution given detection are likely to be elevated above those of an adversary with the environment property variables displayed in Table 5.3.

Perceived Consequences of Failure—C/F

As with the previous environment profile, an adversary who is a member of an action group (such as a hacktivist group) will infrequently engage in an attack objective in which they fear they may fail. This relates to the adversary's perceived probability of success.

Influences on Attack Drivers Through Variables in Environment Profile #2

The following are additional observations regarding the third adversarial attack driver (motivators). Note the number of the drivers as a result in a change of the location variable (within the attacker property).

Target Property: Owner-Influenced Drivers

The attack target, an online voting system operated and developed by the government in power within the country in which the adversary resides, serves as a significant attack driver due to its high-profile nature. This is especially true if the action group (hacktivist group) is orientated around U.K.-specific causes.

Environment Property: Significant Events-Influenced Drivers

For a hacktivist group whose aim is to persuade the public that we are not ready to engage in Internet voting due to security concerns, the occurrence of a general election utilizing an Internet voting system in the United States is likely to motivate the group further because it will provide further justification that "something needs to be done." A significant event in the environment of the adversary (in this case, their country of residence) such as an Internet-based general election occurring in the country in which the adversary resides would provide the perfect opportunity for such a group to convey their message.

Environment Property: Group Association Drivers

The action (hacktivist) group to which the adversary belongs is likely to be the source of the adversary's primary motivator (driver). This is likely to be true for a number of reasons:

1. If the hacktivist group to which our adversary in this profile belongs is oriented primarily around U.K. causes, an event such as an Internet-based general election and the opportunity to disrupt it would be of enough significance to result in considerable pressure on the adversary to take full advantage of the opportunity in support of the group's cause.

2. The adversaries involved may, due to their location (in the United Kingdom) and through a sense of patriotism, believe that they are helping their country by demonstrating a flaw in something as critical as an Internet-based general election voting system—hence justifying an adversarial act and providing additional attack drivers (motivators).

Table 5.5 displays a projected set of environment property variables for adversary of sorts who may threaten the security of the "UK E-Vote" system.

Table 5.5 Environment Profile #3

Profile Query	Answer
Attacker location	St. Petersburg, Russia
Significant world events	Approached by U.K. business
Significant associations	Several U.K.-based businesses
Significant action group associations	None
Additional resource from environment	Finance, if objective met

---

NOTE

The third adversary environment profile we will look at represents an adversary who, although having no links to hacktivist or other action groups, is associated with several U.K. businesses that stands to benefit from the results of the general election falling in one direction rather than another. We postulate that such an adversary may be paid by one of the businesses he or she is associated with to cause the election results to fall in a preferred direction.

Perceived Probability of Detection Given Attempt—P (D/A)

The perceived probability of detection of the adversary whose environment properties include the variables in profile #3 (outlined in Table 5.5) will be significantly less than those of the hacktivist group adversaries.

The reason for a significantly reduced perceived probability of detection given attempt is that it is in the interests of many hacktivism groups for their activities be detected and published in the media. In fact, if detection of such activities did not occur, many such hacktivist attacks would be in vain. This is not true for the adversary whose environment properties are presented in this example. Typically, such an adversary would take extreme measures to prevent detection from occurring, for the reasons explained in the section pertaining to the adversaries consequences of failure.

Perceived Consequences of Attribution Given Detection—C (A/D)

Due to the location variable of the adversary's environment property and the location of the target, the perceived consequences of attribution given detection will be far less than that of the adversary with the adversary environment variables shown in Table 5.4. This is due to the amount of physical separation between adversary and target and the laws (or lack thereof) governing the adversaries' country of residence. As we mentioned earlier, when considering the risks associated with an attack, cyber adversaries frequently refer to bygone attacks by other adversaries where detection and attribution has occurred. In the case of our adversary (whose environment variables are displayed in Table 5.5) who could consider the cases of other Russian adversaries who have been detected and attributed in similar attacks, he or she may worry far less about attribution since in almost every known case of a Russian adversary being detected and attributed, the adversary escaped with few consequences of attribution.

> **NOTE**
>
> Many of the cases in which Russian cyber adversaries have been detected, attributed, and forced to face the consequences of detection involved their extradition to the country in which the attack target resided. In many such cases, this was only possible when the adversary could be first lured into a friendly nation such as the United Kingdom. Example cases include those of Oleg Zezov and Vladimir Levin.

Perceived Consequences of Failure—C/F

In the context of the adversary whose environment property variables are displayed in Table 5.5, failure may come in one of two forms:

- **Detection occurs** If detected, the objective of manipulating data on the attack target to fix the results of the UK E-vote would almost certainly be thwarted.

- **The target cannot be penetrated** In this instance, the adversary does not possess sufficient resources (technical or otherwise) to achieve the objective of manipulating data on the attack to fix the results of the U.K. E-vote.

In either case, a consequence of the failure to achieve an attack objective would be that the adversary would not receive the financial resources from his or her environment (in this case, probably from the sponsoring business on whose instructions the adversary is acting). Due to the high amount of resources the adversary may be forced into investing to ensure success (such as ensuring that detection does not occur), if objective failure occurs, the adversary will almost certainly be left with fewer resources than those which he or she possessed before engaging the attack target.

Influences on Attack Drivers Through Variables in Environment Profile #3

The following observations are a continuation of the discussion regarding the "motivators" attack driver. Note how many of the drivers, significant in previous examples are now of far less significance due to the introduction of a resource driver (motivator) in the form of finance.

Target Property: Owner-Influenced Drivers

In the case of the adversary whose environment variable values are displayed in Table 5.5, there is no data to support the adversary being motivated by the owner variable of target property.

Environment Property: Significant Events-Influenced Drivers

Again, unlike the hacktivist group, which is drawn to the target because of its significance in the context of the cause it supports, the adversary whose environment variable values are displayed in Table 5.5. is unlikely to be concerned with the upcoming U.S. or U.K, general elections. He or she is, however, likely to be influenced by the approach of a U.K.-based company.

Environment Property: Group Association Drivers

In the context of the adversary's objective, the cyber adversary is a lone actor and is therefore not motivated further by any associations he or she might have.

Case Study Conclusions

When we begun this exercise, we asked ourselves two questions. First, we asked whether the concerns that a single adversary or group of adversaries might attack the fictional U.K. E-vote system were well founded. To answer this question, let's take a look at the three adversary profiles side by side, scoring the discussed attack variables in accordance with the deductions in this chapter.

Table 5.6 displays the three adversary profiles side by side, accompanied by scores attached to the deductions made so far. First, let's take a look at the two hacktivist profiles. When considering the inhibitors (or deterrents) associated with the attack targets presented and the payoff if the attacks were to succeed, we are able to characterize that of the two hacktivist profiles, the first profile (Table 5.3) is the more attractive, given the reduced consequence of attribution. If we now consider the risks associated with the more attractive of the two hacktivist profiles, it is apparent that even the more attractive profile carries a high level of risk for a payoff given success that could perhaps be achieved under less risky conditions. In Chapter 2 we alluded to ways that adversaries can utilize increased levels of resource to reduce adverse attack inhibitors such as the consequences of attribution given detection; but unfortunately for the hacktivists, there is data present to suggest that the adversary possesses the kind of resource required to reduce the consequences of attribution, given the observable variables within their environment property.

Table 5.6 U.K. E-Vote Adversary Attack Profile Comparison

Environment Profile #	Probability of Detection	Consequences of Attribution	Probability of Success	Resource Weight	Payoff Given Success
1	0.9	0.6	0.5	0.2	Exposure
2	0.9	0.7	0.5	0.2	Exposure
3	0.9	0.3	0.5	0.2	Financial

Although the adversaries in both hacktivist examples may well possess the technical resources required to achieve the attack objective, the attack inhibitors associated with the attack target create conditions such that the adversaries whose environment property variables are displayed in Tables 5.3 and 5.4 are highly unlikely to go through with such an attack.

Of the three adversary profiles examined, the third (whose environment property variables are in Table 5.5) has an attack profile that is considerably more attractive than the previous two (see Table 5.6). The consequence of attribution is low and the payoff given success is high, making for a highly attractive attack, as long as the adversary can ensure success.

So to answer the first of the two questions: Both hacktivist adversaries in environment profiles #1 and #2 are simply unrealistic. Without additional resources or sufficient motivation to cause the attack inhibitors to be less a concern, the risks associated with the attack are so adverse that they would be found to be unacceptable by the adversary.

Let's now take a look at answering the final question: What will the attacker property consist of for adversaries who have been determined to present a real threat?

When examining the inhibitors associated with the third adversary profile, we determined that for the adversary to succeed in his or her objective, detection must not occur. Although we found that the third adversary profile presents the most real threat against the target given in this scenario, you will notice that an adverse condition remains: the adversary's perceived probability of detection. Since such a condition could lead to an adversary determining that the inhibitors associated with the attack are too adverse, making the attack less attractive, we must examine the ways that the adversary could offset the remaining adverse attack inhibitor to create a more acceptable attack.

Table 5.7 displays the variant weight of resources the adversary in our third environment profile could invest in the attack to offset the remaining adverse attack inhibitor—the perceived probability of detection.

Table 5.7 U.K. E-Vote Adversary Attack Profile Comparison

Profile #	Probability of Detection	Consequences of Attribution	Probability of Success	Resource Weight	Payoff Given Success	Resource Expenditure to Acquisition Ratio
1	0.9	0.3	0.5	0.2	Exposure	N/A
2	0.9	0.7	0.5	0.2	Exposure	N/A
3	0.9	0.2	0.2	0.2	Financial	0:2
3	0.5	0.2	0.4	0.4	Financial	0:1
3	0.2	0.2	0.7	0.9	Financial	1:1

The increased resource invested may include the use of intrusion detection systems (IDS) evading attack techniques or other attack techniques that create less attack noise but are less time efficient (time being a resource). An additional column has been added to represent the adversary's perceived value of outgoing resources in relation to the resources acquired if the attack is successful. In the first instance, the adversary invests few resources, and although the resource expenditure to resource acquisition ratio is highly attractive, the risks associated with the attack remain highly adverse. In the second instance, the resource expenditure is heightened, reducing the probability of detection but also reducing the resource expenditure to acquisition ratio.

In the final instance, the resources used are increased further, reducing the probability of detection considerably but leaving the resource expenditure to acquisition ratio at 1:1—in other words, in the adversaries' eyes, if successful they would be left with an equivalent resource to that which they exhausted through ensuring that the attack is a success.

Table 5.8 displays the three attack scenarios, each with a variant level of resource consumption and probability of detection, listed in the order of preference. It should be noted that although in the initial attack scenario, where the resource expenditure to resource acquisition ratio was at its most preferential, the high probability of detection would make the attack far less unattractive than that with a lower probability of detection and slightly reduced payoff given success.

Table 5.8 U.K. E-Vote Adversary Attack Comparison

Preference #	P(D)	C (A/D)	P(S/A)	Resource Weight	Payoff Given Success	Resource Expenditure to Acquisition Ratio
1	0.5	0.2	0.4	0.4	Financial	0:1
2	0.9	0.2	0.2	0.2	Financial	0:2
3	0.2	0.2	0.7	0.9	Financial	1:1

Summary

The example scenario presented in this chapter demonstrates both how we are able to learn where the real threats to our assets lay and why those threats are very real and not just conjecture or management paranoia. The security and information risk management departments of many large organizations often fail to consider not only the realism of the threats they believe put their business in most jeopardy but the reasons those threats pose such a threat and the ways we can tailor security measures to deter these specific threats. If you are responsible for the management of any kind of asset that is on some level a potential target to a cyber adversary, you are encouraged to think long and hard about who you really believe your adversary is. Based on what you have learned so far, consider why he or she is your adversary and the ways that you can make adversaries' attack as unattractive as possible.

Whatever your role, whether you are responsible for the security posture of an entire organization or a systems administrator fighting from the cyber war trenches; the next time you consider the steps you must take to improve the security of your organization, do not think firewall, do not think application proxy, and do not think source code audit. Sit down with an analog pen and paper and think long and hard about your "attack soup"—who wants to eat it; why they want it, how they're going to get it, and finally, how you can put some flies in it. Remember that one person's flies are the next person's croutons!

## Chapter 6

Bringing It All Together: Completing the Cyber Adversary Model

Topics in this Chapter:

- **Intermetric Component Relationships**

Introduction

Over the last five chapters, we've learned about the adversary model that forms the basis of our characterizations, as well as the component properties of the adversary model and the variables associated with those properties. We examined some of the measures (or metrics) we can utilize to determine the values of certain adversary variables given a set of observable data, such as the data pertaining to an attack or data regarding a potential target for which we are attempting to characterize the threat.

This chapter serves to detail the remaining theory covered by this book, introducing some principles that augment some of the previously documented theories.

Intermetric Component Relationships

As we have seen, when performing the characterization of a cyber adversary, it is often the case that insufficient data is available to satisfy many of the metrics that have been introduced. This situation was exemplified in Chapter 4, where we alluded to several caveats of attack tool and attack technique scoring metrics that stem from a lack of data relating to an attack technique or the specifics of a tool.

Filling in the Blanks

We hypothesize that through an understanding of the variables that impact the result of an attack metric, such as the score given to a specific attack technique, just as we can make determinations about an adversary's resources, attack inhibitors with data pertaining to an adversary's environment property (see Chapter 2), we can also project the most likely values of unknown variables in the same or neighboring adversary objects. Figure 6.1 demonstrates a characterization metric with unsatisfied data inputs.

Figure 6.1 An Unsatisfied Characterization Metric!

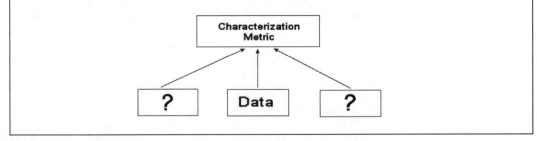

To examine how we can do this, let's use one of the Chapter 4 attack tool caveats as the basis for our example. In Chapter 4, we alluded to a situation in which we are required to characterize an adversary utilizing an attack tool for which we are unaware of the origins, but we are able to observe other variables of the tool, such as its payload.

Our aim is to be in a position where we can predict the likely values of attack tool variables that are unavailable to us, such as the probable distribution level of the attack tool. Figure 6.2 displays such a scenario, where an attempt to utilize the attack tool characterization metric (described in Chapter 4) is being made. As you can see, only one out of three data pieces of the puzzle are available, leaving us with the task of predicting one, the attack tool's distribution levels, and two, any nontechnical perquisites required to leverage the attack tool.

Figure 6.2 Attack Tool Metric Missing Inputs

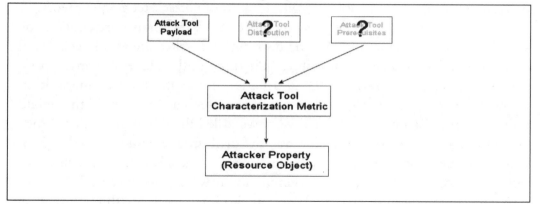

NOTE

Although the number of possible scenarios is almost indefinite and the way that this problem is approached will differ slightly from case to case, using a thorough understanding of the interaction between characterization metrics, determining the appropriate methodology for retrieving the data required should be fairly intuitive.

In the case presented in Figure 6.2, we begin our characterization of the attack tool with the data available to us (i.e. the attack tool payload). Let's begin by looking at projecting the most probable value of the "attack tool prerequisites" variable within our attack tool characterization metric. As we mentioned in Chapter 4, the technique utilized in an attack is often endemic of the attack tools used; by the same token, the attack tool prerequisites will also (more often than not) be endemic of the attack technique used. For these reasons and the fact that attack techniques can, at least in part, be characterized by a tool implementing the respective technique, we are able to glean at the very least a partially accurate idea of the prerequisites of an attack tool. Some more obvious examples include if an attack tool with unknown distribution and prerequisites payload resulted in a user's privileges being escalated to an Administrator user, it would in most cases be fair to say that a prerequisite of the tool utilized was the initial possession of a local user account.

Next up comes the distribution of the attack tool. As we learned in Chapter 4, the distribution of an attack tool is a useful thing to know because it allows us to glean insight into the cyber adversary's capability. As with the nontechnical prerequisites of the attack tool, we again look to our attack technique theory, introduced in Chapter 4, to help us out. Since attack techniques are endemic of specific attack tools, by examining the distribution level of the attack technique implemented by the attack tool—observable through the observable attack payload—we are able to determine the distribution of the attack technique, at least to the extent of whether the implemented attack technique is within the public domain or not. Chapter 3 examined what we called the disclosure pyramid (or cyber food chain); we alluded to the way the disclosure pyramid can be used to make determinations, including those pertaining to the adversary's capability, from their positioning within the pyramid. Just as we can assess capability through positioning in the pyramid, we can also infer capability through the attack technique, inferred from the attack payload, thereby deterring the probable location of the adversary within the disclosure pyramid. As indicated in Chapter 3, the position of the adversary in the disclosure pyramid also acts as a measure of the relative level of distribution of a vulnerability—in other words, distribution increases as the position in the pyramid is lowered.

You might have noticed that one of the attack tool variables established in Chapter 4 has yet to be mentioned—the attack tool's ease of use. This is intentional because the ease of use of an attack tool is not commonly linked to any other attack tool or, for that matter, other adversary variables and therefore cannot be enumerated. To summarize, the ease with which an attack tool is used is not easily enumerated without access to the tool itself.

Table 6.1 details the relationships between tool and technique metric variables.

Table 6.1 Attack Tool to Attack Technique Metric Variable Relationships

Variable	Metric	Relationship	Relation Metric
Ease of use	Attack tool	None	N/A
Distribution level	Attack tool	Pyramid metric	Attack technique
Prerequisites	Attack tool	Attack tool payload	Attack technique

Table 6.2 details the relationships between attack technique and attack tool characterization metrics. Just as we are able to infer the values of unobservable attack tool variables, we are also able to infer the values of attack technique variables.

Table 6.2 Attack Technique to Attack Tool Metric Variable Relationships

Variable	Metric	Relationship	Relation Metric
Ease of Implementation	Attack technique	Attack tool payload	Attack tool
Distribution level	Attack technique	Distribution level	Attack tool
Nontech resources	Attack technique	Prerequisites	Attack tool
Inhibitor reductions	Attack technique	Prerequisites	Attack tool

Internet Metric Relationship Result Reliability Calculations

When performing a characterization of an adversary with an amount of observable data that requires us to attempt to predict the most likely values of unknown variables, it is helpful to be able to assess how accurate our conjecture is.

By analyzing the data inputs used for the characterization of a cyber adversary, we are able to score the quality of a characterization by assessing which of the utilized metric input variables have a proven relationship with other, unknown variables, thereby corroborating one another in cases where the results of their respective metrics "agree."

Figure 6.3 demonstrates how we can establish the accuracy of a characterization by examining the relationships between utilized variables. Note that a score of 1 is given to a variable where it results in the corroboration of another variable. Such a score would occur if the attack tool payload variable was populated to determine the unknown attack technique—ease of implementation variable. A score of 2 is given where an attack variable corroborates two or more other variables, used in the same or neighboring metrics. This would be the case if the *attack tool prerequisites* variable were used to determine both the *attack technique— nontechnical resources required* and *attack technique—inhibitor reductions* variables. Obviously, the more known (observable) variables that have known relationships with other known (observable) variables, the higher the score and an increased characterization accuracy.

Figure 6.3 Characterization Scoring Matrix

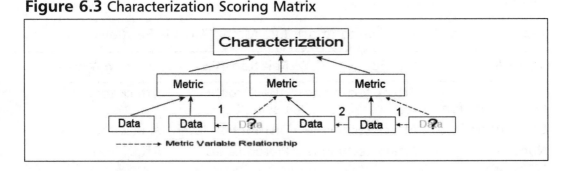

Figure 6.4 demonstrates the example given in Figure 6.2 where the only available input data to the attack tool characterization metric (introduced in Chapter 4) is the attack payload. Although the score for this particular characterization is only 3, based on the metrics displayed, it should be noted that additional metrics would typically be used in a characterization and that the sole purpose of the diagram is to demonstrate the way the scoring system would be used in a real characterization.

Figure 6.4 Characterization Scoring Matrix Based on Figure 6.2

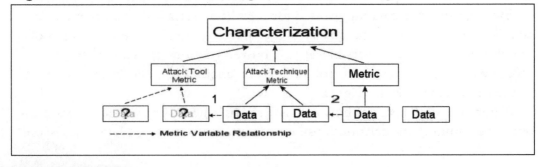

Summary

Adversary characterization methodologies and metrics provide us with a firm basis to begin to answer some of the questions that we put to ourselves early on in this book. These questions included, What is our adversary's capability? What is our adversary's motivation? And, perhaps most importantly, how do we really know that someone is our adversary?

Whether the adversarial data being considered relates to the use of social engineering, insider access to your organization, or an unpublished vulnerability that an adversary possesses, the principles, methodologies, and metrics that we have established apply across the board. The next four chapters examine the realities of dealing with some very real threats, including insiders within large organizations, what the mass media chooses to refer to as cyber terrorists, and the ways that these specific threats can be detected and managed. The amount of data pertaining to an adversary has no bounds, but the principles remain the same. As you read through the remaining chapters, consider what you have learned thus far; consider how what you are reading about fits into the adversary model and how it applies to you and your organization. If you are reading about insiders, consider how their additional resource—their elevated level of initial access to an organization—influences the adversary's perception of the risks attached to an attack as was described in Chapter 5, and how it can make an attack more attractive to the adversary.

## Chapter 7

WarmTouch: Assessing the Insider Threat and Relationship Management

Chapter Contributed by Eric Shaw and Ed Stroz

Topics in this Chapter:

- **The Challenges of Detecting the Insider Threat**
- **Case Illustrations**

Introduction

Columnist Jay Heiser recently drew the attention of the information security community to the need to better understand and incorporate "Layer 8—the human layer" of the Open Source Interconnection (OSI) Reference Model into security thinking. According to Heiser, "The new and exciting infosecurity challenges don't require coders—they require behavioral specialists (Heiser, 2004)." For several years now, we have found that the best approach to security thinking in general, and especially, the assessment and management of a range of cyber attacks includes a broad repertoire of technical, security, legal, organizational, and behavioral science expertise. For example, whereas many cyber adversaries confine their attacks to code, others accompany their messages with verbal communications. These messages often play a vital role in efforts to obtain revenge, commit extortion, instill fear, or impress or coerce their targets. Others enjoy including political statements, justifications or other messages along with their attacks. This chapter describes a behavioral science tool we use to assess the verbal communications that often accompany these activities, including insider acts, anonymous threats, hacker extortion, cyber stalking, and other forms of cyber attacks.

The Challenges of Detecting the Insider Threat

Insiders remain one of the most potentially dangerous and difficult-to-detect threats to the integrity of U.S. government and corporate institutions. In the national security context, the individual insider's access to systems, information, resources and personnel make him, or her, a potentially disastrous force multiplier. Insiders can steal vital secrets, damage critical infrastructure, injure staff, or even turn vital assets directly against his or her country. In the corporate context, insider espionage and sabotage have become a major source of significant business losses (Computer Security Institute, 1997). In both government and corporate settings, disgruntled and disturbed insiders have also assaulted and killed hundreds of fellow employees.

Within the last three decades, opportunities for insider activity have grown, and the difficulty of detecting insider risk has increased. For example, the dispersion of computerized information systems throughout our institutions and society has made once centrally located and controlled information more widely available. But, it has also created proportional vulnerabilities and opportunities for damage. At the same time, the migration of daily business, legal, and personal communications from face-to-face and telephone to online formats has made it more difficult to detect the emotions, attitudes, and intentions of those communicating—important visual and auditory cues are no longer present. This relative decrease in the amount of personal contact between coworkers has made it harder to detect indicators of risk posed by angry, disgruntled, or otherwise threatening individuals. In the workplace, identifying employees who are at-risk for damaging the interest of their organization through espionage, sabotage, theft, assault, or other acts has become more difficult. The growing use of emotion icons in e-mail represents evidence of this problem and a crude, initial effort to restore this lost information.

In the national security context, some of the best available information on individuals who commit espionage comes from a series of in-depth interviews with convicted traitors conducted by the federal government during the 1970s and '80s, referred to as Project Slammer. According to the results of this research, significant symptoms of emotional distress are a detectable side effect of the process of committing espionage. Without exception, the 40 Slammer subjects studied felt dissatisfied with their circumstances, and the majority identified a significant situational stressor present at the time of their decision to spy. Approximately one-third of the subjects described indicators of personal turmoil, which were ignored or dismissed by peers and supervisors. These indicators were not subtle. They included symptoms of extreme anxiety, alcohol intoxication, frequent arguments, hostile comments regarding U.S. foreign policy, undisguised extramarital affairs, conflict with supervisors, inappropriate sexual comments, and acts of sexual harassment. According to Project Slammer, supervisors and fellow employees either ignored or rationalized these signs of disaffection for many reasons. Even when the changes were detected, these coworkers and supervisors often chose not to intervene or intervened in ineffective ways. In Chapter 8, a similar pattern of warning signs are described in the corporate context with insiders who subsequently commit violations utilizing IT resources. This group displayed signs of disgruntlement or distress an average of 11 months prior to the attack. However, these warning signs were not detected, not taken seriously enough, or not well managed.

If such indicators of risk of espionage were difficult to detect and manage in the largely face-to-face work environment prior to the dispersion of computerized information systems, they have become even more difficult to discover now. Although there have been many technical solutions offered to assist investigators in discovering individuals at-risk, they have produced as many problems as solutions. For a recent example, counter-intelligence staff at a U.S. research facility using e-mail security monitoring software detected over a thousand violations of bans on e-mail to restricted countries such as Iran, Iraq, China, North Korea, Libya, and other locations. The sheer number of indicators left these investigators struggling to find a way to prioritize their resources according to risk. They noted that an approach that would allow them to identify disgruntled individuals—people who were violating the guidelines but might also be motivated to do harm—would be a significant contribution and would help them prioritize their efforts.

Clearly there is a need for improved detection and reporting of the risk of such acts. According to recent research featured in this text, many of these acts are preceded or accompanied by corresponding changes in psychological states, attitudes, and behavior. A system that would increase the likelihood of detection and improve the chances that the signs are not underestimated by supervisors or peers would create a real opportunity to reduce the frequency of these and many other damaging acts.

An Approach to the Insider Problem

We have recently produced and are currently testing computer software designed to detect changes in the emotional state and attitudes of individuals from their online communications, indicative of the emotions and attitudes associated with disgruntlement and risk of dangerous behaviors. This patent-pending system, called WarmTouch, is constructed to do the following:

- Collect and analyze computer-generated and transmitted communications.

- Utilize psychological profiling algorithms to evaluate the psychological state of the author with special emphasis on detection of psychological states associated with threatening behaviors.

- Use keyword algorithms to provide information on specific possible behaviors or actions the author might take relevant to this threatening psychological state.

- Use communication-characteristic algorithms to assess possible targets of these potential threatening actions or behaviors.

- Identify changes in the psychological state of an author from computerized communications that indicate an increased risk of potentially damaging actions.

- Be programmed to draw the attention of qualified professionals and authorities to these detected changes in order to more fully evaluate risk potential, thereby increasing the ability of authorities to identify at-risk individuals from large quantities of potentially monitored computer-generated communications.

- Be flexibly programmed to generate specific types of alerts or warnings and analysis depending on user requirements, including recommendations for user actions.

The psychological algorithms incorporated in the system were derived from psychological content analysis methods used in academic research, intelligence, and forensic profiling (Shaw, 2003; Shaw, 2001; Shaw et. al. 1999).

Case Illustrations

This chapter describes several case applications of this tool, including scenarios on insider detection and management and the identification and management of anonymous online and other threats, as well as the tool's use with the management of more routine computer-mediated relationships.

Case 1: Detecting Insider Risk and Deception—A Bank Systems Administrator

Several years ago, a New York bank woke up to find its accounting computers sabotaged. The destruction was so finely designed that every effort to revive the destroyed data was met with a technical obstacle that simply stated, "I'm smarter than you and got here first." Clearly this was the work of an insider, intimately familiar with the system. Days before the destruction, the contract SysAdmin who had designed, installed, and worked with the accounting department on the system for the last 20 months, earning over $500,000 in the process, had quit. Although he had been a model employee for the last two months prior to his departure, the three preceding months had been filled with acrimony. A new supervisor, viewing his overtime costs, noting his refusal to answer to IT management because of his close relationship with the accounting department, had decided it was time for a change.

But her efforts to get this employee to keep colleagues up-to-speed or to document system code were met with angry refusals. According to the FBI agent investigating this case, as the conflict mounted, the subject decided it was time to resign and leave the bank a destructive goodbye note. The investigator believes the subject used the three month period between his resignation and departure to design the elaborate sabotage of the system, while feigning loyalty to cover his efforts.

Having acquired copies of the e-mails between the subject and his supervisor, we wanted to find out if WarmTouch could detect the deterioration in their relationship and the deception campaign the employee used to cover his sabotage.

Figure 7.1 displays simple measures of threat risk associated with disgruntlement derived from actual perpetrator e-mail with his supervisor around three months prior to an attack. The risk assessment utilizes no formula for "normal" or "appropriate" psychological state or attitudes. The subject's scores on measures indicative of psychological states are compared only to his or her own preceding mean scores. A significant change can signal a need for increased attention. Figure 7.1 displays measures for several sample psycholinguistic variables for the specific hostile message being considered on April 10th (the bar on the left) and compares it to mean levels of these indicators in his previous communications with his supervisor. At the figure indicates, these values are more than double this subject's mean scores (the bar on the right), indicating a need for concern.

Figure 7.1 Psycholinguistic Threat Measures: Mean Scores vs. Recent E-mail Four Months Prior to Attack

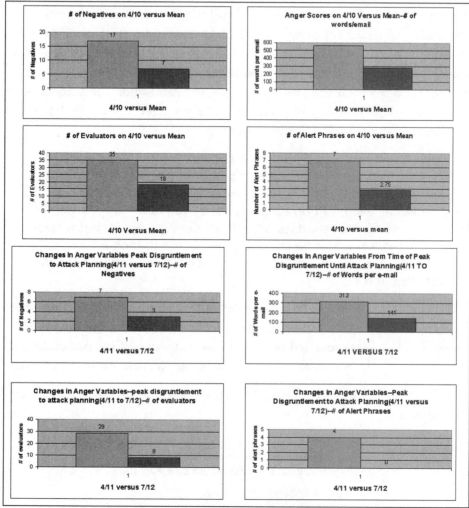

For example, one message to his supervisor in the midst of their conflict included:

> "Until you fire me or I quit, I have to take orders from you. I'll sit with him after I've written some procedures on what he can do. Just like he cannot have LAN supervisor password until he is a trained LAN expert, I won't give him Sybase ROOT access until he has been trained to be of some minimal use. If you order me to give him root access, then you have to permanently relieve me of

any duties on that machine. I can't be a garbage cleaner if someone screws up."

The availability of this data would leave little doubt of the importance of this change in the subject's emotional state. In addition, independent security access to this information would have overcome the frequent problem of supervisor reluctance to report concerns to personnel or security staff.

Figure 7.2 deals with the same case at a later date when the subject deceived his supervisor with charming pleasantries as he prepared his attack. For example, one of these messages included the following:

"Hello, 'Jane'. I would be honored to work until the last week of July, but unfortunately I have a prior commitment which I cannot delay for an additional two-week extension. You can always call me or page me, even if I don't work here... I can look into the possibility of working a few days on and off during August, but a two-week extension won't be enough time for me to look into everything for such a critical and complex system...Thanks for all your trust in me."

Like his supervisor, normal e-mail screening measures would also have been deceived by his cover story. However, the specialized measures used in Figure 7.2 (Psychological Distance) revealed the continued existence of intense underlying hostility, indicating the presence of deception in his pleasant, overt communications.

Figure 7.2 Continued Covert Hostility: Psychological Distance over Time Prior to 8/10 Attack

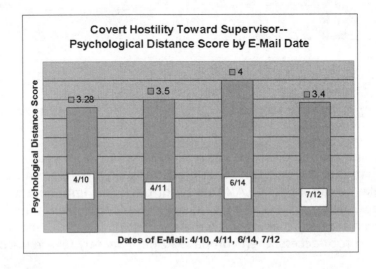

Figure 7.3 demonstrates the persistence of covert hostility as overt hostility diminishes. In this case, we now know that the subject began to actively plan his attack when he stopped sending threatening e-mails and shammed loyalty, an effort at deception that the psycholinguistic measures employed picked up.

Figure 7.3 Psycholinguistic Measurement of Deception: Overt vs. Covert Deception

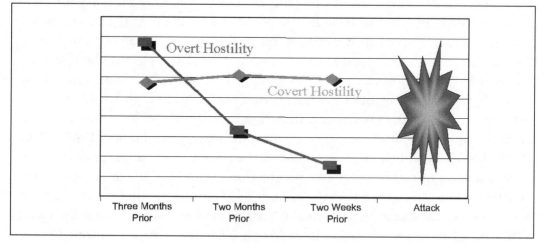

This early test of the software used the communications of a known violator to see if the program could, after the fact, detect changes in his psychological state indicative of risk and penetrate his efforts at hiding his underlying negative attitudes.

Case 2: Robert Hanssen at the FBI

Another, more familiar, example of insider risk is the case of Robert Hanssen, the FBI agent who was arrested in February 2001 for spying for the Soviets. According to the unclassified review of his case published by the Justice Department's Inspector General in 2003 (DOJ, 2003), Hanssen's espionage career spanned three time periods: 1979–1981, 1985–1991, and 1999–2001. Several public reviews of Hanssen's personal and professional life have referred to the emotional stressors that accompanied his spying during this period (for example, see Shannon and Blackman, 2002) and the Inspector General's report also notes his increasing "recklessness" and "self-destructiveness during this period" (DOJ 2003: p. 14). As an additional test of the software, we utilized Hanssen's published communications with his Soviet handlers (Shannon and Blackman, 2002) over the last two periods of his spying to see if the reported levels of anxiety, depression, and general emotional vulnerability reported could be detected across this period in these communications. This involved applying WarmTouch to eight notes written by Hanssen between October 1, 1985 and November 15, 2000[1].

Figures 7.4 through 7.6 display the WarmTouch results for several indicators of Hanssen's emotional state. The measures used for anger were his use of negatives ("no," "not," "never," and so on) and the word "me." The measures for emotional vulnerability—use of feelings, use of the word "I," direct references to others, and use of adverbial intensifiers (terms that exaggerate adverbs, such as "so" in the phrase "I miss you *so* much") were designed to portray the direct, intense communication of emotion to another person. An individual's use of terms that qualify or discount statements (such as "I *think* I'll go" or "I *sort of* want to go") and retract statements (like "but" and "although")—known as retractors and qualifiers—were used to measure anxiety (Weintraub, 1981, 1986, 1989). As Figures 7.4 through 7.6 indicate, there were marked increases in all of these measures of emotional stress over the time period for which there was data available encompassing the last two periods of Hanssen's espionage. For example, contrast these two messages in terms of their emotional content—one from June 1988 and a later communication from March 2000, the year of his arrest. Although neither is bereft of emotional content, Hanssen's depression and fatalism are readily apparent in the second selection.

> "I found the site empty. Possibly I had the time wrong. I work from memory. My recollection was for you to fill before 1:00 a.m. I believe Viktor Degtyar was in the church driveway off Rt. 123, but I did not know how he would react to an approach. My schedule was tight to make this at all. Because of my work, I had to synchronize explanations and flights while not leaving a pattern of absence or travel that could later be correlated with communication times. This is difficult and expensive. I will call the number you gave me on 2/24, 2/26 or 2/28 at 1:00a.m., EDST. Please plan filled signals. Empty sites bother me. I like to know before I commit myself as I'm sure you do also. Let's not use the original site so early at least until the seasons change. Some type of call-out signal to you when I have a package or when I can receive one would be useful. Also, please be specific about dates, e.g. 2/24. Scheduling is not simple for me because of frequent travel and wife. Any ambiguity multiplies the problems. My security concerns may seem excessive. I believe experience has shown them to be necessary. I am much safer if you know little about me. Neither of us are children about

these things. Over time, I can cut your losses rather than become one…P.S. "thank you" was deeply appreciated."

"I have come about as close as I ever want to come to sacrificing myself to help you, and I get silence. I hate silence…Conclusion: One might propose that I am either insanely brave or quite insane. I'd answer neither. I'd say, insanely loyal. Take your pick. There is insanity in all the answers. I have, however, come as close to the edge as I can without being truly insane. My security concerns have proven reality-based. I'd say, pin your hopes on 'insanely loyal' and go for it. Only I can lose. I decided on this course when I was 14 years old. I'd read Philby's book. Now that is insane, eh! My only hesitations were my security concerns under uncertainty. I hate uncertainty. So far I have judged the edge correctly. Give me credit for that. Set the signal at my site any Tuesday evening. I will read your answer. Please, at least say goodbye. It's been a long time my dear friends, a long and lonely time."

Figure 7.4 Changes in Detected Levels of Anger, Emotional Vulnerability, and Anxiety, 1985–2000

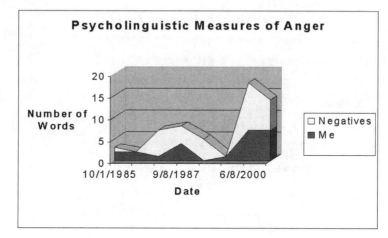

Figure 7.5 Changes in Detected Levels of Emotional Vulnerability, 1985–2000

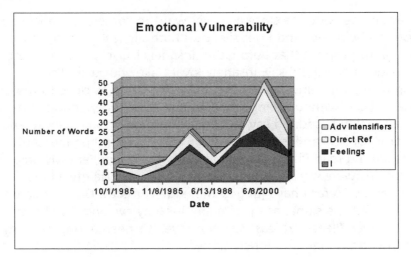

Figure 7.6 Changes in Detected Levels of Anxiety, 1985–2000

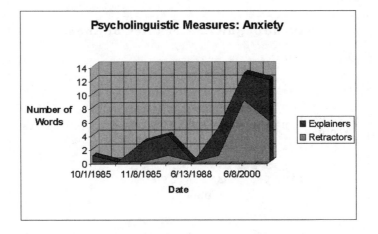

As more employee communications move online, so must means to detect disgruntlement, psychological distress, and deception. As the case of Hanssen illustrated, initial background investigations are not useful to detect employees that become disgruntled while on the job. In addition, disgruntled employees have done considerable damage to organizations and national security before (and after) regular security (even polygraph) updates. The ability to detect changes in employee communications indicative of increased risk of violations, to narrow a field of suspects, or to locate individuals with specific characteristics or vulnerabilities from their online communications could be a valuable assessment tool.

Case 3: Identifying the Source of Anonymous Threats— Are They from the Same Author?

Another frequent profiling challenge involving cyber adversaries is the analysis of anonymous threats. Subjects seeking to extort payments from individuals and companies, terrorize or discredit former colleagues, or seek revenge against organizations often use online channels to pursue their objectives. In addition to assessing the characteristics of these individuals, it is often important to understand whether multiple threat communications are from the same author. This is particularly important if the subject is pretending to send communications from different sources in an effort to magnify the appearance of the threat.

Table 7.1 displays the results of analysis of four anonymous threats sent to an organization in which the author—a suspected insider—threatened to reveal critical client information. The analytical tasks involved determining whether the letters were written by the same author and whether the psycholinguistic characteristics displayed in the notes were consistent with other materials produced by the suspected insider. When the four letters were compared, several consistent patterns were noted indicating one author, including the following:

- The lack of use of personal pronouns ("I," "we," "me")
- The lack of use of negatives and qualifiers
- The unusually high use of direct references and evaluators
- The unusually high use of rhetorical questions

This distinctive pattern left little doubt that the letters were from the same source.

Table 7.1 Scores on Psycholinguistic Variables For Four Anonymous Threat Letters

Threat Date	10/29A	10/29B	11/12A	11/12B	Mean Value
I	0	0	0	0	0
We	0	1	0	0	.25
Explainers	1	0	0	0	.25
Feelings	2	3	1	3	2.25
Me	0	0	0	0	0
Negatives	0	0	0	0	0
Qualifiers	0	0	0	0	0
Retractors	1	2	0	2	1.25
Direct References	9	4	13	14	6.75
Evaluators	17	19	8	13	14.25
Intensifiers	0	5	1	0	1.5
Rhetorical Questions	2	3	2	4	2.75

These distinctive characteristics were then compared to a writing sample from a suspected insider, adding confirming data to support her identification. Data from the system was then utilized to compile a psychological profile of the suspect to assist in the management of her removal from the office and reduce the likelihood of damage to the organization and their clients.

Related applications of WarmTouch with similar e-mail threats have been used to study and then simulate the communication of adversary associates and to design communications, based on profiling results, likely to be most effective with a specific cyber adversary.

Case 4: Extortion Attempt by a Russian Hacker Against Bloomberg Financial

On March 24, 2000, Michael Bloomberg, at that time head, founder, and owner of Bloomberg L.P., a multinational financial communications firm based in New York City, received an unsolicited e-mail from someone identifying himself as "Alex." The e-mail contained an attachment, with a letter from Alex, offering to help Bloomberg "understand some drawbacks of your system." These drawbacks included the claim that the Bloomberg Traveler—a small, portable version of the Bloomberg terminal for sending and receiving financial information and e-mail—was unprotected in terms of its security. Because Bloomberg offers subscribing clients financial reports, analytical software, and a members-only e-mail service through which they can communicate with brokers to trade securities and allows members to store their private financial data on its servers, this security gap was potentially quite significant. In addition, Bloomberg supplies news service to its subscribers and the public worldwide. The subject claimed that he could also place "disinformation" into the Bloomberg news service by entering data under the user name of the editor of this service. He appeared to have access to this editor's user data.

In the e-mail, "Alex" supported this charge by claiming that he had obtained access to all the Traveler's functions and passwords of various Bloomberg employees, including Michael Bloomberg, and was able to send and receive e-mails on behalf of, and in the name of any Bloomberg user. Alex further stated that he could prove his claims with screen shots of this access, and that he was not a "terrorist," but was hoping "…that you'll find my information valuable and kindly propose…adequate payment." While noting that Bloomberg could refuse his help, he closed the letter by stating that "your security and reputation are in your hands."

The tale of FBI, Bloomberg staff, and private security efforts to lure "Alex" (whose real name was Oleg Zezov) from his safe haven in Kazakhstan to a hotel room in London where he was arrested and subsequently extradited to the U.S. reads like a crime novel. On August 10, 2000, Zezov and a traveling companion described as a lawyer named Igor Yarimaka, met with Bloomberg representatives in a hotel room at the Hilton Hotel Park Lane in London. With the Bloomberg staffer in the room were two British police officers—one posing as a security guard and the other working as a translator. Mike Bloomberg joined the group periodically. According to the transcript of the audio and videotape of the meeting, negotiations see-sawed over Zezov's demand for an employment contract prior to revealing the manner in which he penetrated the Bloomberg system. Zezov and his lawyer noted that this contract was needed to protect Zezov from prosecution and also to explain the resulting income to tax authorities in Kazakhstan.

In the course of the negotiations, the law enforcement team got Zezov to admit that he had written the "Alex" e-mails and penetrated the system. Bloomberg refused to give Zezov the employment letter that would have legitimized his attacks and threats. Having accepted the refusal for the employment letter, Yarimaka asked for a verbal contract to cover Zezov's legal exposure and tax liability. This was also refused. The law enforcement team increased the pressure on Zezov to reveal his methods prior to such a contract and Zezov continued to refuse to do so. As the two groups continued to deadlock, the team decided to end the meeting and British police entered the room and arrested the two men.

The team composing the e-mail responses to Alex sought to tempt him with the payment he wanted while getting him to change his reluctance to meet in a location with computer crime statutes or an extradition agreement with the U.S. The team had to monitor Alex's psychological state and be ready to both pressure and mollify him depending on his reaction. He often reacted angrily, threatening to expose the Bloomberg vulnerabilities to the press. At other times he was quite anxious about security guarantees designed to protect his safety and freedom.

Using copies of the e-mails between Alex and Bloomberg, we attempted to determine if WarmTouch could be useful in assessing the levels of anger and anxiety in Zezov as the team attempted to lure him to London.[2] Figure 7.7 displays output directly from the system that groups together the psycholinguistic indicators of anger used across the 20 e-mails sent by Alex. As the figure indicates, Alex's level of anger peaks when things don't go as planned early in the negotiations, but slowly subsides, as he accepts the new plan.

Figure 7.7 WarmTouch Indicators of Anger in Zezov During E-Mail Negotiations

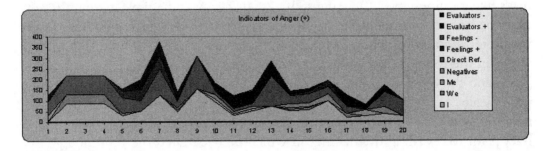

Figure 7.8 displays WarmTouch output for retractors—a primary measure of anxiety, over the same 20 e-mails. In a pattern similar to his anger, Alex's anxiety appeared to peak early but then decline, allowing the Team to "pull him in."

Figure 7.8 WarmTouch Indicators of Anxiety in Alex's E-Mails over Time

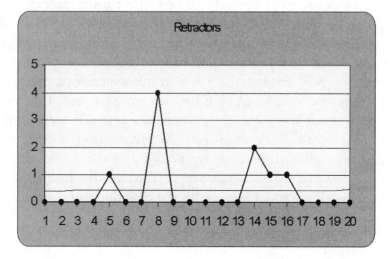

Case 5: Monitoring a Cyber Stalker

Another recent case involving the potential use of WarmTouch for monitoring involved cyber stalking by a former lover and coworker. In this episode, a female employee who refused to restart a relationship with a former lover on his return from overseas was receiving threatening e-mails from an anonymous source. Although the stalker pretended to be of a different race and sex than her former lover, she felt sure the messages were from him. The anger, desperation, depth of felt betrayal, and threatening nature of the communications were of significant concern to the subject and her employer. The military background of the former lover also indicated his ability to make good on his threats. While providing consultation on the case, we also wanted to see if WarmTouch could prove sensitive to the mounting anger the subject was experiencing and especially test the software's capability to predict, after the fact, the subject's move from online to real-world activities. Specifically, just before Valentine's Day, the subject's e-mails grew in length and emotional expressiveness and he also damaged the employee's car.

Figures 7.9 through 7.11 display actual WarmTouch output measures of anger (Figure 7.9) and its components. Figure 7.9 shows the variables we combine to create an overall measure of anger. These measures show a steep increase in value in the subject's e-mail coinciding with his attack on the victim's property at time period 12 (Valentine's Day). Figures 7.10 and 7.11 disaggregate two of these measures. Figure 7.10 displays the number of negatives ("no," "not," "never," and so on), considered one of the most direct measures of anger, that peaked the same day of an attack on her vehicle while it was parked. Figure 7.11 displays the subject's use of the term "me," considered by psychology professionals as a useful, sensitive, measure of victimization, because "me" can only be used as an object of the actions of others. It is very difficult to use "me" in a sentence in which the subject is not passively being acted upon. In our experience, persons who feel extremely angry and victimized by others are among those at greatest risk for antisocial behavior. It was particularly interesting that this measure increased a day prior to the actual attack and before the increase in the other anger measures. This is consistent with recent psychological research (Bushman and Baumeister, 1998) that makes theoretical predictions that feelings of victimization precede and contribute to an increase in the likelihood of aggression.

Figure 7.9 Aggregate Measures of Anger in a Cyber Stalker—17 E-Mails over 2.5-Month Period

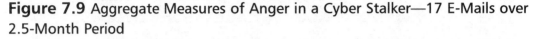
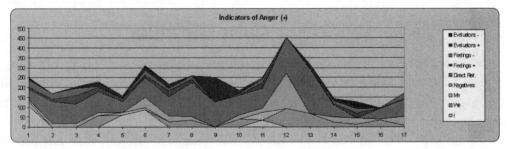

Figure 7.10 Negatives in the E-Mails of a Cyber Stalker

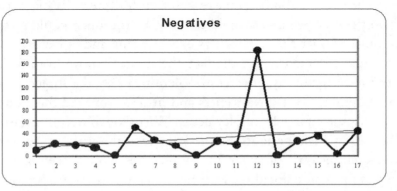

Figure 7.11 Use of "Me" as a Measure of Feelings of Victimization in a Cyber Stalker

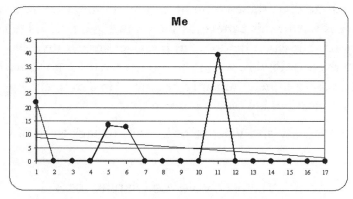

Case 6: Relationship Management

As noted, the shift to online communications has facilitated many forms of relationships, but the loss of visual and verbal clues makes it more difficult to understand the psychology of those with whom we are trying to communicate.

This problem led us to test the feasibility of using WarmTouch's profiling capability to help an individual assess and facilitate his relationships with his superiors, colleagues, and subordinates at work. For this purpose, we asked "Jack," a corporate vice president at a large financial institution, to select three individuals with whom his working relationship was important. He selected his immediate superior, "Bob"; a fellow vice present, "John," with whom he shared a fairly uncooperative and competitive relationship; and "Phyllis," a liaison between him and his customers.

As a first step in our efforts we used WarmTouch to check the emotional tone of the e-mail communications from John, Phyllis, and Bob to Jack. We asked Jack to download these e-mails from a specific time period and asked WarmTouch to tell us the emotional tone of the correspondence by scoring the balance of positive and negative feelings and evaluators (judgments about persons, places, ideas, objects, and so on). We also counted the number of negatives used in these e-mails as a measure of opposition or anger. This produced the graph displayed in Figure 7.12, which charts the distribution of these e-mails by visibility (number of e-mails from each party) and emotional tone of the e-mails, or their valence.

As Figure 7.12 indicates, Jack receives many positive e-mails from his boss, Bob; relatively fewer, less positive e-mails from Phyllis; and he rarely hears from John, but when he does, these communications are negative. Jack's e-mails to his three colleagues mirror this pattern, as shown in Figure 7.13. He communicates rarely with John, but when he does, his messages are negative. He communicates more frequently with Phyllis, whom he reports having a good relationship with, but his e-mails are still predominantly negative. He also rarely "speaks" with Bob, and his communications are barely positive.

Figure 7.12 Visibility and Valence of E-Mails to Jack from Bob, Phyllis, and John

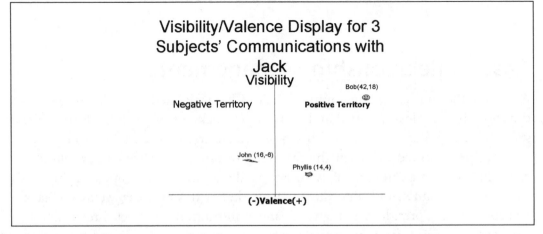

Figure 7.13 Visibility and Valence of Jack's E-Mails to Bob, Phyllis, and John

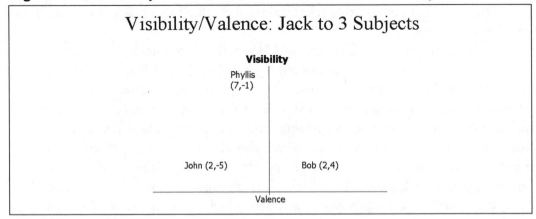

Figure 7.14 summarizes the results of these findings by comparing the relative balance in tone of the e-mails of all four parties. This graph tells us a great deal about Jack's communication and how he can improve it. He needs to increase the frequency and positive content of his communications. After helping Jack understand this problem, we also helped him use WarmTouch to facilitate this change. Before sending e-mails to these three, he ran the content through the system, which told him the balance of negative and positive content, highlighted the words involved, and helped him alter the content accordingly.

Figure 7.14 Comparison of Negative and Positive E-Mail Contents

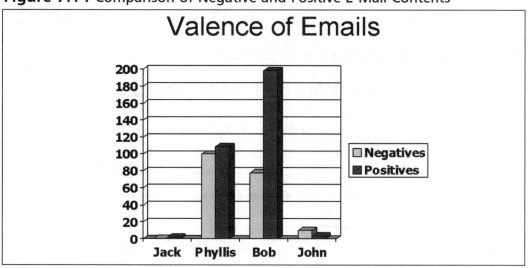

Next, we wanted to see if WarmTouch's profiling capabilities could be of further assistance to Jack. We thought a comparison of some of Jack's characteristics with his colleagues might help him improve his communications. Figures 7.15 through 7.18 display comparative scores for the four employees on several WarmTouch trait "dashboards" covering characteristics such as expressiveness, team player, initiates versus reacts, dogmatic versus flexible, rational versus morale-oriented in decision-making, and sensitivity to the environment. These results told us that Jack has a great deal of common ground with John, and that he is different from Phyllis and Bob in many ways.

Figure 7.15 Dashboard Comparison of Traits

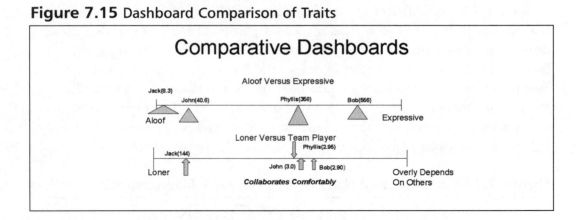

Figure 7.16 Dashboard Comparison of Traits

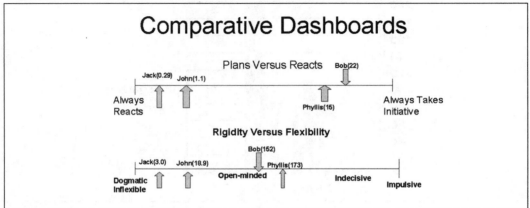

Figure 7.17 Dashboard Trait Comparisons

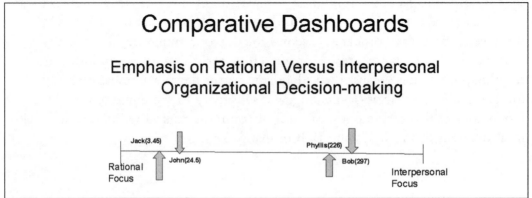

Figure 7.18 Comparison of Parties In Sensitivity

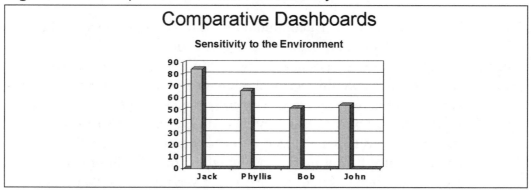

Based on this analysis, some of the recommendations regarding his communication with his colleagues included the following:

- Add more emotionally expressive terms, such as positive feelings and judgments, to all his communications, especially those with Phyllis and Bob, to more closely match their communication style and personalities.

- To improve his communications with John, incorporate their personality similarities in his e-mails—both prefer to operate as individuals versus team players, react to events rather than initiate, have strong values and beliefs, and like to make decisions rationally rather than based on interpersonal or political issues.

- Use his advantage in sensitivity to the environment (the ability to detect subtlety and changes, and perceives shades of grey versus seeing things as black versus white) in his communications.

Jack's use of the system and this advice resulted in improved communications and relations with all three parties, especially John. He used WarmTouch to start sending John detailed e-mails containing factual information with conclusions that emphasized their shared strong values and beliefs but also shared insights based on his sensitivity to technical and political factors in the environment. Rather than pressuring John to take the initiative on common issues, he presented detailed information and gave John time to consider and react. Before sending these communications, he ran them through WarmTouch to ensure the correct emotional and psychological tone and then charted John's reactions using the system.

WarmTouch's profiling and relationship-tracking and management capabilities might be equally helpful for those with important e-mail relationships, such as individuals using online communications for sales, management, or social life.

Summary

The shift of business and personal communications to computer-mediated channels (CMC) has left a void in our ability to detect traditional signals of motivation, personality, emotion, and attitudes, as well as indicators of trust. WarmTouch represents an effort to restore this personal dimension to CMC. Our initial applications have been to the security world, especially the challenges of detecting signs of risk of violations of trust from online communication. Our focus on cyber adversaries has thus far emphasized insiders, authors of anonymous threats, cyber stalkers, traditional hacker extortion, and efforts to discredit or damage company reputations online. We are also exploring ways in which WarmTouch technology can help restore the psychological insights lost in this "colder" medium to assist users in more general and benign forms of personal and professional relationships.

References

Bushman, B.J. and Baumeister, R.F. (1998) "Threatened egotism, narcissism, self-esteem and direct and displaced aggression: Does self-love or self-hate lead to violence?" *Journal of Personality and Social Psychology*, 75, 219-229.

Computer Security Institute (1997) "Computer Crime Continues to Increase, Reported Losses Total over $100 Million," Press Release. March 6, 1997. www.gocsi.com.

Heiser, Jay (2004) "Layer Eight," *Information Security*, page 30, January 2004.

Project Slammer Behavioral Science Team. *(a) Character Traits of Convicted Espionage Subjects: A Report for Investigators*. Newington, VA: Community Research Center (For Official Use Only).

Project Slammer Behavioral Science Team. (b) *Monitoring the Continued Reliability of Cleared Personnel*. Newington, VA: Community Research Center (For Official Use Only).

Project Slammer Behavioral Science Team. *(c) Managing At-Risk Employees: A Report for Supervisors*. Newington, VA: Community Research Center (For Official Use Only).

Shannon, E. and Blackman, A. (2002) *The Spy next Door: The Extraordinary Secret Life of Robert Philip Hanssen, the Most Damaging FBI Agent in U.S. History*, New York: Little and Brown.

Shaw, E. "Saddam Hussein: Political Psychological Profiling Results Relevant to His Possession, Use and Possible Transfer of Weapons of Mass Destruction (WMD) to Terrorist Groups," *Studies in Conflict and Terrorism*, Washington, D.C.: Rand Corporation, September/October 2003.

Shaw, E. "To Fire or Not to Fire," *Information Security*, January 2001.

Shaw, E. Post, J. and Ruby, K. "Profiling the Dangerous IT Professional," *Security Management*, December, 1999.

U.S. Department of Justice, Office of the Inspector General, "A review of the FBI's Performance in Deterring, Detecting, and Investigating the

Espionage Activities of Robert Philip Hanssen," August 2003 (*Unclassified Executive Summary*).

Weintraub, W. (1981). *Verbal Behavior: Adaptation and Psychopathology.* New York: Springer.

Weintraub, W. (1986) Personality profiles of American presidents as revealed in their public statements: the presidential news conferences of Jimmy Carter and Ronald Reagan. *Political Psychology*, 7, 285-295.

Weintraub, W. (1989) *Verbal Behavior in Everyday Life*, New York, Springer.

Footnote

[1] The specific dates of these written notes as published in Shannon and Blackman (2002) were: 10-1-85, 10-10-85, 11-8-85, 6-13-85, 9-8-97, 6-8-2000, 3-14-2000, and 11-15-2000.

[2] These e-mails were obtained from court records.

## Chapter 8

Managing the Insider Threat
Chapter contributed by Eric Shaw

Topics in this Chapter:

- **Prevention**
- **Detection**
- **Insider Case Management**

Introduction: Setting the Stage

Claude Carpenter, age 20, was hired by a noted defense contractor on March 13, 2000, to serve as a Web host and part-time systems administrator on three IRS servers housed in a secure facility within the Department of Treasury's computer center located in the New Carrollton Federal Building in Lanham, Maryland. This system tracks inventory for all hardware and software within the IRS. Within days of starting work, Carpenter was in trouble. Frequent conflicts with his supervisor and peers, late arrivals to work and inappropriate racial comments alienated him from coworkers. Carpenter also abused his access privileges on the system, attempting to impress IRS computer security staff with his ability to detect and plug security vulnerabilities. However, many of these efforts were counterproductive as Carpenter closed access ports designed to be open to system users. In a meeting with his supervisor on April 18, 2000 regarding his poor work performance, Carpenter reportedly became hostile, and his boss referred the matter to the project manager, who advised Carpenter that any further difficulties with his attitude or performance would result in dismissal. But between April 20 and May 17, 2000 Carpenter reported late for work seven times and had other personal conflicts. As a result, management decided to limit his work and system access. On May 18, 2000, following a dispute between Carpenter and a coworker, his supervisor prepared a draft letter of dismissal and sent it up the chain of command. He did not print the letter, give it to Carpenter, or advise Carpenter of its existence.

On May 18, 2000 Carpenter was assigned to a 2:00 pm to 12:30 am shift on one of the servers. He used it to log in to a server he was banned from and open a host file to obtain root access. He then accessed his supervisor's computer profile and edited it so that it read, in part:

> "don't you feel like a dumbass—while you are sitting here on your fat ass, your entire network is being fucked...Connection Fucking Terminated...Fuck with the wrong people gets you nowhere. This is example #1."

He also inserted several lines of destructive computer code but then "commented out" the code in his supervisor's profile so that it would not execute. Carpenter then inserted the same lines of active destructive code into several other servers and set it to execute when the volume of data reached a designated level. He then attempted to conceal his actions by turning off all system logs, removing history files and seeking to have the destructive code overwritten after execution to make it impossible for administrators to determine why the data was deleted.

"Bill" was a 37-year old Automation Technician and Safety and Control Officer at a petroleum processing plant in the southern U.S. He was responsible for the maintenance and repair of all pneumatic, electronic, computer process controls and plant online cryogenic systems. He worked closely with the plant electrical, measurement, and engineering teams to ensure optimum processing conditions.

Bill's new supervisor, concerned that the plant might be closed if improvements in efficiency were not made, sought tighter control over Bill's hours and overtime and pushed him to delegate responsibility to others. Bill resisted these efforts, refusing to keep appointments with the supervisor and to improve his collaboration with employees. In late January 1995, Bill attacked the team leader verbally for behaving like a dictator and stormed out of a meeting. The next day he verbally abused two fellow employees working on a plant repair approved by the team leader that he disagreed with. At a team meeting requested by Bill the following day, he again attacked the team leader for inappropriate technical procedures and stated that "we don't need a soccer coach to coach a football team." On February 14, 1995 Bill was placed on progressive discipline and given a written warning of unsatisfactory performance. The report accused him of the following:

- Withholding pertinent information from other team members

- Overtaking the responsibilities of others rather than coaching them through a problem-solving process

- Making negative statements regarding other team members' performance

- Storming out of meetings

- Harassing and intimidating team members and using profane and abusive language

- Failure to improve his communication, teamwork, and listening skills despite prior warnings

Bill was suspended with pay for four days and told to develop a plan to improve his performance and measure his progress with regard to these issues. When his performance failed to improve and further issues developed, Bill was given a Final Written Warning of Unsatisfactory Job Performance on April 27, 1995. He was suspended without pay for one week and instructed to refrain from any contact with plant personnel or work activities. This letter specifically cited him for failure to make the improvements requested in his February letter, including continuing to withhold information, defying orders to get approval for overtime work, and failing to make the improvements in plant safety and management procedures recommended by a consultant. The letter stated that any further problems would result in immediate dismissal.

Shortly after receiving this letter, Bill refused to provide a team member covering his assignment with a crucial password to a plant safety system. As time progressed without team access to this system, actual danger to the plant increased. It was not until Bill was contacted at home by a senior employee that he provided this password. During this period of suspension, Bill was also implicated in two acts designed to portray his new supervisor's inability to run the plant successfully. The first act involved manipulation of computerized plant safety and control mechanisms from a remote site to create a crisis. The second act involved collaboration with another employee, who shared Bill's frustration with the new manager, to again impact the safety and control mechanisms to produce a crisis. Both these actions appeared designed to demonstrate the supervisor's inability to manage the plant without Bill's input. However, these measures were resolved without Bill's involvement.

Bill's actions while on suspension prompted a collaborative security/human resources/operations investigation of his behavior and its impact on team members and plant productivity. In consultation with a security/mental health professional, the team also discovered that Bill had done the following:

- Spread derogatory rumors regarding his supervisor

- Verbally abused outside repair workers and suppliers

- Made unwanted sexual advances toward, and stalked, a coworker

- Made verbal threats of violence toward coworkers

- Had a belligerent confrontation with a coworker at a group meeting requiring physical intervention from others to avoid violence

- Been suspended two years earlier for bringing a handgun to the worksite

- Recently purchased a 30-round clip for a semi-automatic rifle he owned

- Was asked to leave a coworker's property after shooting an effigy of his supervisor with his rifle

Interviews with coworkers further revealed that:

- A number of them feared for their safety due to his anger.

- A friend saw him as "sick and in need of help."

- Another friend feared that his anger, alcohol abuse, impulsiveness, and access to weapons might combine to create a disaster.

- Another colleague described him as "looking through you."

- A friend expressed concern that he was verbally and physically abusive to his wife who was undergoing chemotherapy.

- A friend described him as increasingly isolated from social contacts.

Carpenter and Bill are two selections from dozens of insider cases that were the subject of study and/or consultation over the last 10 years. This chapter uses these cases and others to explore the challenges of managing insider threats. The chapter is divided into sections on prevention, detection, and management, and follows Carpenter, Bill, and other actual insider cases as they evolved. For this purpose, prevention refers to policies and practices affecting the screening and selection of employees and their assignment to tasks. Prevention also includes policies and practices designed to deter these acts, such as education and awareness training. *Detection* refers to policies or practices that increase the odds that an employee at risk for the commission of such acts will be noticed by personnel in position to intervene. *Management* refers to the manner in which at-risk personnel are dealt with in order to reduce the risk of an insider attack or decrease the consequences of an act, should it occur.

The conclusions and recommendations in this chapter are based in part on a review of 40 insider cases for the Department of Defense carried out between 1998 and 2000, as well as in-depth analysis of 10 additional cases covered between 2001 and 2003. It is also based on 16 years of practice as a clinical psychologist working directly with troubled employees and consulting with corporate security, human resources, and operations managers to assess and guide their management and treatment—ranging from safe termination to rehabilitation. This experience has also involved direct consultation with corporate security and law enforcement in assessing and managing online threats from insiders and outsiders. However, this research is not designed to present a profile of individual insider subjects. The insider phenomenon is too complicated and interactive for such "silver bullets." Our research has consistently found that the insider's story, his or her pathway to the attack, is consistently propelled forward by plot twists and turns that involve interactions with surrounding personnel, institutions, and society. In order to make a contribution to insider prevention, detection, and management, we have, however, concentrated on the insider's presentation in the workplace, especially his or her interaction with peers, supervisors, and the technology involved.

Prevention

This section focuses on key aspects of preventing insider cases, especially screening candidates for hire and educating supervisors and coworkers on the signs of risk. However, a great deal of previous research on employee screening, insider activity, and espionage indicates that many employees turned disgruntled after satisfying periods of employment. There are also serious obstacles to detecting risk in job candidates for whom there may be little or no record of previous computer misuse or other violations. Nevertheless, successful management of the insider threat begins with basic prevention measures.

Screening and Its Weaknesses

Claude Carpenter completed the application for a formal background check prior to coming to work at the IRS. But the demand for IT staff was so pressing that he was allowed to start work prior to the completion of the checks. By the time the review came back recommending against hiring, Carpenter had already attempted to sabotage the servers and been terminated. The recommendation against hiring was due to prior convictions related to drug use and sales. Only after the investigation of his sabotage at the IRS was it discovered that he had reportedly been discharged from previous employment at Patmos International Corporation for drug use and sales, as well as computer system misuse. According to an investigator, Carpenter introduced multiple backdoors into the Patmos system on his arrival. When personnel problems reportedly arose, and he learned that he was going to be fired, he shut down the system and blackmailed the company into paying him to come back and restore system operability. In addition, the investigator reported that Carpenter attempted similar violations at an even earlier employer, Comcast Cable. His supervisor also learned that at the time he was hired to work for the IRS contractor, there was an active FBI investigation of his activities at Patmos. It is noteworthy that Patomos reportedly went bankrupt, in part, because of Carpenter's activities.

Although employee screening can be a major firewall against hiring critical workers with a history of risk factors, it is not a panacea. In the Carpenter case, the delay between his start of employment and the completion of screening provided plenty of time for his employment to degenerate dangerously. In addition, standard screening may reveal legal violations, civil complaints, and debts, but it will rarely surface hacking violations that were not prosecuted, much less active involvement in the hacker community.

Failure to screen for hacker connections or unprosecuted hacker crimes was also a problem in two other cases we examined in-depth for the Department of Defense's (DoD) Personnel Security Research Center. For example, Jesus Oquendo was fired from his previous position for attempting to extort security fees from Web sites after attacking them to expose their vulnerabilities. He ran a well-known hacker site on the Web where information on hacking technique was exchanged. He also was a vocal critic of antihacking legislation on this site. We studied an attack after he had been laid off by his next employer where he used this access to target a subsidiary in order to convince a potential client of the need for his group's security services. This employer performed no background check on Oquendo prior to his being hired. Such a check might have revealed a previous drug bust, but it would not have exposed this unreported hacker extortion.

A help desk employee who worked at Globix Corporation we studied was also hired without a background check, due in part to his brother's employment there. "Rick" was an active 2600 participant and was proud of his hacking accomplishments, especially given his relative lack of formal training. However, it was with the encouragement and active advice and participation of friends from the hacker community that he transferred Globix's proprietary engineering plans to a friend sitting at a courtesy PC in the Globix lobby. This "friend" also happened to be employed by a Globix competitor and was happy to receive and post the specifications on the Web. Globix did not learn of the violation until another hacker from Rick's circle provided the information in an effort to get a job. Rick reported that he was motivated, in part, by Globix's alleged exaggeration of its capabilities in its' advertising. In his interview, he described this as "a fraud against my friend, Globix customers, and the whole planet." Consistent with general hacker philosophy, he and his friend decided that this information had to be shared, so the Globix engineering files were sent via FTP to a site his colleague controlled called "users.informationwave.net/missinglink/Globix/stash/." Globix employees reported the posted documents to include engineering design schematics and technical specifications, correspondence, spreadsheets, contracts, pricing charts, marketing information, and other data that could give competitors a significant advantage in competing for business. Globix staff assessed the value of the information involved at around $500,000. After the content became known to others, company officials reported that Globix also received weeks of attacks from the hacking community and ultimately launched an internal investigation and notified the FBI.

Of the 10 cases we recently explored in-depth, none of the offenders had received background checks prior to entering the workplace. Carpenter was the only subject for whom a check was reportedly processed. Three of the 10 subjects were also hired, in part, due to family connections—a misleading guarantee of lack of risk. As a matter of fact, in many cases family members and peer referrals can form dangerous coalitions against management. This was the case in the episode involving Abdelkader Smires, who attacked his employer after his mentor was fired. Smires joined Internet Trading Technologies, Inc. (ITTI) in January of 2000 and walked into an escalating controversy that pitted his brother and supervisor (and former professor/mentor) against management. All three ended-up leaving the company and Smires reportedly attacked and disabled the trading system as sensitive negotiations broke down.

Although it is clearly better to perform standard background checks than not, employers must be aware of risk factors—such as dangerous hacking history—that may not be tapped by these measures. Other forms of clearance, such as using an agency with access to hacker networks or online checks that examine non-obvious associations from nontraditional areas should be utilized, especially with critical hires. Even when these efforts fail to yield results, it may also be useful to audit a new employee's IT use during a very early probationary period. Carpenter, "Rick," and other hacker subjects tended to turn off security measures and construct various backdoors early after their arrival at their new employers.

Hire A Hacker?

The question of whether organizations should avoid hiring individuals with prior or current hacking background is controversial. There have been no longitudinal studies of hacker performance in the workplace. That 4 out of 10 of the offenders we studied in-depth were current hackers does not bode well, but our sample is far from representative. But the question of whether to hire hackers actually masks larger and simpler personnel security risk issues regarding how to screen individuals for risk and the extent to which screening can be effective.

Our limited case study results do not address the issue or support the conclusion that persons with hacker background alone should be screened out of employment. Of the 4 out of 10 subjects in our forensic sample who were hackers, 2 had histories of criminal activity and previous online violations resulting in damage to their corporations. These two individuals, Carpenter and Oquendo, should have been screened out of employment (Carpenter was, but too late) for their criminal activity, which they attempted to repeat in their new positions. But clearly employment screening for hacking risk and computer misuse in the workplace needs to improve.

But what other criteria could one use to screen out individuals with hacking background? Our previous research has indicated that certain personality factors may increase the risk of insider activity (Shaw et. al., 1998). However, far more individuals have these traits and never commit insider acts than do, so they are of limited value in screening. Our results show that only after individuals with these traits get involved in stressful workplace conflicts may they become dangerous. Like some of the most infamous espionage insiders in the history of the U.S.—who passed initial employment screening measures, including polygraphs, with flying colors—the majority of subjects in our sample became disgruntled on the job. Although screening can eliminate the risk posed by a small proportion of applicants, efforts at prevention probably have to rely to a greater extent, on early detection and aggressive intervention to manage at-risk employees.

Education and Prevention

Education and awareness training are critical to early detection of risk, aggressive intervention and prevention of escalation to insider events. The cases of Bill and Carpenter are good examples of situations allowed to escalate until they reached a crisis where there was significant risk. Our research indicates that successful education and awareness training has several vital components—components that have been missing from many organizations that have experienced insider events. These ingredients include the following:

- Effective policies and practices to prevent insider activity

- Effective policy enforcement measures that are followed to intervene in cases of policy violation and risk

- Persuasive psychological components that encourage employees to identify with the workgroup and understand the potential negative impact of insider activity on their livelihoods and those of their peers

- Real-world cases that employees and supervisors can identify and struggle with, as they role play ways of managing insider challenges

- Instructional materials derived from these actual cases that identify the critical pathway often seen as they escalate from the early stages of employee disgruntlement to attacks and specific warning signs along the way

Effective Policies and Practices

An in-depth review of policies and practices relevant to insider prevention is beyond the scope of this chapter. A review of the 10 in-depth case studies describes the policy and practice gaps that either facilitated employee disgruntlement or were not in place to deter or prevent the insider activity. Policies covering the issue leading to disgruntlement (such as intellectual property disagreements) or which could have deterred or prevented the attack (such as password protection) were missing in six of the nine relevant insider cases we recently reviewed in-depth. (One case involved a hack by a customer/subscriber who was not subject to such policies.) Failure to implement existing relevant policies was a problem in 7 of the 10 cases. The access of the customer/subscriber noted should have been cancelled for nonpayment according to existing policy, which might have prevented the attack. Clearly lack of policy and lack of policy enforcement are still challenges.

But policies and practices to prevent insider actions without accompanying educational plans designed to sell these guidelines are useless. Employees need to understand what these guidelines are and why they exist. But awareness and educational efforts alone will ring hollow if they do not contain relevant policies that are also enforced. Policies that are not enforced undermine the reliability of all other human resource and security policies and practices relevant to insider prevention.

Persuasive Components

Security and human resource policies and practices can be burdensome. It can be intimidating to approach a coworker you are concerned about or report this concern to a supervisor or Employee Assistance Program representative. Even if they are notified, supervisors do not like to report employee problems that suggest they cannot handle their staff. Personnel and security departments often do not have good relationships with operational groups and are often not seen as a

source of assistance. Even as they feared for their safety and the economic viability of the plant, many of Bill's coworkers failed to report their concerns to
authorities and tried to avoid getting caught up in the polarizing conflict
infecting the workplace. Although Rick's direct supervisor was aware that he was
on probation for behavioral problems prior to the attack, his supervisor one step
up was not. There have been a number of attempts in the corporate sector to
make the reporting of ethical concerns and risky behavior easier, including the
use of anonymous hotlines, chat rooms, bulletin boards, and even the old sugges-
tion box. Chapter 7 describes an online monitoring system designed to detect
increased risk of aggression. However, two key cultural components of groups we
have worked with in the past appear critical in overcoming these obstacles and
preventing the escalation of disgruntlement to insider attacks.

The first component is strong employee identification with the work unit as
a group. Like a platoon in combat, a working group that looks after its own to
ensure the survival of the whole group is more likely to be self-policing. A platoon member who is not up to doing his or her job risks group safety and is
more likely to receive needed support and attention and, as necessary, removal
from the unit. If employees at risk identify closely with the workgroup, they are
more likely to seek the assistance they need in order not to hamper the group.
They will also be respected for taking responsibility.

The second component is an understanding that insider activities can severely
damage the group, close a business, lead to layoffs, and otherwise threaten an
employee's livelihood. In this regard, case studies of organizations like Patmos,
mentioned earlier, are a useful educational tool. The case of Bill also involved the
risk of violence by an insider, and it is often difficult to know how disgruntled
employees will express their anger. Good education and awareness programs
address the issue of disgruntlement in general, and therefore seek to prevent all
forms of escalation (Shaw, 1997).

Real-World Cases

Coworkers and supervisors are the frontline sensors most likely to detect at-risk
employees and situations. Effective education programs convey information associated with risk, but they also sensitize employees to their own gut instincts that
something is not right and should be addressed. Effective programs then provide
procedures for employees to do something about their concerns. But to get
employees to overcome obstacles to getting involved, risking confrontations, or
not minding their own business, we have to reinforce the importance of these

gut instincts. To do this, we have to bring them into actual insider scenarios emphasizing the intellectual and emotional experience and decision-making of the coworkers and supervisors that were there.

For example, a behavioral description of Bill as he insulted his supervisor, bullied coworkers, and ignored security sanctions can sensitize employees to academic or intellectual indicators of insider risk. But this profile is even more effective when it conveys the emotional state of the employees who were there. As noted earlier, many of them were chilled by Bill's potential for violence and enraged by his bullying, and they purposely distanced themselves from anything to do with him out of discomfort and fear. Intellectual recognition of risk is vital, but it is the motivating discomfort of such emotions that gets employees to take action.

For supervisors, behavioral profiles of problematic employees and situations are also effective. But they have even greater impact when they are combined with descriptions of the emotional conflicts and decision-making a supervisor experiences when trying to decide what to do about an at-risk employee. For example, Carpenter's former supervisor describes his desires to "salvage" one of the most talented programmers he had ever met, to hold on to a vital team member willing to work undesirable shifts in the middle of an IT labor shortage, to make room for self-taught as well as academically trained employees in his shop. He also describes the many exceptions and dispensations from standard procedure he granted Carpenter. Finally, he admits with guilt and regret that he should have acted sooner, that his altruistic motives were displaced, and that Carpenter manipulated him into ignoring his instincts. This is emotional experience and decision-making feedback that supervisors can identify with and use when the need arises. By bringing employees and supervisors into the thoughts and feelings that others just like them have dealt with in insider scenarios, we better prepare them to recognize and deal with these threats. Traditional brainstorming and role playing used in these programs will then also be more effective.

Effective Instructional Materials

Our research and consultation experience indicates that insider actions do not arise out of the blue but consist of an unfolding story with specific stages involving the interactions of many players. This critical pathway will be described in more detail shortly. The most effective instructional materials will help participants recognize where they are in the often complex, developing story of insider risk, the roles being played by different parties involved, and how to get ahead of the curve.

Insider scenarios are rarely a simple matter of recognizing risk factors and removing the employee from the work environment. For example, in eight of nine of the in-depth cases we examined, there were serious ongoing organizational or personal stressors in play influencing management of the problem. In the case of Bill, his plant was on the edge of being closed for lack of productivity, and his wife was dying of cancer. At Askit.com, where the former CTO attacked the Web site and telephone system and threatened managers, employees were on reduced wages as the company sought to survive after the Internet bubble burst. Organizational and personal stressors often contribute to the occurrence of insider attacks and complicate management's ability to handle these challenges. If the stressors are part of a larger industry or social trend (like the bursting Internet business bubble) employees, supervisors, and senior managers may be suffering similar stress.

In six of the nine cases, there were ongoing social or cultural conflicts that also complicated and intensified case management. These included sociodemographic differences between the subject and other employees and supervisors, as well as educational and financial differences that affected the subject. Perhaps most significantly, in eight of nine cases, the organization had grown extremely dependent on the subject, complicating their ability to manage the case. For example, Bill had constructed very idiosyncratic safety and regulatory controls in the petroleum processing plant he had worked at for 15 years. Few others understood the system in place to safeguard plant physical integrity. Like Bill, the former CTO of Askit.com had the only password to the system he once ruled—in this case the company's Web site and phone system. Complicating case management even further, a number of these subjects exercised independent political power, giving them the ability to outmaneuver or delay their supervisor's efforts. Tim Lloyd's supervisor at Omega Engineering attempted to fire Lloyd before he erased the production database but was stopped by Lloyd's long-term relationship with the owner. Lloyd went on to use his power to eliminate all dispersed backup capabilities in the company's computer system and centralize it under his authority. He was therefore able to rehearse his attack with impunity and be assured of the full destruction of all backups. Bill's father was the former foreman of the plant where he worked and had connections throughout the company, which he used to protect his son. To make matters even more complex, in all nine of the cases we reviewed involving employees, the subject was either terminated or on probation at the time of the attack. As you will learn in the next section, identifying the problem and sanctioning or even firing the employee may not be sufficient to escape attack. It may only open a new chapter in the developing insider struggle.

Detection

Based on our previous research, the key to early insider detection is under-standing how disgruntled employees move down a critical pathway, interacting with their environment in a manner that can easily drive them toward attacks. This section describes challenges to early detection, clues that an employee may be a greater risk for insider actions, and the different pathways various types of insiders have traveled on their way toward aggression.

Detection Challenges

In Chapter 7, some of the new challenges to detecting insider risk are summa-rized. For example, the movement of communication from face-to-face and tele-phone to online formats conceals emotional cues that could indicate the presence of stress or disturbance associated with disgruntlement, Shaw et. al.(1999, 1998) We have also discussed the characteristics of an at-risk subset of IT employees that make it less likely that they will surface their concerns through normal face-to-face channels or deal with disgruntlement in construc-tive ways. These characteristics make it less likely that their concerns will be detected and dealt with appropriately.

For example, prior to exposing Globix's proprietary data, Rick confirmed that he was unhappy about not getting a promotion, getting rejected to work in the engineering department, not getting recognition for using his hacking skills to free up the frozen network when engineers had failed, and not getting credit for using his hacker connections to steer a potential contract Globix's way. When discussing this last incident, he noted that the company's behavior "crossed the line." But he also admits not complaining or taking other internal steps to rectify these perceived injustices. Instead, he confided his dismay to his friends within the hacking community, setting the stage for the problems to come.

Detection Challenges Along the Critical Pathway

After reviewing 40 cases of insider activity, Shaw et. al. (1998) proposed a general pathway or narrative template that described the interaction of a subject's per-sonal characteristics, stressors, interaction with his workplace environment, and other factors, on the path to insider action. Our recent in-depth review of 10 new cases confirmed and highlighted components of this model while adding more specific details depending on the type of subject involved. Awareness of these progressive risk factors can aid employers in detecting problematic persons and situations.

At-Risk Characteristics

The first component of this model is subject at-risk characteristics. As noted earlier, there are many employees who possess these traits who never become disgruntled or consider insider activity. Our findings indicate that these characteristics create a vulnerability to *other factors* along the critical pathway and increase the risk that a subject will interact with his environment in ways that can become problematic. Some authors (Gudaitis, 1998) have taken this approach out of context and characterized it as an effort to construct a "single" hacker profile. This "straw man" argument against using at-risk traits is short-sighted and unscientific. Just because more people have these traits than commit insider acts does not rule out their contribution to the chain of events leading to insider activity. We would not identify an individual with these traits as being at a greater risk for insider activity without the presence of the other factors described shortly. But just because everyone carrying a virus or genetic vulnerability to develop an illness doesn't manifest the syndrome doesn't mean we shouldn't try to understand their vulnerability to the disease. Empirical research, rather than dogmatic assumptions based on personal experience or professional orientation, will be the best determinant of the contribution of these traits.

These predisposing characteristics described in Shaw et. al. (1998) may be summarized in four broad traits:

- **A history of negative social and personal experiences** This history appears to manifest itself in a lower threshold for frustration and a propensity for anger at peers and authority figures.

- **Lack of social skills and a propensity for social isolation** Many subjects appear to lack the social skills that can lead to an increased chance of success in school and social and professional settings. These are not subjects that move freely between the face-to-face and online interpersonal worlds that are so dominant in the social networks of the last decade. These are individuals who experience marked discomfort in face-to-face interactions. They appear to have turned to the computer and computer-based peer groups as a substitute for traditional social networks. Often the computer is used to mediate their social interactions at work. This lack of social skills tends to decrease the odds that the subject will address difficulties in a constructive manner.

- **A sense of entitlement** Many subjects in previous studies appeared to behave as if they deserved special forms of attention and treatment such as exceptions to standard work policies and requirements. These feelings appeared to be derived from a sense that they possessed unique skills or gifts or that past difficulties merited compensation in the form of preferential treatment. This characteristic manifested itself in poor treatment of peers, difficulty adapting to social and professional requirements, and a general need for unusual levels of attention from supervisors and peers. These subjects were often described as "high maintenance."

- **Ethical flexibility** Subjects in previous research appeared to lack the developed moral reasoning or attachment to others that would deter them from ethical violations. Lack of a conscience, lack of empathy for the harm they would be inflicting on others, and lack of loyalty to peers, supervisors, and the organizations affected by their actions were noted. When these characteristics existed, there was a failure to inhibit angry impulses and plans.

Our recent research did not include collection of extensive data on the personal background of our subjects or provisions for direct psychological assessment that would be best suited to determining the presence or absence of these characteristics and their role in the violations described. However, based on the limited information gained on their past histories and the data collected on their behavior and motivation in the workplace connected to these incidents, we found great consistency between these hypothesized traits and descriptors of 8 of the 10 subjects for whom we had data.

These characteristics appear to have played a role in the subjects' progression down the critical pathway.

For example, on interview, Rick reported a long history of difficult international moves due to family financial stresses, being asked to leave his high school in this country, and, just prior to his work problems, the divorce of his parents. He also reported significant frustrations in successfully completing the computer training necessary to become a network engineer. As noted earlier, Rick's frustrations in the workplace began to mount rapidly at Globix when he felt he did not receive the recognition he was entitled to for making important network engineering fixes. But rather than voicing his frustration to management, he withdrew and complained about these problems to his friends in the hacker community. Rick's attitude problems and his inconsistencies at work lead to his being placed on probation several months prior to the attack. He has written at length on how managers must learn to handle hackers in the work environment differently than regular employees, indicating that he feels entitled to special treatment. Confronted by what he felt was false advertising on the part of his company, he felt obliged to correct the alleged misstatement by smuggling out the company's proprietary engineering plans to a hacker friend working for a competitor. He viewed this as getting the truth out and admits placing this value above loyalty or legal obligation to his company.

Another case illustrating this pattern involves an insurance company employee. This man's personal history included multiple arrests for forgery, grand larceny, and disorderly conduct. There were also court records covering complaints in landlord-tenant disputes and a protection order for harassment. Fellow employees described him as easily aroused with a "bad temper." This employee also used his help-desk position to make romantic advances toward a female employee, and illustrative of his lack of social skills, repeatedly ignored and misinterpreted her statements of lack of romantic interest. Despite these rejections, he escalated his pursuit, indicating he could ignore this feedback. After further rebuffs, he reverted to harassment, significantly interfering with the female employee's work and personal life through her email communications. This aggressive behavior is consistent with that of entitled individuals who become enraged at those who reject them. Consistent with this framework, these individual tend to create their own moral guidelines as they go along and frequently feel that they are the victims seeking justice. When confronted with his behavior, the subject denied the charges, even after being caught on video tampering with her computer. After his dismissal from the company, his acts of revenge escalated significantly, including unauthorized visits to the workplace and continued online sabotage.

Based on our in-depth case reviews, Figure 8.1 describes how these personal traits interact with environmental stressors to increase the risk of insider acts. We have found that a subject's negative personal history creates a propensity for anger, especially at authority figures seeking to control their behavior. The anger derived from this previous negative history creates a lowered threshold for frustration when personal or professional stressors are encountered.

Figure 8.1 How Personal Traits Interact on the Critical Pathway

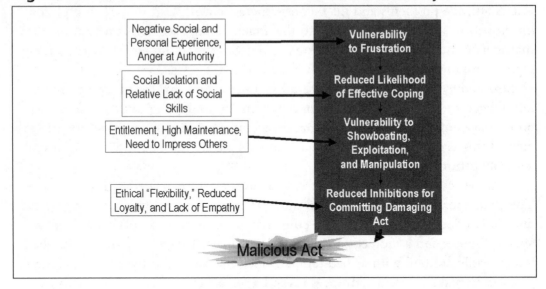

The subjects' lack of social skills then reduces the likelihood that they will react in a constructive manner when these stressors are encountered. Their sense of entitlement—that they are above the rules and needs and deserve special treatment—has several dangerous effects. These subjects appear to need constant reinforcement of their self-esteem in the form of feedback from others, special treatment, and exemptions. As noted, they also react bitterly when they feel rejected or denied the attention they deserve. This need for attention and rejection-sensitivity makes them vulnerable to showing off as well as exploitation by others who will supply this needed reassurance. Finally, their lack of a conscience, loyalty, and empathy reduce normal inhibitions against harming others, making them more likely to undertake destructive actions.

The Next Step on the Critical Pathway: Personal and Professional Stressors

Data on personal and professional stressors was available for 9 out of 10 of our most recent subjects. Table 8.1 describes the types of stressors experienced by each subject. As the table indicates, four of the organizations involved were undergoing significant stress at an institutional level. ITTI was attempting to transition out its software development team in favor of a staff with production experience. The organization employing Oquendo ran out of funds, and its employees were laid–off abruptly, without the back pay they were owed. After the Internet bubble burst, the Internet company employing the CTO in the study also went through massive layoffs, and the subject was placed on partial pay. The refinery plant where Bill was employed was so inefficient compared to the price of its product that it was at risk of closing.

Table 8.1 Personal and Professional Stressors by Subject

Subject By Stressor	Personal Stressor	Professional/ Organizational Stressor
Programmer at Internet trading company	Mentor, brother, and self losing job	Transition to production database team
Insurance co. help desk employee	Romantic rejection, harassment charges	Unknown
Jesus Oquendo	Layoff without pay	Layoff due to lack of funds for startup
Timothy Lloyd	Threatened loss of control of system	Former employee becomes supervisor
Claude Carpenter	Drug addiction, sales, interpersonal conflicts	Probation, threatened termination
Globix help desk employee	Parental divorce, brother leaves company	Failure to get promotion, failure to receive school support, failure to receive acknowledgement for contribution
Former CTO	High levels of conflict with coworker	Loss of pay due to company financial stress, asked to train replacement, conflict with management over severance
"Bill" at refinery	Wife terminally ill, sexual harassment of employee	Conflict with supervisor, threat of loss of control over system, plant in danger of going out of business
Investment banker	Unknown	Placed on probation within one month of promotion

In several of these cases, the organizational stress produced obvious personal and financial stress for the employee. However, six of the subjects had independent personal stressors of significant seriousness. For example, Bill's wife was terminally ill, and the former CTO had had serious conflicts with other employees, Carpenter appeared to be chronically late for work and in constant conflict with coworkers.

Maladaptive Emotional and Behavioral Reactions

As the stress on the employees mounted, our subjects tended to react in ways that increased, rather than helped resolve their problems. Bill at the refinery escalated his conflict with his new supervisor and had to be physically restrained, placed on probation, and asked to leave a neighbor's house due to his intoxication and use of a weapon. The programmer at the Internet trading company refused to provide copies of code to the new employees and walked out on negotiations. After his romantic rejection, the insurance company employee escalated his harassment, actively interfered with the female employee's email communications, and tampered with her computer. As he felt his control over his part of the organization slipping away, Timothy Lloyd physically assaulted a female employee, refused to collaborate with other team members, stole computer equipment, and started lying about his work and personal activities. When confronted with his security and personnel violations, Carpenter became even more aggressive and hostile toward fellow employees, threatened his supervisor and ignored security sanctions. As noted, the help desk employee at Globix withdrew and notified no one of his unhappiness on the job but started to come in late and spend time on nonwork activities in the workplace.

Detection Delays

Column two in Table 8.2 displays results indicating the time period during which the subject was disgruntled compared to his time on the job. Column three describes the elapsed time during which the company was aware of a personnel problem prior to the actual attack. Signs of disgruntlement in the nine subjects where this was relevant appeared from 1 to 48 months before the attack. The time period prior to the attack—during which there were active problems requiring company intervention—ranged from 12 days to 19 months. These results are extremely important for the detection of insider risk because they indicate the existence of a "window" period during which effective employer intervention may, or may not, reduce the risk of an attack. In addition, the findings indicate that this window may be expanded by months, in some cases, if disgruntlement is discovered sooner.

Table 8.2 Detection Issues by Subject

Detection Issue/Case	Time from Disgruntled to Attack (Time on Job)	Time from Active Problems to Attack
Programmer at Internet trading company	2 months (2 mos.)	2 weeks
Insurance co. help desk employee	16 months (34 mos.)	16 months
Jesus Oquendo	1 month (4 mos.)	None visible, deception
Investment banker	7 months (18 mos.)	12 days
Timothy Lloyd	4 years (11 yrs.)	14 months
Claude Carpenter	1 month (2 mos.)	1 month
Globix help desk employee	6 months (19 mos.)	6 months
Former CTO	2 months (22 mos.)	2 months
Bill at refinery	19 months (15 yrs.)	19 months

Subject Escalation

Although detection may often be delayed, management interventions in these cases lead these subjects to escalate rather than cease their dangerous activity. Gudaitis (1998) observed that "the vengeful inside intruder is actively sabotaging after they perceive their organization has done 'damage' to them." Her conclusion is supported by the data displayed in Table 8.3 on the range of management interventions that failed to derail subject escalation. In effect, these efforts are too little, too late.

Table 8.3. Management Interventions Prior to Attacks

Subject	Management Intervention Prior to Attack
Programmer at Internet trading company	Negotiations over pay, options, job, security, then termination of negotiations
Insurance co. help desk employee	Investigation without intervention followed by confrontation of evidence and abrupt dismissal
Jesus Oquendo	Abrupt layoff without back pay followed by efforts to help finance startup security firm
Investment banker	Probation

Continued

Table 8.3. Management Interventions Prior to Attacks

Subject	Management Intervention Prior to Attack
Timothy Lloyd	Counseled by supervisor, transferred, demoted
Claude Carpenter	Probation under threat of dismissal
Globix help desk employee	Probation for lateness, Web surfing
Former CTO	Reduced pay, counseled by supervisor, no consequences
Bill at refinery	Suspension

These interventions ranged from counseling by a supervisor, to negotiations, to suspension. The uniform failure of this range of efforts indicates that by the time this stage of the critical pathway is reached, there may be few traditional standard management options that can prevent an attack, and that an emphasis should be placed on security and psychological management with such employees.

A review of the reported psychological state of the employees suggests that seven of the subjects were so disgruntled at this stage that an attack was inevitable. In the case of Jesus Oquendo, the venture capital firm whose sponsored company was attacked opened itself to this aggression by offering to help Oquendo with his startup. The manager in this case stated that he felt badly regarding the abrupt layoffs by another of his subsidiaries. The termination of negotiations at the Internet trading company when demands became unreasonable appears to have resulted in the attack on the system in order to force the company back into negotiations. As noted, the investment banker did not mean to damage the database affected when he stole proprietary data he felt entitled to. However, the remaining subjects were involved in intense conflicts with coworkers and/or their employers and their online attacks were preceded by other violations.

The case of Bill offers some additional insight into management options under these circumstances. Bill attacked the safety and control mechanisms at the petroleum processing plant where he worked immediately after his suspension. He was intimately familiar with these controls and appears to have attacked initially using remote access and subsequently with the cooperation of a fellow employee. His efforts were reportedly aimed at demonstrating his supervisor's inability to run the plant safely without him. In the initial phases of this case, suspension did not deter the attacks. However, shortly after these attacks a management panel advised by a mental health/security consultant designed an assessment and remediation program for Bill that was successful in preventing further attacks and providing Bill with opportunities to seek employment elsewhere. The investigation of past problems at this facility and psychological counseling were major components of this program that appear to have contributed to the elimination of further attacks.

Detection Indicators and Challenges by Subject Subtype

Earlier work efforts were made to create subject typologies describing the motivation of offenders and their specific attack types. Early efforts by Shaw et. al. (1999, 2000) described a range of hypothesized subtypes with emphasis on their motivation for attacks, as shown in Table 8.4.

Table 8.4 Eight Perpetrator Subtypes

Subject Type	Subject Characteristics
Explorers	Curious individuals who commit violations in the process of learning or exploring the system, mostly without malicious intent; they are unaware that their activities violate company information-security policies (or such policies may not be in place).
Samaritans	Individuals who bypass protocols and hack into a system to fix problems or accomplish assignments, believing their efforts to be more efficient than following approved procedures.
Hackers	Individuals who have a prior history of hacking and continue penetrating systems after they are hired. These individuals have installed logic bombs or other devices in company systems to serve as job insurance when their activities are discovered. (They will defuse the trap in exchange for severance considerations.)

Continued

Table 8.4 Eight Perpetrator Subtypes

Subject Type	Subject Characteristics
Machiavellians	Individuals who engage in acts of sabotage, espionage, or other forms of malicious activities to advance their careers or other personal agendas. They include those who steal intellectual property to become consultants, those who sabotage competitors (or superiors) and those who cause outages to facilitate their own advancement or ability to gain attention. Machiavellians may also use their skills to advance social agendas.
Proprietor	Act as if they "own" the systems they are entrusted with and will do anything to protect their control and power over this territory. They may actively resist threats to their control and are willing to destroy or damage the system rather than give up control.
Avenger	Classic disgruntled employees, who act impulsively out of revenge for perceived wrongs done to themselves.
Career thieves	Individuals who take employment with a company solely to commit theft, fraud, embezzlement, or other illegal financial acts.
Moles	Individuals who enter a company solely for the purpose of stealing trade secrets and other information assets for a competing company, outside group or foreign country.

(From Shaw et. al. 2000)

Subsequent efforts by Shaw (2001, 2002) attempted to expand the described typology beyond motivation to include the subject's behavioral presentation in the workplace and relationships with peers and supervisors. These typologies are not designed to function as templates for identifying employee insiders. As research hypotheses regarding the complex pathway insiders travel toward their acts, they are designed to further case-based research on insider paradigms. As we collect more data, these typologies may be modified or replaced. In the meantime, informed readers, familiar with the scientific process, can utilize this background to help them evaluate specific cases of concern, much like a physician would use current research to evaluate an illness or treatment for his patient.

As shown in Table 8.5, ten offenders in the current study were categorized by perpetrator subtype according to case information available to researchers. As the table indicates, the subjects were equally divided between the Proprietor and Hacker categories, with two remaining subjects classified as Avengers. The insurance company employee described was classified as a Machiavellian turned Avenger because he used his IT skills to pursue a romantic target and to attempt to control and punish her for undesirable responses. His attacks on his former organization's payroll system appeared to be exclusively related to this interaction and his termination for his behavior toward this employee.

Table 8.5 Subject Typology Category

Case/Category	Typology Category
Internet trading programmer	Proprietor
Insurance co. help desk employee	Machiavellian/Avenger
Jesus Oquendo	Hacker
Investment banker	Avenger
Timothy Lloyd	Proprietor
Oleg Zezov (chapter 7)	Hacker
Claude Carpenter	Hacker
Globix Help Desk Staffer	Hacker
CTO of Askit.com	Proprietor
Bill	Proprietor

The classification of subjects by type allows a closer focus on their specific route on the critical pathway and the detection challenges each subject category offers.

For example, the four Proprietors in this research behaved in characteristic ways, consistent with their efforts to retain control of their systems. The Lloyd case is paradigmatic of the Proprietor's pathway, and recent research has highlighted the relatively high frequency and serious threat posed by the "Proprietor" subtype (Shaw 2001). Like many Proprietors, Lloyd appears initially as a model employee. He is knowledgeable, dedicated, and responsive to management needs. Compared to other staff, he is on the cutting edge of a new technology, facilitating group dependence on his skills. However, with this success, he began to operate as if he had personal control and ownership of the company's computer system. He successfully cultivated supportive relationships with senior employees to protect his turf. He successfully resisted manager efforts to dilute or curtail his computer policies and control of the system. He specifically refused orders to train backup personnel, including his supervisor. He appears to have been willing to destroy the system and damage the company rather than give up control. Like other Proprietors, he used his unique system knowledge to construct a long-term strategy to disable the system, if necessary. Often, this strategy banks on the company being unable to run the system without him (and returning as a well-paid consultant). In more extreme cases, there is an effort to destroy the system rather than give up control.

Ultimately, his control over the system also facilitated unique operational security for his plans, including the opportunity for multiple rehearsals of his attack. His attack coincided closely with his termination—his loss of control of the system—as in other Proprietor cases. Finally, he appears to have valued control over the system above his own self-interest as the attack was readily traced to his activities. This level of irrational thinking is typical of Proprietors whose unique position often leads them to overestimate their own abilities and underestimate the abilities of others. This may have been the case with Lloyd's reported plan to use the attack to rejoin the company as a consultant, underestimating the extent and thoroughness of the company's reaction. As more cases of proprietor abuse emerge, the validity of this specific pathway model will be tested. Table 8.6 summarizes these elements of the Proprietor pathway.

Table 8.6 "Steps" along the Proprietor Pathway

"Steps"	Description
1. Initial presentation	Dedicated, skilled, responsive, works long hours
2. Dependency grows	Abilities and dedication foster growing delegation, dependency, and autonomy
3. Personal turf	Increasingly personalizes "turf" and identifies with system as his personal domain, subject to exclusive control, needs his "protection" from less competent
4. Political flanking	Through independent service and relationships with customers, growing ability to flank department supervisors and willingness and desire to expand independence
5. Resistance	Resists efforts to curtail control over system by passive and active means (refuses to train backup, offer access to "unqualified" personnel, or make recommended system changes)

Continued

Table 8.6 "Steps" along the Proprietor Pathway

"Steps"	Description
6. Potential conflict behaviors	Uses unique control to help competitors fail in order to demonstrate his unique skill and lack of expendability; create long-term plan to damage system if he loses control; and ensure operational security of plans; may plan on returning as consultant to save system from the damage he has instigated
7. Proprietor vulnerability	May overestimate his ability and underestimate that of others—to detect plans and operate system without him

The relatively high frequency of Hackers in our insider cases was surprising. However, when the three insider hackers (Oquendo, Carpenter, and the Globix Help Desk staffer) are examined, there are notable similarities in their pathways to the attack. and efforts to avoid detection. These included the following:

- A significant negative personal history. Carpenter and Oquendo had criminal records, and the Globix employee had been expelled from high school and had a history of hacking activity.

- A history of previous computer misuse.

- On arrival or shortly thereafter, neutralization of organizational security devices.

- Ignoring security and personnel protocols.

- Significant self-esteem issues that require unusual attention, make the subject sensitive to slights or generally "high maintenance."

- Personnel conflicts or problems requiring official attention.

- An angry reaction to a company policy or action related to him or his interests.

- A lack of inhibitions about retaliation or revenge for these perceived activities.

The case of Carpenter particularly fits the Hacker subtype described in earlier research. His criminal background is consistent with other hackers studied in this sample, including his history of previous computer misuse and drug offenses.

Like other hackers studied, he set up a system to assure his operational security upon his arrival. This reportedly included the elimination of the history logs and the activation of sniffers to gain access to his supervisor's files. For example, he knew about his termination letter when it was in draft form on his supervisor's password-protected email program. His hacking skills also made him immune to normal security controls and sanctions. He also demanded and received exceptional treatment due to his technical skills, ignored security policies and procedures, and actively fought security interventions designed to curtail his access. He also made unilateral changes to system configurations without prior approval that resulted in system disruptions. When he was finally threatened with termination, he countered by attacking the system. His interpersonal behaviors (arrogance, propensity for conflict with others, resisting authority, ignoring policies and practices) were also consistent with his hacker peers. Table 8.7 summarizes some of these steps along the Hacker's pathway to attack.

Table 8.7 "Steps" on the Hacker Pathway

"Steps"	Description
1. Wires on entry	Neutralizes monitoring and security devices on his PC or workstation, wires turf with sniffers and backdoors to monitor key individuals and systems of interest
2. Evades	Ignores, evades, or neutralizes other security protocols on larger systems on which he operates
3. Initiates changes	Makes system changes without approval, often designed to demonstrate abilities
4. Becomes high-maintenance employee	Growing number of problems related to working within standard rules, interpersonal conflicts; demonstrates need for special treatment
5. Active conflicts	Problems evolve to active conflicts with job and computer-related consequences (access curtailed); often sanctioned by supervisor, which only escalates hostility and resistance
6. Attacks	Attacks designed to get "revenge" for sanctions or perceived mistreatment

Insider Case Management

In the previous sections, we discussed many management functions relevant to insider risk. These included the prevention functions of employee screening, awareness, and education training, and the establishment of effective and enforced policies and practices. Other management functions mentioned under detection included sensitivity to the issues and events along the critical pathway that indicate the potential presence of growing insider risk; disgruntlement and ineffective interventions in dealing with these problems were also highlighted as contributing to an increased potential for insider acts. This section summarizes some of these earlier findings and discusses recommendations to improve management of insider risk. Steps organizations can take to evaluate their ability to prevent, detect, and manage insider risk have been described in greater detail in an article on the insider personnel and security audit (Shaw et. al., 2000).

Table 8.8 summarizes these findings and recommendations. The high rates of gaps in employment and security policies that either lead to insider activity or failed to help prevent or detect it indicate the need for more widespread security policy evaluation and education. An organization concerned about its insider risk potential should immediately run its current personnel and security policies and practices against a selection of these real insider cases. What, if any, policies and practices would be relevant? What would happen if these policies and practices were executed in a hacker case like Carpenter or a proprietor case like Lloyd? The fact that there were even higher rates of policy implementation and enforcement failures suggests the existence of an even deeper problem. Would the employees involved even be aware of the relevant policies and practices? In many of these cases involving implementation and enforcement failures, technical means were not present to enforce the policy, human resources were lacking, personnel did not understand the importance of the policy, or the offenders simply utilized superior system knowledge to ignore and evade enforcement efforts.

Table 8.8 Key Management Findings and Recommendations

Key Findings	Recommendations
Gaps in personnel and security policies and practices	Need for increased education and proliferation of personnel and security policies and practices, audits of policies and practices
High rates of personnel and security policy implementation and enforcement failures	Need for increased education and proliferation of personnel and security policy implementation and enforcement methods, management training in enforcement practices, case management training
Lack of technical and human resources and education for policy enforcement	Improved education and awareness training regarding policy enforcement, improved enforcement auditing, increased corporate self-regulation of policy enforcement to avoid liability, government regulation and legislation
Offender ability to avoid detection of policy and practice violations	Improved education and training of personnel and security personnel responsible for policy implementation and enforcement, improved technical and human resources to assist these personnel
Window of opportunity to intervene prior to attacks	Improved manager, personnel, and security training regarding the risk of personnel problems, need for aggressive detection and effective interventions to reduce risk
Need for improved case assessment and planning	More coordinated information sharing and planning involving HR, Security, and Operations, more in-depth assessment of employees and security risks; need to consider insider actions as possible symptom of organizational problems.
Problems with probation and termination processes	Need for revised probation and termination procedures to decrease vulnerability to attacks, reduce likelihood of attacks during these periods and monitor attack risk more effectively
Subject use of remote access for post-termination attacks	Need to revise remote access policies and practices, especially after detection of subject risk and during probation and termination periods

One of the most important findings of this research was that there was a "window" of opportunity for dealing with the personnel problems affecting these subjects. Although many authors have offered system-based tools for detecting insider misuse (Magklaras and Furnell, 2002; Schultz, 2002), these results indicate that offline personnel issues also provide early warning. These individuals were reportedly disgruntled in some cases for over a year prior to their attacks, and management was aware of these personnel problems weeks if not months prior to the attack. Yet there were consistent intervention problems. In fact, in many cases management actions exacerbated the problem. This finding indicates the need for improved management training and procedures covering interventions with at-risk individuals. A significant part of improving management of disgruntled employees that present a risk of insider activity should be more in-depth and coordinated case assessment.

The case of Bill described in the introduction is a good example of effective case assessment and planning. There were two key elements of the company's intervention that contributed to the quality of the resolution in this case, including avoidance of further sabotage and the prevention of violence. First, the use of an outside consultant allowed Bill to be viewed in the context of peers, family, organization, community, and even the social and economic issues playing a role in the crisis (such as the lowered price of petroleum placing economic pressure on the plant) as these forces advanced over time. The use of the outside consultant also facilitated the examination of organizational problems that had helped move Bill down the critical pathway. These included the company's difficulty adhering to its own policies and practices, its failure to intervene earlier, and the fear that Bill was able to instill across the company to intimidate peers and superiors. The outside consultant was also able to address the political connections that protected Bill from the consequences of his actions and realign company priorities in this crisis. In addition, the clinical background of the consultant allowed the risk assessment and planning process to take account of Bill's personality, alcoholism, depression, risk of violence (Shaw and Post, 1997), and his wife's terminal illness and suicide attempts.

The second key element of the assessment was coordination among the different parties and departments involved, including Operations, HR, and Security. With the parties sitting around the table comparing notes, new information was discovered and shared, better contingency planning was developed, and more detailed and in-depth solutions to the multidisciplinary challenges Bill presented were also agreed to and enforced. This coordinated team approach also made it easier to consider the difficulties in the case as symptoms of larger issues affecting the organization in a post-incident review. Case assessment and planning with Bill can be contrasted with the Lloyd case. In that situation, conflicts between his line supervisors and management delayed a solution and allowed Lloyd time to plan and execute his attack. Lloyd also had a complex medical and psychiatric background that was never considered in the assessment and planning process.

In addition to case assessment, Table 8.8 portrays several problems with the probation and termination processes in these cases. Most notably, after the employee had left the work site due to termination or was placed on probation, there was a failure to block his access to the system, facilitating the high rate of remote attacks. Nor was the access of employees on probation remaining onsite effectively curtailed or monitored. The high rate of these attacks post-termination indicates the need for a careful review of personnel and security issues prior to the termination of at-risk employees. In addition, it may be beneficial to reexamine policies and practices related to remote access. Although remote access can increase productivity, organizations may need safeguards (such as the right to onsite inspection) to ensure that this access is not abused, especially post-termination. Termination of remote access may also be keyed to other forms of personnel violations.

Summary

Many standard personnel and security policies and practices require adaptation to the new IT-dominated environment. Standard prevention, detection, and management practices—when used—do not appear to measure up to current insider challenges. They do not screen out employee candidates with nontraditional risk background or successfully detect those at risk in a timely fashion. Nor were effective personnel and security policies and practices in effect and/or enforced in a manner that facilitated early detection of risk or successful intervention in our cases. Our results thus far also indicate strongly that getting the disgruntled employee out the door is no guarantee of security from attacks.

Our approach to understanding the evolution of insider threats in this environment has been to attempt to follow the people, systems, institutions, and communities involved as they interact to contribute to increasing insider risk over time. Our emphasis in this latest stage of research has not been on developing in-depth offender personality profiles but on a more detailed, pragmatic understanding of how persons around the subject experienced his behavior in the workplace. This is a scientific research venture designed to shed light on a growing financial and national security issue by accumulating and analyzing case study data (Kaarbo and Beasley, 1999). It is not a simple-minded effort to create a set of insider personality templates to aid investigators. As more data is acquired, the practical application of these results may become clearer. In the long run, it is our belief that "nothing is more practical than a good theory."

References

Gudaitis, T. (1998) "The Missing Link in Information Security: Three Dimensional Profiling," *CyberPsychology & Behavior*, Volume 1, No. 4, pps. 321–340.

Kaarbo, J. & Beasley, R. (1999) "A Practical Guide to the Comparative Case Study Method in Political Psychology," *Political Psychology*, Vol. 20, #2, 369–391.

Magklaras, G.B. and Furnell, S.M. (2002) "Insider Threat Prediction Tool: Evaluating the Misuse," *Computers and Security*, 21,1: 62–73.

Schultz, E. (2002) "A Framework for Understanding and Predicting Insider Attacks," *Computers and Security*, 210:526–531.

Shaw, E. "Profiling the Corporate Information Technology Insider," Defense Personnel Security Research Center, Monterrey, Ca. September 30, 2002.

Shaw, E. " To Fire or Not to Fire," *Information Security*, January 2001.

Shaw, E., Post, J. and Ruby, K. "Managing the Insider Threat: The Personnel Security Audit," *Information Security*, July 2000.

Shaw, E. Post, J. and Ruby, K. "Profiling the Dangerous IT Professional," *Security Management*, December, 1999.

Shaw, E.D, Ruby, K. G., and Post, J.M. "The Insider Threat to Information Systems," *Security Awareness Bulletin*, Number 2-98, pp. 27–47, Security Research Center of the Defense Security Service. Monterey, Ca, 1998.

Shaw, E.D. and Post, J. "Threats of Workplace Violence: The Role of the Mental Health Professional on the Law Enforcement and Security Team," *The Police Chief*, March 1997.

## Chapter 9

The Cyber Adversary in Groups: Targeting Nations' Critical Infrastructures

Chapter contributed
by Marcus H. Sachs

Topics in this Chapter:

- Historical Context

- Increasing Threats and Vulnerabilities

- Identifying and Characterizing the Cyber Threat

Introduction

A *critical infrastructure* is a vital physical or cyber asset or system, the destruction of which would destabilize a national economy or way of life or jeopardize national security. Some examples of these infrastructures are energy grids, transportation systems, telecommunications networks, emergency first responders, healthcare facilities, and government organizations. In today's highly connected world, a nation's critical infrastructures depend on the reliability of two key systems, which are also considered critical infrastructures: the electric power grid and communications networks.

Attacks on either of these systems have the potential to cause ripple effects in other infrastructures and could, in the worst case, lead to a national economic collapse. Fortunately, both the electric power grid and the communications networks in the United States are now very mature, having their roots in the 19th century. In both cases, redundancies and backups are in place to ensure their reliable operation in the worst of disasters. In the United States and most other countries, the federal government regulates these industries and provides funding for safety systems, surge capacity, and backup capabilities.

A relative newcomer to the infrastructure community is the global Internet, a massive "network of networks" that sprang from a loose collection of academic, private, military, and government computer networks in the 1970s and 1980s. In less than 20 years, the Internet grew from fewer than 10,000 hosts to tens of millions of hosts worldwide. In the recorded history of humankind, there has never been such explosive growth in a new method of communication. Critical infrastructures' dependence on the Internet is growing annually and will surpass the dependence on the traditional telephone system within the next decade.

The Internet is largely unregulated, controlled by rules that are more like technical guidelines rather than rigid government-enforced laws and agreements. Many of the technical standards were written in the early 1970s, when the number of connected computers was only in the hundreds, yet these standards are still prominently in use today. There are no government backup plans, no mandated safety features, and no restrictions on who can connect to the Internet. The only requirement is that users follow the basic technical requirements set forth in documents known as Internet *Requests for Comment*, or RFCs. However, software and hardware manufacturers, governments, private industries, and individuals frequently violate even that requirement.

Because of critical infrastructures' growing dependence on the Internet for the movement of information and data, nations are in jeopardy of becoming victims of economic or national security attacks manifested via attacks on the Internet itself. Threats to the Internet are increasing rapidly, whereas the rate of developing new methods for detecting and averting these threats in real time is growing very slowly.

NOTE

The National Strategy to Secure Cyberspace, published by the White House in February 2003, identified the Critical Infrastructures as one of five areas that were of concern. The Strategy recommended that the infrastructure sectors work together to share the burden of finding and reducing cyber threats and vulnerabilities:

"When organizations in sectors of the economy, government, or academia unite to address common cyber security problems, they can often reduce the burden on individual enterprises. Such collaboration often produces shared institutions and mechanisms, which, in turn, could have cyber vulnerabilities whose exploitation could directly affect the operations of member enterprises and the sector as a whole. Enterprises can also reduce cyber risks by participating in groups that develop best practices, evaluate technological offerings, certify products and services, and share information. Several sectors have formed Information Sharing and Analysis Centers (ISACs) to monitor for cyber attacks directed against their respective infrastructures. ISACs are also a vehicle for sharing information about attack trends, vulnerabilities, and best practices."

So how does a nation characterize these threats to protect against them and thus ensure the reliable operation of critical infrastructures? How does a digital economy built on standards that are not much more than simple gentlemen's agreements avert what appears to be a certain cataclysmic conclusion? Is more government oversight and regulation needed, or will the Internet ultimately self-regulate through a process commonly called *industry governance*?

To answer these questions, this chapter reviews a few significant events over the past quarter century that brought us to the situation we currently face. In addition, the chapter takes a look at the different types of threat we know of today as well as future threats that are slowly becoming clear as we gain a better understanding of what the Internet phenomenon means.

Historical Context

At the end of 1979, fewer than 1,000 hosts were connected to a few large computer networks collectively known as "the Internet." Most of the pieces of the domestic Internet during this time connected via circuits leased from various telephone companies, with AT&T being the largest carrier. AT&T had enjoyed a near monopoly on long-distance telephone service for almost a half century in the United States, but that status would soon change.

Challenged by several companies accusing the phone giant of monopolistic practices, the U.S. Department of Justice filed an antitrust suit in 1974 against AT&T for anticompetitive behavior, seeking the breakup of the Bell System. After many years of hearings and negotiations, both sides settled on a divestiture plan in 1982, to take effect on January 1, 1984. Divestiture ultimately opened domestic long-distance competition to several companies, including MCI Communications and Sprint.

In the early 1970s, the Federal Communications Commission (FCC) granted MCI permission to build and operate a limited number of microwave links separate from those operated by the Bell System. After divestiture, MCI's small network grew into a coast-to-coast system that competed directly with AT&T's long-haul microwave system.

Another challenger to AT&T in the 1970s, the United Telecommunications Company, had a different approach. Instead of building microwave links, this company's methodology was to bury thousands of miles of fiber optic cable to interconnect cities across the United States. By 1980, United Telecommunications had established UNINET as the world's third largest packet switching network and was laying fiber optic cable coast to coast as rapidly as the company could acquire right-of-way access. Following divestiture, United Telecommunications launched the first domestic all-fiber, all-digital long-distance telephone service, in 1986. The system was marketed under the Sprint brand name.

Without a high-speed backbone, the Internet was doomed to the relatively slow speeds offered by copper wire. Thanks to the development of Sprint's fiber optic network (and many others that followed), Internet speeds in excess of several billion bits per second—several orders of magnitude higher than what was possible with copper—were within reach. The availability of fiber, combined with a growing commercial interest in the new data networks, set the stage for massive Internet growth throughout the 1990s.

Missing in the mid-1980s was a "killer application," an essential ingredient necessary to fuel the coming network explosion. A scientist in Switzerland invented such a killer app in 1989. Looking for a way to link documents across multiple systems and networks, Tim Berners-Lee proposed a "hypertext" system that eventually spawned what is now called the World Wide Web.

The General Public and the Internet

The creators of the Internet in the early 1970s did not envision today's nearly exclusive commercial and personal use of the invention. The core protocols, switches, mechanisms, and software that underlie the Internet were developed and perfected for a networked culture envisioned to be open and cooperative. The idea of harming the network or using it for hostile purposes was beyond consideration. After all, who would want to harm a capability as powerful as the new global network of computer resources? It was hard enough just to build and operate the early networks; intentionally causing disruptions was counter-productive.

That mindset began to change in the late 1980s and early 1990s as more users gained access to the Internet. Many of the newcomers were not computer scientists or researchers. They were "regular people" looking for ways to expand the use of personal computers widely available in offices and homes. The Internet offered a new communications medium, and access to systems outside the user's office or home was an exciting concept. Natural curiosity led to growing interest in seeing how far one could go on the Internet—to explore the endless amounts of data and information that had previously been unavailable to the average user.

Unfortunately, when access to any resource or facility previously off-limits or not available is granted on such a broad basis, abuse of the privilege will occur. This behavior is well understood in the physical world. Take, for example, a new highway or mass-transit rail system, or even a new office building. Unless tightly controlled, curiosity seekers will attempt to gain access as soon as possible, even before construction has finished or while final testing is still under way. Drivers will attempt to take a shortcut on new highways that are not yet open to the public; curious commuters will stay on a subway past the last station to see what a new line looks like before it is open for service. Except when confronted by a security guard, inquisitive future occupants will roam through unfinished buildings or office complexes.

In terms of the Internet, further complicating the situation was the explosive growth of Internet commercialization through the 1990s, reaching a peak with the "dot–com bubble" in early 2000. By the end of that decade, millions of users were connected on the global network using computers more powerful than the best mainframes or supercomputers of only 10 years earlier. Only a fraction of those users had any idea how the computers worked or how they were programmed. Still fewer had any concept of the power that a single computer represented.

NOTE

According to the FCC, by 2000 there were 7.1 million high-speed lines connecting homes and businesses to the Internet:

- 5.2 million of these lines were residential and small business subscribers.
- 4.3 million of theses lines provided services at speeds of over 200 kilobits per second (kbps) in both directions.
- 2 million lines were via DSL, and 3.6 million via cable.

- High-speed subscribers were reported in 75 percent of the nation's zip codes, covering all fifty states, the District of Columbia, Puerto Rico, and the Virgin Islands.

Increasing Threats and Vulnerabilities

Although network viruses, worms, denial-of-service (DoS) attacks, and unauthorized remote access increased in frequency through the 1990s, there was no corresponding defensive or security change in the culture of the Internet user. Antivirus software was introduced in 1988 to address the growing problem of viruses being spread by floppy disks. Through the mid–1990s, the main threat vector from malicious software remained via infected diskettes, but most computer users did not use antivirus software. This was partially due to a lack of awareness and because of the drop in performance that most users experienced when using antivirus protection.

Likewise, the use of firewalls prior to the late 1990s was not as widespread as it is today. Most home users and small to midsize businesses did not have a firewall or even know what one was. Unfortunately, today a significant percentage of home users still connect to the Internet without enabling some type of firewall protection.

Finally, the concept of updating and patching software to prevent security breaches has taken a number of years to be understood by the general public. Even today, a large number of Internet users do not keep their system software updated or patched. Many believe that it is not necessary or that there is no threat. Others do not understand what the blinking "Update" icon in the system tray means. Unfortunately that is as dangerous as ignoring the "Check oil" warning light on a car dashboard.

These three areas—antivirus protection, firewalls, and software patching—are essential for providing a baseline of security to Internet users. Large numbers of users today do not understand how to use these techniques, making the spread of malicious software and other methods of attack trivially easy. The exponential annual growth of broadband or high-speed residential connections makes the situation even worse. The Internet and the infrastructures that depend on it are at risk of a catastrophic failure event occurring in the near future. Figure 9.1 reflects the number of incidents reports to the CERT/CC from 1988 through 2003.

Figure 9.1 Incidents reported to the CERT/CC from 1988 through 2003 (source – CERT/CC)

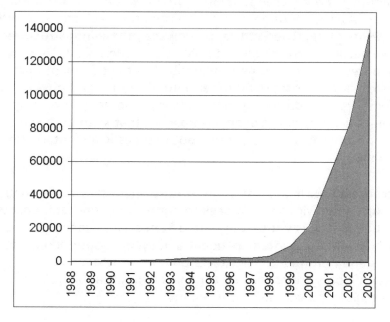

Critical Infrastructure Vulnerabilities

In the mid-1990s, the Clinton Administration launched an initiative to assess the impact of the Internet on the nation's economy and its underlying infrastructures. As part of this effort, the President's Commission on Critical Infrastructure Protection studied the critical infrastructures and found numerous significant vulnerabilities. In Fall 1997, the commission proposed a strategy for protecting the nation. Its report, *Critical Foundations: Protecting America's Infrastructures*, called for a national plan to assure the security of the United States' increasingly vulnerable and interconnected critical infrastructures. The report noted that critical infrastructure protection is a "responsibility shared by both the public and the private sectors."

A subsequent white paper the White House published in Spring 1998 to accompany Presidential Decision Directive 63 (PDD 63) explained that the nation's military and economy were increasingly reliant on certain critical infrastructures and on cyber-based information systems:

> Many of the nation's critical infrastructures have historically been physically and logically separate systems that had little interdependence. As a result of advances in information technology and the necessity of improved efficiency, however, these infrastructures have become increasingly automated and interlinked. These same advances have created new vulnerabilities to equipment failures, human error, weather and other natural causes, and physical and cyber attacks. Addressing these vulnerabilities will necessarily require flexible, evolutionary approaches that span both the public and private sectors, and protect both domestic and international security.
>
> Because of our military strength, future enemies, whether nations, groups or individuals, may seek to harm us in non-traditional ways including attacks within the United States. Our economy is increasingly reliant upon interdependent and cyber-supported infrastructures and non-traditional attacks on our infrastructure and information systems may be capable of significantly harming both our military power and our economy.
>
> —The Clinton Administration's Policy on Critical Infrastructure Protection: Presidential Decision Directive 63, May 22, 1998

PDD 63 recognized that the United States needed to develop the means to protect the nation's critical infrastructures from intentional acts that would significantly diminish its capabilities. Some of the items identified included:

- The federal government's ability to perform essential national security missions and to ensure the general public's health and safety

- State and local government's ability to maintain order and to deliver minimum essential public services

- The private sector's role in ensuring the orderly functioning of the economy and the delivery of essential telecommunications, energy, financial, and transportation services

PDD 63 also recognized that "any interruptions or manipulations of these critical functions must be brief, infrequent, manageable, geographically isolated, and minimally detrimental to the welfare of the United States."

The administration's directive proposed the creation of five new resources:

- **A national coordinator** whose scope included not only critical infrastructure protection but also protection against foreign terrorism and threats of domestic mass destruction.

- **A National Infrastructure Protection Center (NIPC) at the FBI** created to fuse representatives from FBI, DOD, USSS, Energy, Transportation, the Intelligence community, and the private sector into an unprecedented attempt at information sharing among agencies in collaboration with the private sector. The NIPC was charged with providing the principal means of facilitating and coordinating the federal government's response to an incident, mitigating attacks, investigating threats, and monitoring reconstitution efforts.

- **Information Sharing and Analysis Centers (ISACs)** were encouraged to be built by the private sector in cooperation with the federal government and modeled on the Centers for Disease Control and Prevention.

- **A National Infrastructure Assurance Council** was to be drawn from private sector leaders and state and local officials to provide guidance to the policy formulation of a national plan.

- **The Critical Infrastructure Assurance Office** was to provide support to the national coordinator's work with government agencies and the private sector in developing a national plan. The office was to also help coordinate a national education and awareness program as well as legislative and public affairs.

Of these proposed capabilities, all but the NIAC were implemented by the end of the decade. All these functions ultimately became part of the U.S. Department of Homeland Security in 2003.

Throughout this process, the primary risk that was identified was an attack on the cyber networks, the common thread connecting all the critical infrastructures. It was also noted that the reliable operation of the electric grid and the power system are fundamental to the operation of the critical infrastructures. However, the Internet is accessible worldwide, making it a likely avenue for an adversary wanting to disrupt or degrade these systems.

The publication of PDD 63 in the spring of 1998 marked a turning point in the understanding of how dependent the nation was becoming on the Internet. It laid the foundation for organizations that ultimately were incorporated into the Department of Homeland Security. It also predicted that terrorist organizations might someday attack U.S. critical infrastructures. The thinking at that time was that a future attack on the United States would come via bits and bytes, not via airplanes flying into buildings.

Terrorist Attacks of September 2001

A simultaneous cyber attack on the critical infrastructures did not accompany the terrorist attacks on September 11, 2001. Imagine the amount of damage if, at the same time terrorists attacked buildings in New York City and Washington, D.C., cyber attacks took place against the communications systems used by the police, fire, and other emergency response teams. What would the national reaction have been if the local urban mass-transit systems, national rail-switching networks, or the Federal Aviation Administration's flight-tracking system were concurrently disrupted or disabled?

We were fortunate that the events of that morning were limited to only three geographic areas. Did Al Qaeda plan to add cyber attacks as a force multiplier but was unable to or chose not to? We may never know the answer. What we do know is that computers discovered in Al Qaeda safe houses in Pakistan a few months after the attacks contained detailed information about many domestic infrastructures, including maps, photographs, and technical data about their operations and interdependencies. What were the terrorists planning? Were additional critical infrastructure attacks coming?

In spite of the tragic loss of human life and physical property, many lessons were learned in the aftermath of the attacks. For example, a single central telephone office located adjacent to the World Trade Center complex serves most of Lower Manhattan's office buildings. Hundreds of thousands of telephone lines connect to the Verizon building at 140 West Street, along with several million data circuits. Next to the building, in WTC 7, were two of Con Edison's electric substations that served most of the Lower East Side and virtually every building from Duane Street to Fulton Street to South Ferry. The collapse of WTC 7 late in the day on September 11 instantly destroyed both substations.

Fortunately, the Verizon building did not collapse, but along with many other buildings bordering the WTC complex, it suffered significant damage. Steel I-beams and other heavy debris punctured many sections of the walls facing the WTC complex, penetrating deep into switching rooms and offices. When WTC 7 fell, a large section of that building's steel frame came to rest against the Verizon building, causing additional damage.

Not visible in many of the photos taken that day was the chaos under the sidewalks and streets. The fiber optic and copper cabling entering the Verizon building from below the streets was physically damaged by large steel girders that pierced the sidewalks to a depth of several feet. Millions of gallons of water from broken water mains, steam lines, and the Hudson River rushed into the underground conduits and chambers that carried not only the telecommunications cables but also pneumatic mailing tubes, electrical cables, and other infrastructures.

The damage extended to a number of blocks around the WTC complex. Several large bundles of underground fiber optic cables just outside the Verizon building were literally sliced in half by the debris, then encased in water, mud, and steam escaping from broken high-pressure lines. Due to the severe damage to the underground conduits and tunnels, Verizon and Con Edison quickly decided to restore operations using a street-level network. For many weeks after September 11, the sidewalks of the area around the World Trade Center complex became the pathways for miles of power and communications cables.

Years of telephone company mergers and acquisitions largely reduced the redundancy previously engineered into the networks. For example, the New York Stock Exchange had designed over a dozen separate communications paths, with roughly half of them terminating at the Verizon building and the remainder traveling over diverse routes to other switching centers further north. On September 11, there were still over a dozen "separate paths," but they were only virtual—all but one physically terminated in the Verizon building.

Many large metropolitan areas have two major central telephone-switching centers, a remnant of the days when AT&T dominated the telephone market. Since the terrorist attacks, many urban businesses have reexamined the physical paths that their communications circuits take to their local switching office, ensuring that they are not paying for what really amounts to "virtual" diversity.

The loss of communications towers and infrastructure, combined with a massive overload in calls, disrupted the cellular telephone service in Manhattan on that day, making it virtually unusable for most of the day. The loss of cell phone service affected both individuals attempting to call business partners or family members and first-response organizations that had grown accustomed to using the cellular telephone service as a primary means of communication.

Remarkably, although both the landline and cellular telephone systems suffered significant loss of service in the area around the WTC complex, most Internet users in adjacent buildings were able to instant message or use e-mail to communicate during the crisis. Due to the multiple cross-connections and web-like fabric of the Internet, data automatically routes around physically damaged sections. Fortunately, there were no direct attacks on the Internet mechanisms that morning in conjunction with the physical attacks.

The past few years have brought many "wakeup calls" to the vulnerabilities of our critical infrastructures and dependence on the cyber networks. The terrorist attacks in September 2001 were by far the most severe recent example, but two other cyber events, frequently referred to as "wakeup calls" or "watershed events," inside the U.S. Department of Defense deserve mentioning.

Eligible Receiver and Solar Sunrise

At about the same time that the President's Commission on Critical Infrastructure Protection was developing its report in 1997, the U.S. Department of Defense (DoD) conducted a highly classified no-notice exercise. Code-named Eligible Receiver 97, the drill's purpose was to imitate a foreign cyber attack on the Defense Department and to test the department's planning and crisis action capabilities. Over a period of a few weeks in June of that year, a team of government hackers portraying a hostile country successfully invaded multiple military computers and networks. The ease with which they gained access shocked officials and revealed significant vulnerabilities in DoD information systems.

The exercise was real—there was an actual attack on key DoD information systems, using known vulnerabilities and resulting in genuine disruptions noticed by some system administrators. The attacks were launched from commercial

Internet accounts and used tools and techniques derived from open source research. During the exercise, the attack team members gained root or administrator access to dozens of computer systems; were able to read and modify e-mail, files, and passwords; and were even able to disrupt some telephone services.

Several key observations were made at the conclusion of the exercise:

- Informational and operational security practices were poor and were significant contributors to the overall DoD vulnerabilities.

- Gaining attribution for an attack is nearly impossible, and usually inaccurate.

- The DoD had nearly no means to detect or assess the impact of cyber attacks.

- The few existing methods of detecting, reporting, and reacting were too slow compared with the speed of cyber attacks.

- No special tools or techniques were needed beyond those available through open source channels to severely degrade or disrupt DoD computers and networks.

NOTE

At the time of the exercise, there was a general understanding of the increasing vulnerabilities and resulting risks to the security of the DoD networks, but little was done to change the way that business was conducted. Many senior leaders felt that since the findings were from a simulation, they did not reflect the true nature of the threat. The consensus was that "real" access to the DoD systems was possible only via specially crafted attacks. That view would change about a half year later.

In early February 1998, the United States was preparing for potential military action against Iraq in response to United Nations weapons inspection disputes. While those preparations were under way, a subtle attack against DoD computer networks began. The attack pattern looked like preparations for a larger attack against all the department's information and communication systems.

Appearing to come from sites in Israel, France, Germany, Taiwan, and the United Arab Emirates, the attacks targeted Air Force, Navy, and Marine Corps computer systems worldwide. The intruders used a well-known vulnerability in the Solaris operating system and followed the same attack profile against each target:

- Scanning and probing networks to find vulnerable systems
- Exploiting the vulnerability
- Loading a sniffing program to gather usernames, passwords, and other data
- Returning at a later time to harvest the sniffed data

The DoD and other government agencies went into 24-hour emergency response mode, installed intrusion detection systems on key networks, and began an intensive forensics effort to determine the source of the attacks. Investigators began calling the case by its new code name—Solar Sunrise. Several leads were followed, but it was unclear if the attacks were coming from Iraq, a terrorist group, a foreign intelligence agency, or perhaps some hackers hired to gain access to DoD systems.

For the DoD, the parallels between the February 1998 attack and the June 1997 exercise were unnerving. In both cases, the department had no effective indications or warning system, meaning that they were unable to see either of the attacks coming. Intrusion detection systems were available but were not widely deployed and not well understood. There was no departmentwide plan or organization for defending against computer network attacks. Identification of cyber threat groups, profiles, and motivations was nearly nonexistent.

After weeks of investigating, the attackers turned out to be a pair of teenagers in California. A teen in Israel was their guide. Known as The Analyzer, he eluded capture for a few weeks and even granted interviews to reporters while on the run. The teen's motivations centered on ego, power, and the challenge of breaking into Defense Department systems rather than a desire to disrupt the operations aimed at Iraq. The attacks did not cause any serious damage to DoD systems, but due to the interdependency of the civilian and military logistics databases and networks with the department's unclassified computer networks, the potential for impact during the heightened tensions with Iraq was very high.

New Organizations and New Discoveries

Nineteen ninety-eight was a year of significant awakening in both the military and the civil sectors of the U.S. government. In the spring of that year, the

Clinton Administration published PDD 63 and launched the first of several organizations that would eventually become central components of the Department of Homeland Security in 2003. The National Infrastructure Protection Center became part of the Department of Justice, and the Critical Infrastructure Assurance Office joined the Department of Commerce.

The private sector also established the first of several sector Information Sharing and Analysis Centers, each connected with a counterpart office in the federal government. ISACs are a mechanism for the private and public sectors to create partnerships for sharing information about physical and cyber threats, vulnerabilities, and detected events that threaten the critical infrastructures. The ISAC model grew slowly over the subsequent years, but in February 2000, distributed DoS attacks against major e-commerce sites energized the sectors into action.

The Defense Department, reeling from the results of Eligible Receiver 97 and Solar Sunrise, took quick steps in 1998 to respond to the growing threats in cyber space directed at DoD computer networks. A new organization, the Joint Task Force for Computer Network Defense, began operation at the end of the year, following several months of deliberation over its function, design, and placement within the department. Like most cyber defense organizations of that time, the JTF-CND focused initially on identifying and reducing the technical vulnerabilities of computers and computer networks within the networks under its control.

Concurrent with the creation of the JTF-CND in late 1998, the Pentagon also proposed an idea that the DoD examine its networks not just for vulnerabilities in software or a lack of defensive technologies such as firewalls or intrusion detection systems, but also for Web sites and other online resources that exposed sensitive information to the Internet. That proposal came to life in early 1999 with the creation of the Joint Web Risk Assessment Cell, a reserve unit that drilled on the weekends in cyberspace rather than at a Reserve Center. The JWRAC was colocated with the JTF-CND and eventually became part of the JTF under a restructuring effort a few years later.

Beginning at first with the DoD's DefenseLINK web site and then extending to all of the DoD's online resources, the JWRAC confirmed what a foreign Information Warfare officer was quoted as saying in early 1998:

> I am amazed at the amount and content of open-source material available over the Internet from U.S. military and other government agencies... An enemy of the U.S. does not need to have specific war/operations plans when so much info about U.S. doctrine is openly available.
>
> —JWRAC briefing, November 27, 2001

During the first year of operation, the team examined hundreds of DoD Web sites and found significant amounts of information that should not have been available online, such as classified documents, detailed exercise participant information and lessons learned, and For Official Use Only documents and messages. Other items they found included operations plans with annexes detailing logistics, equipment, and manpower data, briefings intended for select audiences, detailed personal data, organizational charts, photos, and other information that should not have been online.

Most of the individual items were unclassified by themselves, but in aggregate a significant amount of classified information could be gathered simply using an online search engine and simple keywords. The remainder of the federal government did not address the same information vulnerability in its Web resources until after the September 2001 terrorist attacks. Even today, a rich amount of information useful for an adversary conducting pre-attack reconnaissance on the critical infrastructures remains online in government and private sector Web sites.

Identifying and Characterizing the Cyber Threat

Publicizing a formal cyber threat identification and characterization methodology is a new area for the DoD and the federal government. Until the late 1990s, any discussion of foreign cyber offensive capabilities, the means and techniques used to gain attribution for a cyber attack against government computers, or the fact that there even was a cyber attack against government computer networks remained classified.

With the establishment of the NIPC and JTF-CND in 1998, that mindset began to change. Both organizations began studying and analyzing the specific types of groups or organizations that might likely conduct an attack against the critical infrastructures or government computer networks. They found that at the national level, over 100 countries had an information operations capability, at least 20 had targeted the United States in the past, and several had capabilities equal to ours. They also found that tens of thousands of Web sites contained cyber tools useful for a cyber attack and that millions of computer users possessed the skills to employ them in such a manner as to cause significant damage to Internet components and mechanisms.

The findings supported earlier research that a rough ranking of the existing threat groups was possible, ranging from the least common in terms of numbers but most capable to cause damage to the most common but least capable to cause widespread damage:

- Nation states (least common, most potential for damage)
- Terrorists
- Spies, including corporate espionage
- Organized crime
- Insiders
- Hackers (most common, least potential for damage)

NOTE

Another finding was that all six of these groups were both increasing in numbers and increasing in capabilities. Unfortunately, the organizations also found that the defensive community is not growing, nor is it becoming more adept in defensive operations at anywhere close to same rate.

All these groups represent overlapping sets of threat actors, and gaining attribution on specifically who or what organization is responsible for a particular attack is extremely difficult. Intrusion detection systems, firewall logs, and antivirus software will not tell the system administrator the name of the intruder. A teenage hacker or a skilled foreign government can activate a buffer overflow attack against a vulnerable application that renders a covert root shell listening on a high TCP port. The techniques and tools used by all six of these groups are typically the same, but the motivations and intentions vary widely.

Nation States

A subject that was highly classified only a few years ago but is now in open discussion is the capability and intent of nations to conduct offensive cyber operations against each other. Chapter 10 explores, in depth, a few of the larger and more obvious threats, such as Russia, China, and others. Nearly all countries connect to the Internet, and most know that information control via computer networks can be a far more powerful weapon than guns, ships, or missiles. The cost of waging an information war against larger and wealthier countries is extremely low, and access to information on how to conduct computer attacks is easy to find.

Information warfare is not always destructive or disruptive. Some of the best cyber attacks have been against the minds of the humans that use the computer systems rather than against the computers and networks themselves. Instead of physically attacking the communications infrastructure or launching malicious code attacks against the computers themselves, this class of attack aims at influencing what a person thinks or does after receiving information from a computer-based system or network.

Direct attacks or disruptions of the cyber backbone would cause significant problems with the operation of the critical infrastructures. However, imagine the chaos that would ensue by injecting false information into the cyber control systems of an energy distribution system. Economic conditions, rather than consumer demand, control the flow of electricity in power grids. The price of energy determines how much electricity flows from a generator to a particular consumption area. Disrupting the barter and sale of energy by injecting false energy values into the computerized energy sales system could have an extremely serious effect on the balance and flow of electricity in a national grid.

The likelihood of a nation attacking another nation with cyber weapons is very low, largely due to the probability that the attack can cause serious side effects to their own Internet-based networks and because of the potential for swift retaliation once the attack is discovered and attributed. However, the amount of potential damage to the critical infrastructures is remarkably high if a nation decides to use the Internet as a path for an attack. For this reason, it is imperative that infrastructure owners and operators protect their systems from a cyber attack and have a means for rapid restoration of operations should an attack occur.

Terrorists

There is a great deal of hyperbole about cyber terrorism and the possibility that terrorist groups like Al Qaeda might strike next via the Internet rather than via a physical attack. Although the likelihood of a standalone cyber attack is low, a cyber attack in conjunction with a physical attack is very likely and could be an extremely effective force multiplier.

The number of organized terrorist groups grows annually, largely because of the apparent success of Al Qaeda in September 2001 and because of growing distrust and dislike of anything "western" or "American" by societies that support this type of violence. Formerly seen as a bunch of thugs with guns and bombs and very little technical capability, the terrorist group model changed when evidence was uncovered that Al Qaeda and other groups actively recruit members with advanced degrees and operate very complex communications systems.

Terrorist groups are not likely to attack the Internet or computer networks in a destructive fashion unless the attacks would amplify the effects of physical attacks. The Internet's global reach and availability are far too valuable as a communications tool for these groups. If the likelihood of Internetwide damage is low, disruptive attacks on specific targets such as a rail-signaling system or a healthcare system are likely scenarios when coordinated to occur simultaneously with a physical attack.

Although not an attack in the destructive sense, there is mounting evidence that terrorist groups take advantage of the complexity of the Internet for fundraising and money laundering. Several recent high-profile investigations revealed online sales of drugs, weapons, and even pirated computer software resulting in profits traceable to various terrorist groups. It is possible that some of the recent rise in phishing e-mails, spam, and other online fraud schemes relate to moneymaking operations connected with terrorist groups.

Espionage

Governments and businesses around the world spy on each other for a variety of reasons. Most espionage operations focus on gathering intelligence about the activities of an opponent to guess his next move or for the early detection of a new weapons system or technology. Other reasons include monitoring an opponent for contract or treaty compliance or simply to maintain awareness of the activities of key individuals. Theft of trade secrets or classified information is also a common practice.

Prior to the advent of the Internet, these types of intelligence-collection operations required years of training for the individuals serving as spies and the possibility of torture or death if captured. Today the risk to human life is much less and the amount of information available via the Internet much more complete. Why risk a human life if all or most of the information needed about an opponent is available online? This technique only works against opponents that are active information publishers, but in today's highly connected world, there are very few that are not.

Gathering intelligence by itself will typically not have a physically destructive or disruptive effect on the critical infrastructures. Many infrastructure owners openly publish data about their systems, and the online search engines provide easy access to billions of documents and files around the world. However, armed with the technical knowledge of infrastructure interdependencies and potential weaknesses, an opponent can focus an attack with much greater precision.

Organized Crime

The Internet of today has many parallels with the Wild West culture of over 150 years ago. Many groups on the Internet operate outside the reach of the formal legal system. There are even groups that function like cyber vigilante posses, hunting down online criminals in return for bounties paid for successful convictions. Government law enforcement organizations seem to be powerless to stop online gambling, pornography, fraud, and sales of illegal substances. For some Internet users, it seems like everybody is wearing a six-shooter and that law enforcement is a job for the citizens rather than the sheriff.

Fueling the online criminal world is the rapid growth of spam e-mail containing fraudulent offers and links to counterfeit Web sites. Most of these sites attempt to collect personal finance information such as credit card numbers or bank account information. Some offer deals "too good to be true" that often turn out to be just that. This is in contrast with the primary online organized crime effort of only a few years ago—pornography.

To get the spam e-mails into a wider number of inboxes, organized crime groups in the past year increasingly turned to the use of viruses and worms to deliver malicious software that creates rogue mail servers. The growth of broadband and high-speed Internet connections in homes and small businesses as well as the increased use of vulnerable peer-to-peer software makes this technique easy and cheap. With millions of home computers "always on" and connected to the Internet, the odds of finding a few thousand unpatched computers with no antivirus protection is very good. These weakened computers make excellent spam remailers.

Support of efforts at money making or perhaps laundering are the most likely reasons organized crime groups would attack a critical infrastructure. These groups rarely engage in online destructive behavior except perhaps to attack an opponent's system or resources. Some examples of organized crime attacks on infrastructures might include attempts at electronically rerouting a package or delivery, manipulating financial networks, or altering the value of a commodity such as electricity, to profit from the change.

Insiders

A critical infrastructure insider is not necessarily an employee of the company or organization that manages the system. In the context of cyber threats, insiders are those who have access to the computers and computer networks and have knowledge of the value of the information contained within them. This group naturally includes most employees, but it can also include business partners, family members, customers, suppliers, and, in rare cases, competitors. The term *insider* by itself does not imply maliciousness or hostility. It only means that the person has access and knowledge, and most insiders are generally not intentionally malicious.

A technique known as *social engineering* helps malicious outsiders gain inside access to organizations with otherwise strong technical security postures. Posing as a legitimate employee or pretending to have authorized access, social engineers take advantage of vulnerabilities in human social customs and courtesies. If they are able to convince a legitimate insider of an organization to allow them to have access to a physical or cyber resource, they are then elevated to insider status since they now possess the two key items—access and knowledge.

Insider cyber threats are either intentional or nonintentional, and within those two groups they can be destructive or nondestructive. An example of a nonintentional, nondestructive insider threat is an employee who forwards sensitive e-mails to a home account to work on them overnight. Normally these employees mean no harm, but no one has explained to them the risk they are creating by forwarding internal e-mails to themselves via a public e-mail system. Nonintentional and potentially destructive insider threats include users who install peer-to-peer software on company computers when they do not know that it is against company policy to do so.

On the other end of the scale, an intentional and (directly) nondestructive insider threat includes actions taken to remove proprietary or classified information from an organization with the intent to pass it along to an adversary or competitor. Intentional and destructive insiders—for example, a disgruntled system administrator who deletes important data from the organization's file servers just before resigning—are the worst case.

Several recent cyber crime surveys point to the insider as the number-one threat facing organizations with computers and computer networks. Because of the complexity of computer networks and the normally small ratio of support staff to users, insiders have many opportunities to cause severe damage. Malicious insiders are and will remain the highest threat to the reliable operation of critical infrastructures.

Well-financed groups such as terrorist organizations or nation state-sponsored offensive cyber organizations will use insiders as a means of gaining access to systems well protected from the Internet. Many infrastructure operators have security systems designed to protect their networks from technical attacks originating on the Internet but lack sufficient detection mechanisms that can alert on malicious insider activity. This is an area where additional education for system administrators as well as senior management staff will be a wise investment.

Hackers

The most common and most visible threat to computers and computer networks connected to the Internet is the malicious hacking subculture. Unfortunately, many system administrators and advanced computer users consider themselves members of the general hacking scene, which makes it difficult to differentiate between those who have malicious intentions and those who do not. The tools used by both "white hat" (nonmalicious) and "black hat" (malicious) groups are identical. For example, white-hat hackers use vulnerability scanners to find and fix security holes to prevent unauthorized access; black-hat hackers use the same tools to find and exploit security holes to gain unauthorized access. Further complicating matters is that many malicious hackers are also key security staff members in various organizations, including many critical infrastructures. The generally accepted term for those who wear both white and black hats is a *gray-hat hacker*.

Many hackers, white, black, or gray, get their start as teenagers. It begins with a friend showing them a neat computer trick, or perhaps they stumble onto a hacking Web site while surfing the Internet. In other cases, the teen finds that he or she is the resident computer expert at home and at school and becomes interested in learning more about how the systems and networks work. Teenagers are naturally curious and most shun adult authority, making the lure of becoming a malicious hacker very tempting.

Adults and particularly parents of teenage hackers do a very poor job of explaining to the adolescents the dangers of malicious computer activity. Our society glorifies illegal computer activity through movies and television dramas. The media places convicted cyber criminals on a pedestal, praising the fact that after doing jail time, many have successful careers as cyber security "experts." We should not admire these people. Instead, we should treat them the same way that we treat other convicted lawbreakers.

As in the physical world, adolescents online seek to join groups with common interests and desires. Once in a group, a teen has a natural tendency to want to achieve some sort of status or rank and to advance that status as the membership continues. For malicious hacking groups, "ownership" of Internet resources such as Web servers, routers, or armies of compromised home computers useful for conducting distributed DoS attacks brings increased status. The underground hacking scene has its own currency, trading passwords of compromised computers, valid credit card numbers, and "zero-day" computer exploits—tools that leverage obscure or hidden security holes in software for which there is no available patch or update. There are even titles and ranks, ranging from *script kiddie* at the bottom to *über hacker* or *elite* at the top.

Some hacking groups seek to increase their group's status by defacing Web sites or leaving other obvious markings around the Internet. Like inner-city gangs with unique symbols and slogans, these online gangs have their own markings as well as territories and property considered their home turf. There are also gang battles and "hacker wars" that are not unlike urban gang fights and conflicts. Innocent third parties get caught in the crossfire and their sites suffer from the equivalent of online graffiti and vandalism.

In rare cases, hacking groups might organize as *hacktivists,* or hacking activists, to target online resources of organizations that they oppose. In even rarer cases, organized crime organizations or terrorist groups seeking to pay for unauthorized access, online vandalism, or computer network disruption have contacted individual hackers to contract for the service. Teenage hackers make especially lucrative targets for this behavior, since the lure of money and the fact that they are underage overweigh any fear of criminal arrest and conviction.

Most critical infrastructure owners view malicious hacking groups, gangs, clubs, and individuals as a nuisance rather than a significant threat. In many cases, this attitude is proper, since most of these groups tend to prey on weakly configured systems and networks. Defending against common malicious hackers is as simple as keeping systems up to date, using good firewalls and intrusion detection systems, and following industry best practices for system security.

Summary

Sometimes investigators get lucky and find clues the cyber trespasser left behind in files, leading to a quick arrest and conviction. Like many physical criminal investigations, success in tracking down and finding the person or group behind a cyber incident is largely dependent on evidence left behind at the crime scene. Clues are available in the techniques or tools that the intruder used to gain access, commonalities across multiple break-ins, or interception of communications between the intruder and his or her peers who brag about the unauthorized access.

Because of the difficulty in gaining attribution, the DoD and many government agencies characterize all intrusions as representative of hostile intent from a foreign country until proven otherwise. Hackers and other curiosity seekers attending recent information security conferences receive that message frequently from government officials. Investigators regularly rule out terrorist and nation state-sponsored groups early in a cyber incident investigation, but the significance of the government's position cannot be overemphasized.

Many feel that the bottom group, the hackers, is more a nuisance than a threat to critical infrastructures. However, there is a general fear that eventually one or more hackers will get "lucky" when experimenting with a new tool or technique. Like Thomas Huxley's proposal that an infinite number of monkeys typing on an infinite number of typewriters will eventually type all the works of Shakespeare, there is a good probability that one of the large number of hackers banging away on computer keyboards will someday type the magic sequence of keystrokes that causes significant damage.

To address the problem of attribution and threat identification and government's relative inability to provide early indications and warning of a coming cyber attack, the Department of Homeland Security and other government agencies advocate that system administrators focus on their own system vulnerabilities rather than the threat. This makes sense, because most administrators have full control over vulnerability mitigation and reducing their exposure to the Internet. However, they have little or no influence over the threat groups and generally have no way to predict their next move.

Vulnerability reduction is not always easy, and analysis of weaknesses frequently circles back to identifying the types of threats that might attack a particular system or network. Many system administrators and security professionals are stuck in an endless loop. They try to figure out whom or what is their most likely adversary, but they cannot. They want to orient on a threat, but they are incapable of properly identifying or characterizing it. They then cannot move forward on developing a defensive plan to counter the threat.

When unable to identify cyber threats and adversaries, system administrators and managers of critical infrastructures should instead focus on vulnerability reduction. After all, if no systems are vulnerable to an attack, there cannot be an attack. With the threat vector (the vulnerabilities) reduced or eliminated, threats cannot manifest themselves. Organizations with defensive postures that are threat oriented rather than vulnerability or exposure oriented often overlook this simple rule.

The critical infrastructures are vulnerable to attacks from many angles, including both physical and cyber. Interdependencies between the infrastructures place all at risk, such that a successful attack on one system will likely affect other systems not directly attacked. As we grow more dependent on cyber infrastructures, we need to become more aware of the risks of cyber attacks and modify the way that we design, install, operate, and maintain all our infrastructures, not just the critical ones.

On an international level, several organizations have addressed the growing need for a "culture of security" that must take root to enable our future digital economy and way of life to be successful. One excellent example is a document published by the Organization for Economic Cooperation and Development. The *OECD Guidelines for the Security of Information Systems and Networks* are available online from the OECD Web site at www.oecd.org. The guidelines suggest the need for a greater global awareness and understanding of security issues, with a focus on security in the development of information systems and networks.

The guidelines contain nine complementary principles for participants at all levels, including policy and operational levels:

- Awareness
- Responsibility
- Response
- Ethics
- Democracy
- Risk assessment
- Security design and implementation

- Security management

- Reassessment

Designed for nontechnical decision makers and leaders, the OECD guidelines suggest that awareness, education, information sharing, and training can lead to the adoption of better security understanding and practices. Other international organizations such as the United Nations, the Organization of American States, the Asian-Pacific Economic Council, and the European Union support the principles developed by the OECD.

Threat identification is crucial to protecting the critical infrastructures, but so is the identification and correction of vulnerabilities and exposures. Adoption of a "culture of security" mindset by all will greatly increase the operational capability and reliability of critical infrastructures and will enable future generations to enjoy the benefits of a globally connected society.

## Chapter 10

Characterizing the Extremes—Terrorists and Nation States

Chapter contributed
by Matthew G. Devost

Topics in this Chapter:

- The Nation State Cyber Adversary

- International Terrorists and Rogue Nations

- Physical Insider Placement

Introduction

Nation states and terrorist organizations represent the high end of the cyber adversary spectrum. An attack launched by either of these entities will target critical infrastructures using methods designed to inflict maximum damage against their targeted asset. The targets of attacks launched by national states and terrorists are also likely to be very similar and will focus on critical infrastructures such as banking and finance, electric power, transportation, telecommunications, and health and government services.[i]

A wide variety of factors influence a nation state's or terrorist's intentions and capabilities to use cyber attacks. Although a nation state might have the technical capability to wage an attack on critical infrastructures, there are many deterrents, ranging from fear of escalation into conventional conflict to economic blowback, that reduce their intentions to launch an attack. Likewise, a terrorist organization certainly has the intentions to launch sustained cyber attacks against critical infrastructures, but does not necessarily posses the technical capacity to engage in such an attack.

This chapter evaluates those decision elements that will influence terrorist and nation state cyber attack potential. It looks at attractors and deterrents to attack and technical capabilities, and it provides insight into how we might characterize and differentiate these two distinct high-end cyber adversaries.

The Nation State Cyber Adversary

The concept of national security has evolved in recent years to include attack and defense of the IT components of critical infrastructures. Many nations have developed programs to accommodate this evolution from both offensive and defensive perspectives. Government officials have estimated, in congressional testimony, that more than one hundred nations are currently developing information warfare programs in some capacity[ii]. There are several interesting dynamics that influence the characterization of the nation state cyber threat, which can be nominally broken down into two categories: attractors and deterrents.

The nation state decision-making process is prejudiced by the nation's role in the global community (economic, military, and cultural) and is more likely to be influenced by the deterrents to attack than the attractors. Given the potential costs of engaging in a sustained cyber attack against the critical infrastructures of another nation state, the attractiveness of launching the attack is significantly reduced. The exceptions to this rule will exist when one or more of the following has occurred:

- An attack can be launched with guaranteed anonymity.

- The nation state acts irrationally due to poor decision making by individual leaders.

- The nation state is presented with a desperate situation such as fear of or presence of conventional conflict, economic failure, or leadership crisis.

Nation State Cyber Adversary Attractors

Cyber attacks launched by nation states are likely to be characterized as information warfare attacks, which creates a unique dynamic because the term "warfare" carries different connotations and commitment than those of the word "attack." Politically and strategically, there are many attractions to state-sponsored information warfare. It is low cost, timely, not location specific, provides no early warning, is not taboo, inflicts low human life costs, and can be waged in complete anonymity. Each of these must be examined at length to gain perspective on the nation state threat.

Low Cost

Information warfare is relatively cheap to wage, and you get a high return on your investment through the use of information warfare techniques. Expert estimates in the mid-90s indicated that it would cost less than $100 million to reduce the Unites States to information rubble. That amount is incredibly cheap when compared to the cost of conventional military weapons. Later estimates noted that the cost to develop a capable nation state cyber attack capability was less than $100 million. This makes offensive information warfare attractive to entities such as third world states and offers them the same basic capability to inflict damage on information infrastructures as second and first world nations.

Timely and Not Location Specific

Information warfare is timely, and it is not location specific. Information warfare can be waged at the "drop of a pin" (to steal an analogy from the telecommunications industry). There is no early warning system for information warfare; you don't know it is coming and so you must always anticipate it. This creates a high level of paranoia. No radar can pick up a long distance phone call from overseas, yet that one phone call may cause more monetary damage than a dozen planes carrying conventional ordinance. The first World Trade Center attack is a perfect example. The damage to the flow of information, estimated at over $1 billion,[iii] proved to be more costly than the structural damage inflicted on the building. Viruses can be imported into the United States through information networks, telephone lines, or on simple floppy disks, which typically do not attract the attention of U.S. customs inspectors.

Although a well-planned information warfare attack might take several years to orchestrate, it can occur instantaneously. To uncover plans for such an attack would involve a great deal of investigation and intelligence, or in many cases, a stroke of luck. Most of the actors would be invisible, both to the victim and to each other. Most of the preparatory work for lower levels of information warfare can be done outside the traditional territorial boundaries of the victim nation.

Anonymity

Information warfare can be waged anonymously. Anonymity is the nature of new technologies, especially telecommunications. An anonymous attack creates two problems. Not only has a state's national security been breached, but there is also no one to hold accountable for the attack. This makes information warfare a very attractive tool to covert operators. However, given the nature and intent of terrorism, it is highly unlikely that terrorists will remain anonymous while engaging in information warfare, since it is in their best interest to claim the damage they have inflicted.

Political dilemmas arise in the victim state when citizens demand retribution. The government has no target. The result will be political instability as citizens focus blame on the government for allowing this to happen. It might even be possible to collapse a particular political system with prolonged, systematic anonymous attacks.

"We need computers in our lives, but we do not trust them." Winn Schwartau calls these conflicting feelings "binary schizophrenia." When used anonymously, information warfare plays on feelings of binary schizophrenia, causing insecurity and chaos. In this regard, anonymous information warfare is comparable to the German blitzkrieg of World War II. It makes an impact on the citizenry as well the government. Targets can be strategically selected to generate the maximum amount of chaos and insecurity possible.

Minimal Loss of Human Life

Information warfare can also be waged to minimize the amount of human life lost within a target nation. This makes information warfare techniques politically attractive since there are no global taboos associated with waging war against machines. Jeff Legro gives three reasons why states might restrain from using certain weapons or means of warfare. He argues, "Countries may pursue restraint because popular opinion vilifies certain weapons; because leaders calculate that escalation would damage their domestic and international political support; or because states fear retaliatory attacks."[iv]

How does information warfare fit within this framework? Because information warfare causes low levels of human casualties and structural damage, there is little reason to believe that popular opinion will vilify it. In fact, populations will not even know information warfare is being waged against them until it is too late. Even at that point, very few people will understand the methods used. Therefore it is highly unlikely that information warfare will be considered an inhuman way to pursue diplomacy by other means.

There is also little reason to believe that using information warfare will be politically damaging to the aggressor country. Information warfare's potential anonymity assures that the aggressor will be identified only if they wish to be. When information warfare is waged by one nation against another without anonymity, the political outcomes would resemble those of traditional warfare. Strategic alliances could be formed, and some states could chose to remain neutral, though it is highly unlikely that neutral states will be able to avoid the global economic aftershocks of high-intensity global information warfare.

If waged without anonymity, it is very likely that a victim nation would respond to information warfare with retaliatory strikes. In this regard, fear of retaliation or escalation will act as a deterrent to using information warfare. However, the first strike advantage of information warfare might neutralize any fears regarding retaliation using counter-information warfare, leaving victim nations with the difficult decision of responding with conventional military force.

First Strike Advantage

In information warfare, there is a huge first strike advantage, but only if the goal is unlimited destruction, and anonymity is utilized to prevent a conventional response. There is a high correlation between the extent to which a nation damages its enemy's information capabilities and their ability to respond using purely information warfare techniques. A nation can execute this first strike anonymously if it so desires, thus delaying retaliation indefinitely.

The first strike advantage of information warfare complicates matters further by creating a security dilemma in which those countries exercising the greatest amount of restraint will likely incur the most damage. In information warfare, a first strike decreases the likelihood and may even prevent an adversary from responding. The strategic advantages of waging a first strike means that nations will always keep a finger on the trigger. In an anarchic international system, hostilities or conflict might escalate quickly into information warfare in an effort to generate a strategic advantage over one's adversary. If conventional conflict is inevitable, whoever destroys their adversary's information systems first gains a strategic advantage in battle.

Offensive Nature of Information Warfare

Information technology and computer systems are vulnerable by nature. Therefore, taking defensive measures against the information warfare threat will always be difficult and costly. Improving the defense of information systems also contributes to the security dilemma since decreasing one's susceptibility to information warfare increases the attraction of using information warfare offensively. There are, however, as will be examined in the next section, several deterrents to waging state-sponsored information warfare among technologically advanced nations that will entice states to pursue defensive postures. In order to neutralize the security dilemma presented by defensive postures, states may share defensive technologies to ensure that a defensive equilibrium is maintained. This serves a dual purpose: a relative balance of power is maintained among states; and the offensive threat of rogue states or terrorist entities is reduced. Though states will want to maintain offensive "just-in-case" capabilities, security is best maintained, due to the nature of the threat, by developing defensive capabilities.

Nation State Cyber Adversary Deterrents

Among technologically advanced nations, there are several deterrents to waging information warfare. Factors such as economic interdependence, fear of escalation, and lack of technical expertise detract from the advantages of state sponsored information warfare

Economic Interdependence

Perhaps the most useful definition of economic interdependence in any discussion of information warfare is the one put forth by Richard Cooper. He uses the term to "refer to the sensitivity of economic transactions between two or more nations to economic developments within those nations."ᵛ Focusing on economic sensitivity allows us to disregard conventional measures such as trade surpluses and deficits and look at the interlinked effects of economic stability between interdependent nations.

Our focal point, from the information warfare perspective, must be upon the extent to which interdependent nations will feel the economic aftershocks of economic instability. Should the U.S. fall victim to information warfare directed at our financial institutions, what effect would it have on the economic stability of the European Community or Japan and the Pacific Rim nations? If interdependence is to act as a deterrent to information warfare, levels of interdependence must be high enough as to ensure that the costs of waging information warfare outweighs the benefits. According to Rosecrance and Stein, the interdependence of the financial system is now formal because we have vested interests in not letting the reserves of foreign currencies drop below a certain threshold, which would harm our own economy.[vi]

With the realization that information warfare has potentially devastating economic effects, interdependence will act as a disincentive to state-sponsored information warfare. Economic interdependence introduces new complex variables into offensive information warfare strategies. Joseph Nye notes that there is power to be derived from making oneself less interdependent with other nations.[vii] This is especially true where information warfare is concerned. The effectiveness of offensive information warfare is increased as benefits exceed costs. One benefit of less interdependence with the target nation is that economic aftershocks will have fewer effects on the aggressor's economy. Decreasing economic interdependence might be seen as a precursor to waging information warfare, but is not a readily realizable goal for most technologically advanced nations. Reducing levels of economic interdependence is costly for two reasons: the benefits of interdependence can no longer be extracted and distributed among the citizenry, perhaps decreasing a nation's prosperity; and domestic political constraints can disrupt the nation's internal balance of power. The domestic sectors of society that benefit from interdependence (multinational corporations, financial institutions, and other investors) will likely logroll interests to prevent the breaking of interdependent links.[viii]

A decreasing level of economic interdependence also contributes to the intensity of security dilemmas and increases the likelihood of escalation. Decreasing economic interdependence might be interpreted as a threatening posture, especially if one nation is more susceptible to attack than the other, as is the case with the United States and most of its trade partners. Increasing economic interdependence, however, might be seen as increasing relative security, especially for the nations most susceptible to attack. This creates difficult policy decisions since traditional forms of negative foreign policy, like economic sanctions, become less effective and perhaps even threatening. If one nation is perceived as a threat, the most effective way of deterring that nation from attacking is to make the costs of information warfare exceed the benefits. This can be done by threatening to use conventional military force or increasing levels of economic interdependence.

Also, interdependence does nothing to prevent states from waging information warfare against specific corporations of economic sectors to increase comparative advantage in those areas. Since such actions are being taken by allies of the United States such as Germany, France, and Japan[ix], interdependence becomes an ineffective deterrent. Fear of escalation (a result of attack detection and attribution) will act as a more effective deterrent, or at least will place limits on the extent to which limited information warfare can be waged. Fear of escalation relates to the cyber adversaries' perceived probability of detection and attribution given an attempt, and the consequences given detection and attribution given an attempt, as described in Chapter 3.

Fear of Escalation

It has already been demonstrated that the military culture will probably use information warfare methods as a strategic supplement to conventional methods in any military conflict and that the escalation of information warfare is likely. But does the reverse hold true? Will information warfare escalate to conventional military conflict? In the context of the nation state cyber adversary, in order for fear of escalation (consequences of attack detection and attribution) to act as an attack deterrent, information warfare must be allowed to escalate into military conflict. A country will not wage information warfare, especially against a country with strong military capabilities, if they fear that the situation might escalate into military conflict if the attack is detected and attributed.

Under these circumstances, information warfare becomes highly politicized, and the domestic bases of power can be compromised. It is important that political leaders declare ahead of time the value of information systems and assure the international community that conventional military tactics, even though they involve the loss of human life, will be used to counter information warfare attacks.

Given that information warfare causes minimal loss of human life, response will be difficult for nations without strong information warfare capabilities. The urge to respond using Industrial Age warfare techniques will be great, but justifying such responses will be difficult unless the value of these information systems is declared before they are attacked. A White House official stating that the U.S. reserves the right to respond to information warfare attacks with conventional means may seem a little drastic, but information warfare is not to be taken lightly by nation states. This type of warfare erodes a nation's strength, destabilizes its economy, and threatens its autonomy. Such responses might be necessary and will certainly be advocated by many policy makers should the circumstances arise. In order for the fear of escalation to work as a deterrent to information warfare, this position must not only be advocated, but also adhered to.

Stated U.S. policy allows for both in-kind response (such as offensive computer network attacks) *and* conventional military response to information warfare attacks. This policy is designed to deter those nations envisioning information warfare attacks as an alternative to conventional warfare. However, it should be noted that these factors do very little to deter a rogue state or nation from using an information attack to gain strategic advantage within a conventional war theatre or to provoke a conventional response. A possible example of future state-sponsored initiatives exists in a document entitled "Unrestricted Warfare" written by Qiao Liang and Wang Xiangsui from the People's Republic of China. Enunciated doctrines such as unrestricted warfare combined with the potential for anonymous attacks mandates additional consideration of this threat, particularly in a political environment where an anonymous attack is likely to be blamed on multinational terrorists (such as Al Qaeda).

Qualifying the Nation State Threat

Having evaluated the factors that impact the nation state decision cycle for engaging in cyber attacks, the following sections provide an overview of specific nation state perspectives on information warfare.

China

China has emerged as one of the most proactive nations in the world with respect to computer network attack/defense and information warfare concepts. They have developed doctrine and training programs, and have conducted actual information warfare exercises.

Some of the likely mechanisms that would be used as part of a Chinese information warfare attack are discussed in the following analysis:

> "If technology finds expression in arms and equipment, then information systems and even electrons can be strategy carriers. A good strategy can "serve as a type of invisible fighting capacity; may make up for inadequate material conditions to a certain extent; may narrow a technological or equipment gap between an army

and its enemy; and may make up for a shortage of information, fighting forces, or poor information operational means."

Although many of these strategies are focused on disrupting military systems, the potential for attack against civilian infrastructure targets is proposed as a major thesis of the book "Unrestricted Warfare." In addition, China has an active hacker community, for which there is much speculation that the hackers actual operate under the influence, if not the control, of the state government. An attack from China might resemble "death by a thousand cuts" as opposed to a targeted nation state attack generated by government resources, making the characterization of each adversary involved highly impracticable (see Chapter 9, Group Characterization).

Russia

The Russian government has also expended resources examining and preparing for the information warfare threat. However, the Russians also recognize the potential "blowback" or unintended consequences associated with a wide-scale attack, and the level of economic interdependence between the United States and Russia acts as a substantial deterrent to attack.

The Russians define information weapons as follows:

> "An information weapon is a specially selected piece of information capable of causing changes in the information processes of information systems (physical, biological, social, etc.) according to the intent of the entity using the weapon." [x]

Russia equates information warfare capability development with maintaining their nuclear capabilities, and to this end proposed an amendment to the United Nations to reduce the potential for attack. Russia has also stated, like the U.S., that the use of information warfare attacks against them will be responded to using the full means of attacks available, including, as stated here, nuclear:

> "The use of IW means against Russia will categorically not be considered a non-military phase of a conflict... Russia retains the right to use nuclear weapons first against the means and forces of IW, and then against the aggressor state itself." [xi]

This statement creates a strong requirement for secure systems within a nation to prevent them from being "framed" for an attack against Russia that is launched from compromised systems within their borders.

Other Nation States

Although two individual nations have been directly referenced here, it should be noted that numerous nation states possess the capability, if not the intent, to target the critical infrastructures of several highly developed nation states. Several countries actively research and utilize information operations techniques in support of other conflicts or national initiatives. For example, much has been written regarding France's use of advanced technologies to support state-sponsored industrial espionage activities. Additionally, Israel has one of the most active hacking and security communities in the world and, given the right political climate, may seek to utilize information attack capabilities. Such activities from countries considered allies become much more likely if they believe that they can conduct them anonymously, or in such a way that the resultant effects are attributed to one or more of their own enemies.

Also indicative of the emerging potential for nation state threats is the increasing number of attacks from emerging nations such as Korea, India, Pakistan, and others. Although most of these attacks are believed to be the work of unstructured hackers, we do not have a mechanism for absolute attribution or adversary characterization that can discount the potential for state-sponsored activity.

International Terrorists and Rogue Nations

There are no strong indications that traditional terrorist groups will abandon conventional tactics in favor of cyber-terrorism attacks. However, the threat of cyber terrorism remains a high-profile concern. In a recent survey of U.S. mayors, nearly 50 percent indicated they were concerned with the concept of such attacks, while only 30 percent indicated concern with a nuclear attack.[xii] Despite the lack of solid open-source evidence, cyber terrorism should be viewed as a critical emerging threat for several reasons.

First, our ability to detect cyber capability is severely limited due to the nature of the attack tools used. Given long-term planning cycles (three to five years for an attack in some cases), it is quite possible that a terrorist organization is currently seeking to develop a capability for future attacks. Although cyber terrorism hasn't been added as a formal terrorist capability, we know acquiring such a capability is on their radar screens. In addition, the proliferation of hacker tools that can be launched using a user-friendly graphical interface has also lowered the technical barrier required to obtain attack capabilities. In the past, these tools were only believed to have a substantial impact on Internet Protocol networks. However, in today's environment some of America's most critical infrastructures have been irresponsibly connected to public IP networks, making them susceptible to attack.

Secondly, we must recognize that terrorist groups are being influenced by a younger, more technical membership and that they understand and successfully use technology in an operational capacity. There is evidence that terrorist organizations have gained both education and training to use information technology, as part of a program to acquire a cyber-terrorism capability or to support the infrastructure for logistics, planning, and communication for future conventional attacks.[xiii] Given appropriate attention and resources, multinational terrorist organizations are capable of developing a critical infrastructure cyber-terrorism attack capability and have indicated intent to do so.[xiv]

Additionally, given constraints on physical travel, financial, logistical, and support networks imposed on terrorist organizations through a cooperative war on terrorism, it becomes much more attractive to pursue cyber attacks. The more successful the U.S. and its allies are at preventing physical terrorist attacks, the more attractive cyber attacks become because they require no physical travel and can be launched simultaneously from distributed geographic locations (known as networked warfare). In fact, it is likely that attacks would be launched from geographic staging areas and compromised hosts to ensure that we cannot respond conventionally to the attack. In this scenario, organizations might be viewed as an attractive target for the sole purpose of obtaining access to systems (with high bandwidth availability) to be used in multistaged attacks against other organizations. See Figure 10.1 for examples of rogue nations.

Figure 10.1 Examples of Rogue Nations

Examples of Rogue Nations
(State sponsors of terrorism identified
by U.S. State Department)

Cuba
Iran
Iraq (before CPA)
Libya
North Korea
Sudan
Syria

Single-issue terrorist organizations like the Earth Liberation Front (ELF) and the Electronic Disturbance Theater (EDT) have adopted cyber terrorism as a viable companion to continued physical attacks and could serve to inspire international terrorists if their actions are successful. For example, in 1998 the Animal Liberation Front (ALF) issued the following warning:

> "We will take offensive actions to damage animal abusers on the Internet in any way possible…This may include denial of service attacks, virus attacks, e-mail bombing, and hacking Web servers. We have already cracked numerous computer systems and borrowed useful data; in the future we will also destroy data."[xv]

Activists that specifically target IT infrastructures have also emerged and have launched isolated inconsequential "hacktivist" attacks. As their level of sophistication and membership grows, they are likely to launch additional attacks. It is likely that any adoption of cyber terrorism by multinational terrorist organizations will be spearheaded by the successes of single-issue terrorists against isolated targets. (For specific discussion of single-issue terrorist/hacktivist threats, please see the following section.) Alternately, a small cell of a multinational terrorist group may develop an attack concept that is pursued in parallel with planning for continued physical attacks or to conduct an attack to augment the impacts or a traditional attack.

In recent discussion, one government official noted the following:

> "Software tools for network intrusion and disruption are becoming globally available over the Internet, providing almost any interested U.S. adversary a basic computer network exploitation or attack capability," Vice Admiral Thomas Wilson said. "To date, however, the skills and effort needed for adversaries to use tools and technology effectively, such as intensive reconnaissance of U.S. target networks, for example, remain important limits on foreign cyber attack capabilities."[xvi]

However, a recent article in the Washington Post noted that members of terrorist organizations are conducting electronic reconnaissance and mapping critical infrastructures, most likely to launch an attack in support of or to augment a conventional physical attack.

Additionally, the Institute for Security Technology Studies at Dartmouth University has offered the following:

> "Separate Islamic fundamentalist terrorist groups have become in many ways a loose, global network of terrorist entities. These entities sometimes work together and sometimes in isolation. They embrace the concept of asymmetric warfare: the use of unconventional tactics to counter overwhelming conventional military superiority. The hallmarks of their operations are surprise, scale, and drama. They use both human couriers and encrypted satellite phones. Further, the C.I.A has already identified two known Islamic terrorist organizations, Hizballahand HAMAS, with the capability and greatest likelihood to use cyber attacks against our infrastructures."[xvii]

It also appears that unstructured hackers are increasingly involving themselves with terrorist organizations and nation states, aligning themselves with a cause (such as anti-American sentiment). Collaborating with terrorist organizations provides gratification and validation for hacking initiatives that may be attractive to some parties. Recent cases of American citizens being recruited as holy warriors and converting to Islam help support the notion that some individuals with hacking skills may join or terrorist organizations for political or religious reasons. In addition, recent cases of conversion such as John Walker Lindh, Aukai Collins, and Jose Padilla demonstrate that the demographic for recruitment and conversion is very similar to the demographics within the unstructured hacker community.

Financial incentives also serve to help recruit hackers into performing actions for terrorist organizations. Reportedly, some unstructured hackers have been recruited by individuals affiliated with terrorist organizations. In 1999, a hacker using the moniker "Chameleon" was approached by Khalid Ibrahim, believed to be a member of the Pakistani terrorist group Harkat-Ul-Ansar that has ties to those responsible for the killing of journalist, Daniel Pearl in early 2002. During the interaction, Ibrahim provided a $1,000 cashier's check in an attempt to purchase network architecture information about Defense Department networks.[xviii]

Terrorist organizations have also paid for information obtained through electronic infiltration to aid in physical attacks. In the fall of 1999, a young hacker using the moniker "ne0h" was approached online by a Middle Easterner requesting architectural schematics to an Airbus A300. In exchange for the promise of $10,000, the hacker provided the plans but was never paid. It is believed by some that those documents were instrumental in perpetrating a December 1999 Indian Airlines hijacking to Kandahar, Afghanistan.[xix] In February 2001, the same man, who promised double the initial payment in exchange for schematics of additional aircraft, approached the same hacker again. The hacker refused on the basis of a previous nonpayment. All requested schematics turned out to be for aircraft identical to those used during the terrorist attacks of September 11th, 2001. One recent article noted the following:

> "It is unlikely that a terrorist organization like al Qaeda currently possesses the capability to launch a sustained cyber terrorism attack against critical infrastructures. The ability to launch a sustained attack with national strategic implications requires extensive planning and expertise that would take years to acquire, although well-funded terrorist organizations would have the capability to pay other parties to conduct electronic attacks."

However, it is possible that an isolated cyber-terrorism attack would be used in one of the following scenarios:

In Parallel with a Physical or WMD Attack

It is likely that terrorist organizations will seek to enhance the impacts of conventional attacks through the use of cyber-terrorism attacks. The objective of the attack would be to reduce our response capability thus increasing the impact of the physical attack. For example, a terrorist organization might seek to disrupt emergency response communications or in the event of a chem/bio, nuclear, or radiological attack, they might seek to disrupt key weather data that would be used to calculate the dispersion of harmful material for the creation of evacuation areas and/or evacuation routes.

To Decrease Confidence in Critical Infrastructures/Psychological Operations

Isolated attacks against critical infrastructures could be used to create panic and decrease public confidence in critical infrastructures. Attacks against financial, transportation, or vital human services would cause significant panic and impact our economic security.

To Cause Physical Damage and/or Loss of Human Life

Cyber-terrorism attacks against select infrastructures could be used as an alternative to conventional physical attacks to facilitate the accomplishment of traditional terrorist goals such as the loss of human life and destruction of property.[xx]

Single-Issue Terrorist Organizations/Hacktivists

Unfunded terrorists are threat agents driven by ideological or political goals, but who, in most cases, do not have the intent or resources to impact public safety, utilize weapons of mass destruction, or inflict sustained infrastructure attacks. Agents in this threat category may seek to temporarily disrupt critical infrastructure operations to make a political statement, file lawsuits to prevent operation of systems or networks, or engage in the theft and/or distribution of sensitive information.

Since the attacks of September 11, 2001, single issue terrorists, including those prone to using violence, have been displaced due to an increasing association of the concept of "terrorism" with radical Islamic fundamentalism bent on launching attacks seeking maximum casualties and consequences. Those groups that engaged in calculated political violence in support of a particular issue or objective, are less inclined to utilize such techniques for fear that such attacks would be associated with international terrorists and would attract the attention of those perpetrating a war on terrorism. As those groups seek other means to pursue their objectives, cyber attacks become increasingly attractive.

The term "hacktivists" has been coined to describe a class of issue-oriented activists who have adopted hacking as a cost-effective alternative to their traditional protest mechanisms. Although they are generally less dangerous than unfunded terrorists, the line between activism and terrorism is becoming blurred by groups such as the Earth Liberation Front, which started as an activist group but has evolved into one of the leading domestic terrorist organizations in the United States.

Although unfunded terrorist groups and hacktivists may lack substantial monetary resources, this does not mean attacks from this threat category are always harmless. The Internet itself provides a mechanism whereby these agents can force temporary coalitions around current events. In fact, we see increasing instances of these grass-roots activists demonstrating their allegiance to one cause or another by relatively autonomous actions that, in the aggregate, can cause serious disruption. There are also no clear limits to the extent with which these groups will be satisfied with their results. If vulnerabilities allowing unfunded terrorist organizations or hacktivists to cause more serious harm to the critical infrastructures present themselves, these groups may take advantage of them.

> "The cyber attacks arising from the events of September 11 reflect a growing use of the Internet as a digital battleground. It is not at all unusual for a regional conflict to have a cyber dimension, where the battles are fought by self-appointed hackers operating under their own rules of engagement. A rash of cyber attacks has accompanied the conflict between Israel and the Palestinians, the conflict over Kashmir, and the Kosovo conflict, among others. According to iDefense, over 40 Hackers from 23 countries participated in the Israeli-Palestinian cyber conflict during the period October 2000, when the cyber battles erupted, to January 2001. They also reported that two of the pro-Palestinian attackers had connections to terrorist organizations. One of these was UNITY, a Muslim extremist group with ties to Hezbollah. The Hackers launched a coordinated, multiphased denial of service attack, first against official Israeli government sites, second against Israeli financial sites, third against Israeli ISPs, and fourth, against "Zionist E-Commerce" sites. The other group, al-Muhajiroun, was said to have ties with a number of Muslim terrorist organizations as well as bin Laden. The London-based group directed their members to a Web page, where at the click of a mouse members could join an automated flooding attack against Israeli sites."[xxi]

The most likely attacks from this threat agent will be in the form of Web defacements and denial of service attacks against Internet connection points, particularly those associated with public Web servers. Although these attacks will do little to impact the operation of the organizations from a safety perspective, they could have a negative impact on the confidence of the public, thereby impacting congressional support.

Any organization or facility involved in any testing or advanced medical research involving animals, companies producing hazardous materials, luxury goods, or involved in housing or constructions projects could be directly targeted by single-issue animal rights groups such as the Animal Liberation Front or Earth Liberation Front. Typically, the Animal Liberation Front has targeted companies and facilities that perform animal testing with physical attacks, including attacks against individual employees and key organizational personnel. To this extent, cyber attacks become attractive to facilitate the performance of physical violence. Under this scenario, a single-issue group like ALF may seek to exploit vulnerable systems that provide physical facility security/access control (to obtain access to set animals free or perform acts of destruction/violence) or systems that contain employee information, especially those systems that provide home addresses and/or personal information such as social security numbers.

The best insight available into the emerging tactics deployed by these groups can be obtained by examining the actions of a group called Stop Huntington Animal Cruelty (SHAC). Huntington Life Sciences is a private company performing animal testing and research services in Europe. It is, without doubt, the most hated company in the world by animal rights organizations. The SHAC group was founded with the sole intention of putting Huntington out of business. Their tactics have been varied and increasingly sophisticated, and they publish doctrine and tactics to facilitate attacks by their members/supporters against identified targets.

For example, when the Oklahoma-based Legacy Trading Company registered to trade the Huntington stock as a "market maker." SHAC, having identified stock traders as viable targets, began posting information regarding Legacy and its CEO on their Web site to intimidate them to stop trading the stock. SHAC supporters bombarded Legacy's office and its CEO's home with hundreds of phone calls per day, mass email campaigns, snail-mail campaigns, and small physical protests outside the CEO's home. Using these tactics, SHAC claims to have forced seven of eight market makers to drop the stock, with Legacy as the sole holdout.

With Legacy resisting group intimidation, they expanded the scope of their attack to include alleged electronic attacks against neighbors (breaking into their computer systems and uploading destructive code for example) and the posting of names and social security numbers on their Web site, almost directly calling for intimidation through identity theft.

Clearly, these groups are increasingly sophisticated and present an emerging threat to anyone engaging in animal research activities. They have demonstrated a willingness to not only attack the organization but also employees and key personnel. Although the actions of these groups is, by nature, overt, the tactics used are covert as members of the group are heavily deterred by the fear of discovery and apprehension. In fact, these groups are likely to favor tactics that decrease their attack capability and reduce the impact of the action if those tactics provide a reduced potential for individual attribution.

In addition, these groups favor group actions, or those campaigns that demonstrate strength in numbers as group attacks reduce the potential for individual discovery. For example, these groups will sponsor denial of service campaigns that are announced in advance (thereby eliminating the element of surprise) to demonstrate the level of support for the political objectives of the attack.

The Al Qaeda Threat— Kill With a Borrowed Sword

Just as it is difficult to characterize Al Qaeda in general, it is difficult to characterize their potential for orchestrating a cyber attack. Terrorist organizations like Al Qaeda tend to broadcast their intentions. Therefore, given today's network dominant environment, it is of no surprise that statements regarding targeting intentions have started including the potential for cyber attack. In fact, Omar Bakri Muhammad   went so far as to declare that

> "In a matter of time you will see attacks on the stock market...I would not be surprised if tomorrow I hear of a big economic collapse because of somebody attacking the main technical systems in big companies."

If our measure of the cyber adversary threat from Al Qaeda is determined by looking at the combination of intent and capability to conduct attacks, what does that say for the Al Qaeda threat? Surely Al Qaeda posses the intent to attack, but does it also posses the capability?

According to terrorism expert Brian Michael Jenkins, it is useful to think of Al Qaeda as having the intent to use any weapons at their disposal:

> "Operationally, al Qaeda is committed to spectacular violence without limits. By placing jihad in the context of a defensive war against American crusaders and their allies, who are guilty of perpetrating, instigating, or condoning continued mass atrocities

against Muslims (in Palestine, Iraq, Afghanistan, Bosnia, Chechnya, and other fronts) jihadists are permitted to wage a like war against them.

Moreover, since the jihadists see Allah as the ultimate dues ex machina in this contest, it would be unimaginable, even blasphemous for them to reject capabilities that Allah puts before them including weapons of mass destruction."[xxii]

Although it is not clear that Al Qaeda focuses on issues of "grand strategy," it is quite apparent that their attacks have become more strategic in nature. For example, the attacks in Madrid, Spain of 2004 appear to have been perpetrated with the sole purpose of influencing the outcome of the election and reducing the level of Spanish support for military operations in Iraq. Therefore, cyber attacks become attractive to the extent that they can disrupt social integrity within the target nation causing public panic, fear, and distrust in critical infrastructures or making the cost of foreign policy objectives economically unbearable.

Although Al Qaeda is unlikely to posses a significantly sophisticated cyber capability, it can employ some of the common threat/tool vectors that are observed in use by other cyber adversaries. The following sections provide an overview of the capabilities that might be utilized by a cyber terrorist adversary such as Al Qaeda. Keep in mind that the capabilities terrorists deploy are unlikely to be influenced by their potential for attribution. Terrorists will use the full range of capabilities available to them, often viewing the possession of a capability as an obligation to use it. A cyber attack may be viewed as a simple extension of a suicide bombing with the individual perpetrator operating on the assumption that his/her individual identity will be discovered and is willing to accept that outcome as an upfront cost of engaging in the attack. Contrast this with a nation state's inherent preference to engage in attacks where the potential attribution is minimized and one of the best characterization mechanisms might be an immediate analysis at how well the attackers are covering their tracks.

Direct Compromise

Direct compromise is one of the most fundamental attack capabilities. A direct compromise can occur against a variety of systems with varying implications and be directed against artifacts, including workstations, servers, and infrastructure components such as routers and telecommunication switches.

Many direct compromise tools exist within the public domain and are thus obtainable and utilized by the full range of threats. Public Web sites are the most common source of direct compromise attack tools and techniques. Most have been written to provide an automated attack/testing capability for a given vulnerability.

The potential impact from direct compromise varies somewhat depending on the nature of the direct compromise exploit and the nature of the target system. On a system afforded no protection from known vulnerabilities, the direct compromise exploit may allow for full system compromise of critical infrastructure components that can be used to deny or degrade service or compromise the integrity of the information the system contains or processes.

Here, the issue of connectivity is critical. The fact that a compromised system is not itself a critical component does not mean that the compromise is unimportant. In fact, most sophisticated attacks deliberately avoid critical systems in the initial phase in order to avoid discovery via security countermeasures. Instead, an innocuous test system or other seldom-used system is compromised and used as a base of operations/attack platform. From this relatively safe location, the entire connected network can be mapped, observed, and eventually attacked.

It is also critical to note that sophisticated attackers do not always attack with their most sophisticated tools. Attackers virtually always choose the path of least resistance as long as they can do so without detection. Therefore, even a nation state attacker with sophisticated tools will take advantage of obvious direct compromise opportunities if they are present.

Indirect Compromise

Indirect compromise occurs when an insecure system (compromised in a preparatory attack) contains sensitive information pertaining to another information system or has a trusted relationship with another information system. For example, a system might hold password information for other system(s) or may be in some way "trusted," allowing for remote login to other system(s) without authentication. Indirect compromises are often cited as part of the classic domino effect, where compromise of one system leads to cascading compromise of multiple interconnected systems. Indirect compromises can occur against a variety of information systems, including workstations, servers, and infrastructure components such as routers and telecommunication switches, with varying implications.

The potential impact from a successful indirect compromise is similar to that of direct compromise and is highly dependent on the nature of the target system (asset) and the architecture of its surrounding network. Other key determinants of indirect compromise vulnerability are the extent to which remote login capability exists on the network, and the policies regarding quality and protection of passwords.

In addition, indirect compromise is an especially attractive tool within organizations that do not provide adequate segmentation from the Internet or within the functional enclaves of the organization (such as accounting and administration). Therefore, the compromise of the most insignificant or insecure system can lead to full compromise of critical systems on the network.

Compromise Via a Customized Attack Tool

This attack category is used to signify an advanced attack capability, possessed by a reasonably sophisticated adversary that is able to invest significant resources in the development of a customized compromise tool to target a specific asset. These tools often exploit unpublished vulnerabilities, which the target asset will have no prior knowledge of and therefore a greatly reduced capability to mitigate against. Within the security community, programs taking advantage of undisclosed vulnerabilities are typically called "zero-day" exploits, the zero referring to the number of days that a given issue has been public.

Over the past several years, the number of zero-day exploits for unpublished vulnerabilities has increased significantly as security experts scrutinize widely used public protocols, protocol implementations and other software applications. In the past years, multiple vulnerabilities have been discovered in protocol implementations such as those of SNMP (Simple Network Management Protocol) and SSL (Secure Socket Layer), in applications such as Lotus Notes and Microsoft Internet Explorer, and within core operating systems components such as those within Microsoft Windows NT/2000/XP, the Linux Kernel, and AT&T Unix—many of which were known to members of the underground hacker communities months, if not years, prior to their public disclosure and vendor remediation.

Even systems with stringent configuration control guidelines and solid security implementations are subject to compromise via a customized attack tool, as attackers have the element of surprise in their favor. For example, during the summer of 2000 an exploit was announced that described several methods for compromising the Lotus Domino server, which is widely used within industry and government.[xxiii] Although no exploit code was released, it is probably safe to assume that threat agents attempted to reproduce the exploit. There is a whole subculture of hackers and security experts tracking zero-day exploits with literally hundreds queued up for potential attack.

Physical Insider Placement

This category addresses the deliberate placement of a person inside an organization to gain access to internal information and network resources. This allows circumvention of perimeter security controls or access to a closed network with no external connectivity. In this regard, mechanisms discussed in Chapter 7 for differentiating insider motivations become essential. Models such as Warm Touch can be augmented to allow for the detection and characterization of insiders that do not emerge on the network over a period of time under the psychological influence of internal factors, but rather systematically probe and compromise an internal network.

The term "insider" also merits discussion. Today's information technology environment often includes a network infrastructure designed to accommodate geographically diverse organizations as well as outsourcing of key functions. This means that "insider" placement must include not only placement of personnel within the physical boundaries of the enterprise, but also placement at contractor locations, outsourcing facilities, and even network operation or service centers that support the enterprise network.

As one expert noted, the Aum Shinrikyo cult had extensive IT support contracts within the Japanese government and industry.[xxiv] Furthermore, Aum Shinrikyo executed these contracts as subcontractors to other firms, making it almost impossible for the organizations to know who was developing the software. As subcontractors, the cult could have installed Trojan horses to launch or facilitate cyber terrorist attacks at a later date. The Aum Shinrikyo cult, (now Aleph) serves as a useful demonstration of how extensively an organization can penetrate the IT environment of a specific target.

Evidence has also emerged that training programs within known terrorist organizations train individuals in the use of standard office tools such as word processors and spreadsheets. The implication of this information is that individuals associated with terrorist organizations are acquiring the skills required to obtain positions that might provide lowest common denominator access (such as regular users and temporary employees) to the targeted network. If electronic insider access is gained, the threat agent could plant backdoors or conduct network mapping. If physical insider access is obtained, the threat agent could connect unauthorized devices to the network to create an access point for external threat agents to access via Internet tunneling or via dial-up access. During a recent cyber terrorism threat conference, a scenario was described involving physical insider access and the placement of "black box" hostile devices on the internal network that could be accessed via a wireless connection.

Insiders can compromise the integrity, confidentiality, and availability of information and services, and an insider intentionally placed with malicious intent is likely to successfully exploit all three.

Data Interception/Sniffing/Info Gathering

The interception/sniffing/info gathering attack category includes a variety of mechanisms through which agents can gain information about target systems and networks. Though these attacks are generally passive in nature, they provide invaluable guidance in the planning and execution of later attacks. Software and hardware sensors can be employed. This function can be regarded as analogous to military "reconnaissance in force."

The information gathering phase can also be used in direct support of advanced malicious code that seeks to develop "hit lists" of vulnerable computers that are attacked during the first phase of a worm's release, thereby maximizing the initial damage and speed with which the worm spreads.

Malicious Code

Malicious code attacks occur when external entities attempt to install unwanted code on a victim's computer, either via direct compromise or by deceiving users into executing the code on their systems. Typically, this code is designed to adversely affect the performance of target machines, provide sensitive or personal information to attackers, or even provide a remote facility through which the attacker can control the compromised host.

One of the most destructive and increasingly popular threats to computer networks worldwide, malicious code attacks require little expense to create, propagate quickly, and generate enormous exposure for their authors. According to the Riptech Corporation Q1/Q2 – Internet Security Threat Report, attacks on networks were up 28 percent since the beginning of 2002, and were projected to grow at an annual rate of 64 percent per year.[xxv] It is estimated that in a single incident, the Code Red worm, first released in July and August 2001, infected millions of servers and caused $2.6 billion in damages.

Malicious code attacks can be either direct or indirect, as discussed in the following sections.

Direct Malicious Code Attacks

Direct malicious code attacks occur when hostile entities place active or dormant malicious code into custom or commercial off-the-shelf (COTS) software before it is released, either surreptitiously or under the auspices of a legitimate work order, and execute code on the infected machines after it has been distributed. In one instance, attackers sent compact discs to unsuspecting corporate insiders containing tunneling software to assist them in a future attack.[xxvi]

Although not as prevalent as indirect malicious code attacks, direct malicious code attacks are especially difficult to detect, in that they are usually embedded in legitimate code and distributed with new internal software releases, inside of network protections.

Indirect Malicious Code Attacks

Indirect malicious code attacks, including viruses, Trojans, and worms, are typically self-propagating executables, distributed by a source via IP connections to other, nonspecific IP addresses, mail, or messaging accounts, with the intent of causing a variety of errors to the anonymous target computers. Attacks can create many problems for infected machines, from degradation in performance to divulgence of personal information to complete loss of systems capabilities or content.

Denial of Service Code

This tool category encompasses single-source denial of service activity. Denial of service is typically defined as "An attack on a network with the purpose of overwhelming the target with spurious data in order to prevent legitimate connection attempts from succeeding." Contrasted to attacks whose purpose is to penetrate the target system, denial of service (DoS) attacks do not reveal sensitive data to the attacker. Examples of denial of service attacks are SYN flooding and ping of death."[xxvii]

Distributed Denial of Service

This tool category encompasses multisource denial of service activity, typically defined as "a denial of service attack launched against a site from multiple sources."[xxviii]

"Generally, the attacker will place client software on a number of unsuspecting remote computers and then use these computers to launch the attack. A distributed denial of service attack is more effective than a simple denial of service attack and is more difficult to prevent. Trin00 and Tribal Flood are examples of distributed denial of services attacks."[xxix]

Two of the most disconcerting features of DDOS attacks are their capability to propagate, and the difficulty with which target systems can defend against them. As an Internet Relay Connection (IRC) chat recording where Mafiaboy, a known perpetrator of devastating DDOS attacks to Yahoo, eBay, and Amazon.com, said, "U just pin em so hard they can't even redirect," he continues, going on to say that he had even bigger targets in mind for future attacks. "I'm thinking something big," he writes. "Maybe www.nasa.gov."[xxx]

On October 21, 2002 the Internet root server backbone suffered what was characterized as one of the largest DDOS attack against the backbone to date. This demonstrates that DDOS attacks are increasingly likely, not only against individual organizations, but also the Internet infrastructure.

Directed Energy

This category of threats is used to describe High Energy Radio Frequency (HERF) weapons and other directed energy threats to information systems.

International security experts have warned this was a real threat, but validated case studies documenting the use of these weapons do not exist in the public domain.[xxxi] Regardless, the threat assessment methodology accounts for this type of attack due to its potential impact.

Physical Threats to Information Technology Systems

The reality of physical threats has been driven home by the events of September 11, 2001. When evaluating threats to one's information technology environment, it is important to recognize the viability of the physical threat and to evaluate the impact a physical event would have on the continuity of business operations.

Physical threats may manifest themselves in the wide range of attacks from "bomb" threats causing the evacuation of a key facility to large conventional truck bombs. In our assessment methodology, we categorize over one hundred types of physical attacks, each with its own implications and impact. As noted with the IRA attacks against London Square mile, physical attacks may be launched with the intention of impacting the infrastructure, not the general population, and contingencies for this type of attack must be developed.

Differentiation of the Cyber Terrorist Adversary

Given that cyber terrorists are likely to employ some of the same capabilities and tools as other cyber adversaries, it becomes increasingly difficult to engage in characterization activities during or after an attack. Perhaps, the best method for determining if terrorism is an objective of the attack is to evaluate the attractiveness of the target based on the following:

- Is the target of the attack an infrastructure that would disrupt social integrity (such as power, water, telecommunications, banking, and finance), and is the attack being launched in a sustained manner?

- Does the attack coincide with a physical attack?

- Does the attack promote a specific political or strategic objective?

- Does the attack introduce the potential for loss of human life?

- Does the attacker fail to take measures to reduce the potential for attack attribution?

If one or more of these criteria are met, the adversary could (but not necessarily) be a cyber terrorist, raising a whole plethora of response considerations.

In order to address the full range of cyber adversaries, modern organizations must look at the attractiveness of the various attack capability vectors from the full range of adversaries. For example, the following matrix in Figure 10.2 might be used to provide a summary of the adversaries/capabilities facing a potential nation or critical infrastructure component. In this notional example, "H" is used to designate a high likelihood of threat.

Figure 10.2 Notional Threat Matrix

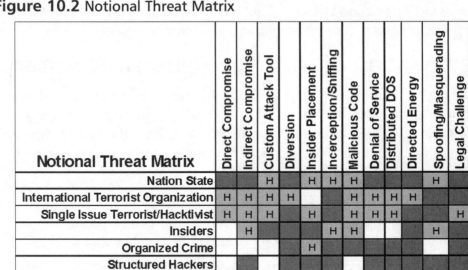

Notional Threat Matrix	Direct Compromise	Indirect Compromise	Custom Attack Tool	Diversion	Insider Placement	Incerception/Sniffing	Malicious Code	Denial of Service	Distributed DOS	Directed Energy	Spoofing/Masquerading	Legal Challenge	Physical Threat
Nation State			H		H	H	H				H		
International Terrorist Organization	H	H	H	H			H	H	H	H			H
Single Issue Terrorist/Hacktivist	H	H	H		H		H	H	H			H	
Insiders		H				H	H				H		
Organized Crime					H								
Structured Hackers													
Unstructured Hackers	H												

Summary

Given the anonymous nature of electronic attacks, cyber adversary characterization is a daunting task, but it represents a crucial and lacking component of current risk management practices. There are a few certainties we can derive from the analysis presented in this chapter.

First, sophisticated cyber adversaries do exist in the form of nation states and terrorist organizations.

Secondly, both the intent and the capability to launch sustained attacks on critical infrastructure exist. However, at this point in time, intent and capability for sustained attacks do not exist within the same adversary. For example, a nation state like China currently has the capability for sustained attacks, but not the intent, and terrorist groups like Al Qaeda have the intent, but not the capability (for a sustained attack against a critical infrastructure).

In addition, the attacks launched by nation states and terrorists are likely to resemble attacks from other cyber adversaries, with two exceptions. First the targets of the attack are likely to focus on critical infrastructure or force projection (military logistics) systems. Secondly, the sustainability of the attack is likely to exceed anything launched by other cyber adversaries thus increasing not only the impact of the attack itself, but also increasing the psychological and potential for disruption of social integrity.

Finally, the dynamic nature of networks and adversaries means that everything is subject to rapid change. Although I might pen today that those with the intent lack the capability and those with the capability lack the intent, it might not be true by the time these electrons hit the printed page.

Therefore, our models for performing cyber adversary characterization must be highly adaptive and robust so as to provide maximum benefit for those engaging in risk management and protection of information systems and critical infrastructures.

Footnotes and References

[i] I am greatly indebted to colleagues Neal Pollard, Don Hewitt, Jim Little, and James Kirkhope for their insight and critical thinking on the issues discussed in this paper.

[ii] "Prepared Testimony of Mr. Jack Brock, Director of Government and Defense Information System, General Accounting Office before the Senate Subcommittee on Financial Institutions", Washington, D.C., May 18, 2000.

[iii] Bowman, Stephen. When the Eagle Screams: America's Vulnerability to Terrorism. (New York, Carol Publishing Group, 1994)

[iv] Legro, Jeffrey W. "Military Culture and Inadvertent Escalation in World War II," International Security, vol. 18, no. 4, Spring 1994, 108.

[v] Cooper, Richard N. "Economic Interdependence and Foreign Policy in the Seventies," World Politics, Jan. 1972, 159.

[vi] Rosecrance, Richard and Stein, Arthur. "Interdependence: Myth or Reality?" World Politics, vol. 26, no. 1, 1973, 1-27.

[vii] Nye, Joseph S. Understanding International Conflicts. (New York, Harper Collins, 1993), 166

[viii] See Snyder, Jack. Myths of Empire: Domestic Politics and International Ambition. (Ithaca: Cornell University Press, 1991).

[ix] See Schweizer, Peter. Friendly Spies: How America's Allies are Using Economic Espionage to Steal Our Secrets. (New York, Atlantic Monthly Press, 1993).

[x] Liang, Qiao & Xiangsui, Wang. "Unrestricted Warfare", *Beijing: PLA Literature and Arts Publishing House*, February 1999.

[xi] Thomas, Timothy L. "China's Electronic Strategies", *Military Review*, May-June 2001.

[xii] Thomas, Timothy L. "Chinese and Russian IW", *Foreign Military Studies Office*

[xiii] ibid.

[xiv] "Mayors Doubt Readiness For Attacks", Mimi Hall, USA Today, June 12, 2002

[xv] Vince Cannistraro, former chief of counterterrorism at the CIA (in a November 2002 Computerworld article), indicated that "... many Islamic fundamentalists, some of them close to al-Qaeda, have developed expertise in computer science. 'And some are well schooled in how to carry out cyberattacks,' Cannistrarosaid. 'We know from material retrieved from [al-Qaeda] camps in Afghanistan that this is true.' " (as referenced in "Examining the Cyber Capabilities of Islamic Terrorists", Dartmouth Institute for Security Technology Studies, March 2004.

[xvi] "Cyber-Attacks by Al Qaeda Feared", The Washington Post, June 27, 2002

[xvii] Windrem, Robert. "Eco-extremists Using E-mail Bombs", *MSNBC*, October 24, 1998.

[xviii] Wilson, Vice Adm. Thomas, Testimony before Senate Select Committee on Intelligence, March 6, 2002.

[xix] "Examining the Cyber Capabilities of Islamic Terrorist Groups", Dartmouth Institute for Security Technology Studies, March 2004.

[xx] McKay, Niall. "Cyber Terror Arsenal Grows", *Wired Online*, October 16, 1998.

[xxi] Morgenstern, Michael, Global InterSec LLC Company Briefing, September 19, 2002

[xxii] Devost, Matthew G. & Pollard, Neal A. "Taking Cyberterrorism Seriously: Failing to Adapt to Emerging Threats Could Have Dire Consequences", *TRC Analysis Paper*, June 27, 2002.

[xxiii] Denning, Dorothy E. "Is Cyber Terror Next?", *Social Science Research Council*, November 1, 2001.

[xxiv] Jenkins, Brian Michael, "Looking at al Qaeda from the Inside Out", Defense Adaptive Red

Team Working Paper #03-4, December 2003.

xxv "Security Experts Warn of Holes in Lotus Domino", *CNN Online*, August 2, 2002

xxvi Denning, Dorothy E. "Is Cyber Terror Next?"

xxvii "Riptech Internet Security Threat Report," *Riptech Corporation*, Volume II, July 2002.

xxviii Denning, Dorothy E. "Is Cyber Terror Next?"

xxix Abreu, Elinor Mills. "Experts Say Computer Hacking Becoming Easier", *Reuters*, August 2, 2002.

xxx This tool category encompasses single-source denial of service activity. Denial of Service is typically defined as "An attack on a network with the purpose of overwhelming the target with spurious data in order to prevent legitimate connection attempts from succeeding. Contrasted to attacks whose purpose is to penetrate the target system, denial of service (DoS) attacks do not reveal sensitive data to the attacker. Examples of denial of service attacks are SYN Flooding and ping of death."

xxxi Definition taken from Checkpoint Security VPN Guide - http://www.checkpoint.com/vpn-guide/d.html

xxxii Ibid.

xxxiii Burke, Lynne, "Hot on the Trail of Mafia Boy", *Wired Online*, February 15, 2000.

xxxiv "Russia Worries About HERF Gun Proliferation", *ITAR-TASS*, December 23, 1998. The article provides just one example of a public domain articles detailing the threat with no direct evidence provided. Garage-developed versions of these weapons have also been demonstrated on popular broadcast news magazines such at *60 Minutes*.

## Chapter 11

Conclusions

Topics in this Chapter:

- A Look Back

- Kevin D. Mitnick Attack, Weighed and Measured!

A Look Back

In Chapter 1 we heard how the infamous Kevin Mitnick penetrated the information systems of a small software firm in the Californian San Fernando Valley. His objective in the attack was to retrieve a network sniffer designed to operate on networks using a proprietary computer networking protocol named DECNET, designed by Digital Equipment Cooperation (DEC). Although Kevin's objective in the attack was to acquire access to a network sniffer, his ultimate objective was to use it on DEC's own internal network (called EasyNet) to capture authentication credentials to access DEC's engineering network, on which was stored the proprietary source code for DEC's Virtual Memory System (VMS) operating system.

Kevin D. Mitnick: Attack, Weighed and Measured!

Let's now reflect on the detailed attack against BadgerComp systems. What were Kevin's real motivations? What was he getting out of the attack, and what variables were present that made his attack such a success?

Kevin's Environment Property Examined

At the time of Kevin's attacks, the general level of awareness in the United States of the ways that information systems, such as those Kevin compromised, could be attacked was low compared to today's levels. The Internet was only just beginning to take shape, and people's general focus was on what they could create with this new technology and not what people could break into. Many groups of computer enthusiasts such as those to which the infamous John Draper (or "Captain Crunch") belonged engaged targets such as telephone switches in the mindset that what they were doing was simply exploring a new technology and therefore was justified. In this light, Kevin felt relatively comfortable engaging in what was, in fact, putting his freedom on the line for sheer entertainment value—something that he says did not fully sink in until after the fact.

A secondary impact of the environment that existed at the time of the attack was that most people involved in information technology were so focused on building (and not breaking) things that they were too short-sighted to see the inevitable threats that loom over all computerized systems to this day. People would run services such as network file systems (NFS) without considering who might attempt to access their sensitive data. The first firewall was a yet-to-be-fired neural rod in its inventor's brain, and the need to characterize the cyber adversary was not even a consideration, since there was simply no awareness that a "cyber adversary" could exist.

Environment Property Influences on Attacker Resources Object

As we have already discussed, the environment surrounding Kevin was one of assumed trust, and the general level of awareness of cyber attacks was, to all intents and purposes, nonexistent. But how did this affect the resources to which Kevin had access? Let's examine this question by first taking a look at the individual resources utilized in his attacks against BadgerComp's computer systems.

Initial Target Reconnaissance

The initial phase of Kevin's attack against Badger Computer Systems involved the enumeration of the targets: BadgerComp's telecommunications and computer system infrastructure. This task involved his knowledge of the telecommunications infrastructure—in particular, his ability to determine which telephone numbers terminated at the same private branch exchange (PBX) as BadgerComp's primary voice telephone number. With this information, Kevin was then able to determine which of the enumerated telephone numbers represented voice, fax, and data—the data numbers obviously being of most interest in the context of the proposed attack. The resources required to achieve this goal were as follows:

- Kevin's deep knowledge of PBX systems and other telecommunications infrastructures, which he almost certainly acquired through associations within his environment and past experience.

- The equipment required to perform his initial reconnaissance. Kevin often acquired equipment through his associations and through "dumpster diving"—an act carried out by many adversaries to attain data and technology artifacts from the waste disposal points of large corporations, which regularly dispose of large quantities of deprecate technology.

Acquisition of the DEC VAX/VMS Update Tape

The ease at which Kevin acquired access to the VMS update tape was a direct result of the lack of awareness of cyber crimes in the environment around him. When he phoned DEC, the call recipients sought no authentication that he was in fact a DEC customer or that he even owned a system to run the software on. The chances are that the trust model at DEC was such that if you knew the telephone number to call to get update tapes, you were presumed to be a DEC customer. Furthermore, chances were good that the purpose for which Kevin had intended the update tapes had yet to be realized by either DEC or his target, Badger Computing.

Modification of the VAX/VMS Update Tapes

The modifications Kevin made to the VAX/VMS update tapes were heavily based on several patches for VAX/VMS binaries, authored by the Chaos Computer Club (CCC), a Berlin-based group of highly prolific computer security enthusiasts who remain active to this day. The CCC VMS binary patches provided Kevin with a road map to make the modifications he needed to make to the binaries contained on the DEC update tapes. Although at the time, the CCC patches were not widely available, Kevin was able to obtain access to the patches through several associations that already had access to the relevant code. After acquiring access to the CCC patches, Kevin proceeded to modify the VMS binaries using a technique similar to that used by CCC in their VMS patches. Authoring his own backdoor code to give him dial-up access to the VMS server, Kevin was then able to make the required modifications, utilizing his knowledge of VAX Assembler.

In addition to the modifications of data on the DEC tapes themselves, Kevin was also able to shrink-wrap the DEC tapes to appear almost identical to their original packaging. This ability came from an associate within his environment, who provided access to the relevant equipment. As insignificant as access to a shrink-wrapping machine might seem, it played a critical role in the success of his attack against Badger Computer Systems. So, in the context of the VAX/VMS binary updates and the physical tapes, his ability to make the required modifications stemmed from the following environment property impacts:

- Kevin's associations leading to the acquisition of the CCC "guideline" VAX/VMS patches

- Kevin's associations leading to a resource to shrink-wrap the VMS tapes in an identical manner to their original packaging

- Kevin's prior knowledge of VAX Assembler, which we can fairly safely presume resulted from one or more influences within his environment

Delivery of the DEC Update Tapes

The attack techniques Kevin used to deliver his backdoor onto Badger Computing's systems exploited the company employees' lack of awareness of the possible threats the DEC update tape presented. Although the tape itself was indeed a genuine DEC update tape, complete with original packaging, Badger made no apparent effort to verify either the origins of the delivery or the authenticity of data contained on the update tape. As far as Kevin can recall, DEC provided no form of checksums to allow companies to verify the authenticity of files provided on update tapes—a common practice today, especially among open source development communities.

To summarize, the relevant resource Kevin possessed—allowing him to deliver his backdoor onto the systems of Badger Computer System—was based on his ability to take advantage of the assumed trust BadgerComp placed on the update tapes, which were apparently from DEC.

Resource Summary

And so, the resources shown in Table 11.1 were available to Kevin, all of which came about as direct result of the environment around him. The resources are displayed next to their respective environment source object (as documented in Chapter 2).

Table 11.1 Environment-Influenced Resources

Resource	Respective Environment Property Object
Knowledge of PBX systems and other telecommunications infrastructures	Associations object
Computer equipment	Associations/intelligence sources
Original DEC VAX/VMS update tapes	Political/cultural (trust culture)
CCC VAX/VMS guideline patches	Associations/intelligence sources
DEC VAC/VMS tape shrink-wrapping	Associations/intelligence sources
VAX Assembler knowledge	Associations/knowledge

This information shows how important it is that you carefully consider the environment of the cyber adversary when performing both theoretical and post-incident ("real") characterizations.

The environment-related resources in Table 11.1 result in the resource elements shown in Table 11.2, which exist within the resource object of the attacker property.

Table 11.2 Resultant Attacker Object Resources

Resource	Respective Attacker Property, Resource Object Elements
Knowledge of PBX systems and other telecommunications infrastructures	Knowledge element/initial access (?)
Computer equipment	Technical (skills) element
Original DEC VAX/VMS update tapes	Technical (skills) element
CCC VAX/VMS guideline patches	Technical (skills) element
DEC VAC/VMS tape shrink-wrapping	Technical (skills) element
VAX Assembler knowledge	Technical (skills)/knowledge element

Environment Property Influences on Attacker Inhibitor & Driver Object(s)

The influences on Kevin's attack inhibitors would have been heavily influenced by the variables associated with the political/cultural object within his environment property. As previously discussed, a high level of trust was endemic of the culture at the time of his attacks against the computer systems of DEC and BadgerComp. This climate would have impacted multiple inhibitor elements in a number of ways, as detailed in the following sections. Take note of the way the resources (detailed previously) to which Kevin had access also impact on his attack inhibitors; this is another example of a relationship between characterization metrics (as alluded to in Chapter 6).

Perceived Probability of Detection Given Attempt

Kevin's perceived probability of detection given attempt would have been low due to the cultural attitude to trust the security of information systems such as those that were compromised at Badger Computer Systems. Kevin was fully aware of the fact that the employees of BadgerComp would not think to suspect the legitimacy of the package he delivered. Why would they? They had no idea of what their adversary looked like, or even that they had an adversary!

Perceived Probability of Attribution Given Detection

The final phase of Kevin Mitnick's attack against BadgerComp would have raised Kevin's perceived probability of attribution given detection to its highest point. Since the final phase involved being face to face with a BadgerComp employee, detection would have resulted in immediate attribution if anything went wrong. This is perhaps the primary differentiation between the instances where Kevin was attacking BadgerComp for the thrill of the hack or if he had been doing it for malicious purposes. In the case of the latter, the chances are that Kevin could have utilized an unwitting agent to deliver the package to the BadgerComp offices; this, of course, would have taken away the thrill but would have significantly reduced Kevin's perceived probability of attribution given detection. Of course, this is not something that he was concerned with doing as the price of attribution was traded off directly against the thrill value of the attack. In his own words: *"I put my freedom on the line for the sheer thrill of the hack"*.

Perceived Probability of Success

Kevin knew that because of the general lack of awareness for cyber adversaries and the techniques that they might use, that the chances of his attack proving to be a success were extremely high. The resources to which he had access at the time would have further heightened his perceived probability of success.

Summary

The success against the attack directed at the computer systems of BadgerComp rested wholly on a lack of understanding for the threat that adversaries such as Kevin Mitnick pose, and the value which adversaries such as Kevin place on assets such as those held by BadgerComp.

As we enter a new era, we begin to recognize the existence of new threats to our well being, the need to understand the nature of those threats becomes a natural progression. As small as BadgerComp were when they were subject to the antics of Kevin Mitnick, they played a vital part in a much bigger operation and failed to realize the value that the resources held on their systems could have to an adversary such as Mitnick.

This serves as a lesson to all, that no matter how insignificant you think you are, whether you are a member of government agency, a nuclear power plant employee or a private user of a home computer, we must all take a step back and take a long hard look at not if we would become a target, but *who* we would become a target for.

And Now for Something a Little Different!

Many of the case studies we examined in previous chapters detailed incidents impacting large private organizations and took the form of isolated incidents, only having an impact on no more than one organization. In Chapters 9 and 10, we alluded to the possibility that a cyber adversary may be used to augment a traditional act of terrorism, espionage, or other significant organized crime that would impact multiple large organizations, entire countries, or even continents. At this writing, there are no examples of such a case study within the unclassified domain that can be properly corroborated. For that reason, there is no real way we can document such an adversarial act. However, do not fret. The following pages contain an excerpted chapter, "Return on Investment," authored by Fyodor at insecure.org, from the book *Stealing the Network: How to Own a Continent*. In the form of a techno-thriller type novel, this book documents some of the ways an organized group, such as those we alluded to in Chapters 9 and 10, could go about taking over many of the computerized infrastructures of a large country to augment a traditional criminal act. At the end of the chapter (the "Aftermath"), you will find the characterization of the cyber adversary featured in the chapter, utilizing some of the metrics introduced in this book.

## Chapter 12

Return on Investment
by Fyodor as "Sendai"

Like many professional penetration testers, Sendai was not always the wholesome "ethical hacker" described in his employer's marketing material. In his youth, he stepped well over the line between questionable (grey hat) and flat-out illegal (black hat) behavior. Yet he never felt that he was doing anything wrong…

Sendai did not intentionally damage systems, and was only trying to learn more about UNIX, networking, security, phone systems, and related technology. Yet the law might consider some of his actions to be unauthorized access, theft of services, wire fraud, copyright infringement, and trade secret theft. In the rare times that Sendai thought of this, he found solace in the words of the Mentor's Hacker Manifesto: "Yes, I am a criminal. My crime is that of curiosity." Surely his innocent motives would prevent prosecution. Besides, his teenage arrogance assured him that the government and targeted corporations were too dumb to catch him.

This perception changed dramatically in 1989 and 1990 when the "Operation Sundevil" raids took place. Well-known security enthusiasts, including The Prophet, Knight Lightning, and Erik Bloodaxe, were raided and many more were indicted. The popular Phrack e-zine was shut down while its editor faced trial. Sendai worried that he, too, might be swept up in the persecution. After all, he had been active on some of the same bulletin boards as many suspects, performing similar activities. Sendai was never targeted, but those nine months of stress and paranoia changed his outlook on hacking. He was not exactly scared straight, but he ceased treating network intrusion as a game or casual hobby. In the following years, Sendai became much more disciplined about hiding his tracks through multiple layers of indirection, as well as always wiping logs, even when it was inconvenient. He also began to research his targets and methods much more extensively. Failing to fully understand a system could cause him to miss important defenses and lead to detection. A side effect of this more methodical approach to hacking is that Sendai substantially broadened his network security knowledge and skill set.

Sendai did not recognize the growing value of this skill set and clean record until he was offered the "ethical hacking" job at a well-known auditing firm. The burgeoning Internet was creating such intense demand for security professionals that the firm asked few questions about his past. Using his real name, they were unaware that he even used the hacker handle Sendai. He did have some reservations about commercializing his hobby, not wanting to be seen as a sell out. Despite these concerns, Sendai accepted the position immediately. It sure beat his previous technical support day job! Soon he was living in the security world during both days and nights. The job provided legitimate access to exciting enterprise technologies, and he could hone his hacking skills without risking arrest. Bragging about his exploits led to bonuses instead of jail time. Sendai had so much fun cracking into systems for money that he eventually ceased much of his nocturnal black hat network exploration.

Playing the Market

Sendai's new position pays far more money than his modest lifestyle requires. After tiring of watching the money stagnate in his checking account, Sendai opens a brokerage account and begins to dabble in investing. As with hacking, Sendai learns everything he can about investing. Interestingly, he finds many parallels between the two disciplines. Many books and articles suggest filling a portfolio with funds that passively track broad indexes such as the S&P 500. This insures diversity and reduces the risk of bad timing or stock-picking mistakes. Sendai discards this advice immediately. It sounds too much like the conventional wisdom that computer and telephone users should restrict themselves to advertised behavior, and stay ignorant about how the systems work. Sendai prefers stretching system capabilities to extract as much value as possible, based on a comprehensive understanding. In other words, he wants to (legally) hack the financial markets.

Sendai soon discovers another aspect of investing that is familiar to him. Successful active trading is all about obtaining relevant information before it is widely recognized and reflected in the stock price. This is similar to the security market, where the value of an exploit degrades quickly. The Holy Grail is a zero-day exploit, meaning one that is not publicly known or patched. Attackers who possess such an exploit can break into any system running the vulnerable service. The attack is unlikely to be detected, either, because administrators and IDS systems are not watching for what they do not know exists. Once the vulnerability is published and a patch is created, the exploit value decreases rapidly. The most secure installations will quickly upgrade to be invulnerable. In the coming days and weeks, most organizations will patch their systems. Soon, only the least security conscious networks will be exploitable, and they are probably vulnerable to many other attacks anyway. As other hackers (and in many cases worms) compromise the remaining vulnerable systems, the exploit value continues to dwindle.

In the security world, Sendai sometimes gains zero-day knowledge through friends in the scene and private mailing lists or IRC/SILC channels.

Other times, he finds them himself by auditing software for bugs. Auditing produces the best zero-day exploits because the bugs are exclusively his, until he discloses them (or they are independently discovered elsewhere). To find an impressive and generally useful vulnerability, Sendai tends to look at widely deployed and frequently exploitable software like Microsoft's IIS webserver, Sendmail smtpd, OpenSSH, or the ISC BIND DNS server. In the more common case that Sendai wants to break into a specific company, he looks for the most obscure software run on the target network. This specialized software is unlikely to have gone through the rigorous testing performed against more popular packages. An alternative approach to obtaining zero-day is to buy it from the controversial organizations that openly broker such information. Sendai has never resorted to this, for both ethical and financial reasons. He still believes some information wants to be free.

The flow of valuable investment insights is similar to security information. Someone with the right insider connections or a willingness to pay extravagant fees to research boutiques can learn information before it moves the market. Unable to partake in these options, Sendai decides to do his own research. Some of the most valuable preannouncement data are company earnings and mergers, acquisitions, or big partnerships. After a couple hours of brainstorming, Sendai comes up with several ways to use his security and networking expertise to his advantage.

Information Leakage at the Packet Level

Because Sendai cannot think of above-board ways to learn public companies' private earnings information directly, he looks for attributes that may correlate strongly with earnings. One idea is to study the SSL traffic to e-commerce sites. The amount of encrypted traffic they generate is often proportional to the number of sales during that period. This begs the next question: How will Sendai measure a company's SSL traffic? They certainly will not tell him. Breaking into a router barely upstream of the target host would give him access to this data, but that is quite illegal and also requires substantial custom work for each target. Sendai wants a general, unobtrusive, easy, and legal way to determine this information.

Eventually, Sendai thinks of the fragmentation ID field in Internet Protocol (IP) packets. This unsigned 16-bit field is intended to provide a unique ID number to each packet sent between machines during a given time period. The primary purpose is allowing large packets, which must be fragmented during transit, to be reassembled properly by the destination host. Otherwise a host receiving hundreds of fragments from dozens of packets would not be able to match fragments to their original packets. Many OS developers implement this system in a very simple way: they keep a global counter and increment it once for each packet sent. After the counter reaches 65,535, it wraps back to zero.

The risk of this simple implementation is that it allows bad guys to remotely determine traffic levels of a host. This can be useful for many sinister purposes, including an extraordinarily stealthy port scanning technique known as Idle Scan.[1] Sendai will use it to estimate daily orders.

He decides to test whether popular public e-commerce sites are actually vulnerable to this sort of information leakage. He visits the online sites of Dell and Buy.Com, following the order placement path until reaching their secure sites. These sites are designated by the https protocol in the URL bar and a closed padlock icon on his browser. They are ecomm.dell.com and secure.buy.com. Sendai uses the open source hping2 program (freely available from www.hping.org) to send eight TCP SYN packets, 1 second apart, to port 443 (SSL) of the specified host.

Using hping2 and the IP ID Field to Estimate Traffic Levels

```
# hping2 -c 8 -S -i 1 -p 443 ecomm.dell.com
HPING ecomm.dell.com (eth0 143.166.83.166): S set, 40 headers + 0 data bytes
46 bytes from 143.166.83.166: flags=SA seq=0 ttl=111 id=8984 rtt=64.6 ms
46 bytes from 143.166.83.166: flags=SA seq=1 ttl=111 id=9171 rtt=62.9 ms
46 bytes from 143.166.83.166: flags=SA seq=2 ttl=111 id=9285 rtt=63.6 ms
46 bytes from 143.166.83.166: flags=SA seq=3 ttl=111 id=9492 rtt=63.2 ms
46 bytes from 143.166.83.166: flags=SA seq=4 ttl=111 id=9712 rtt=62.8 ms
46 bytes from 143.166.83.166: flags=SA seq=5 ttl=111 id=9974 rtt=63.0 ms
46 bytes from 143.166.83.166: flags=SA seq=6 ttl=111 id=10237 rtt=64.1 ms
46 bytes from 143.166.83.166: flags=SA seq=7 ttl=111 id=10441 rtt=63.7 ms
--- ecomm.dell.com hping statistic ---
8 packets transmitted, 8 packets received, 0% packet loss
```

```
# hping2 -c 8 -S -i 1 -p 443 secure.buy.com
HPING secure.buy.com (eth0 209.67.181.20): S set, 40 headers + 0 data bytes
46 bytes from 209.67.181.20: flags=SA seq=0 ttl=117 id=19699 rtt=11.9 ms
46 bytes from 209.67.181.20: flags=SA seq=1 ttl=117 id=19739 rtt=11.9 ms
46 bytes from 209.67.181.20: flags=SA seq=2 ttl=117 id=19782 rtt=12.4 ms
46 bytes from 209.67.181.20: flags=SA seq=3 ttl=117 id=19800 rtt=11.5 ms
46 bytes from 209.67.181.20: flags=SA seq=4 ttl=117 id=19821 rtt=11.5 ms
46 bytes from 209.67.181.20: flags=SA seq=5 ttl=117 id=19834 rtt=11.6 ms
46 bytes from 209.67.181.20: flags=SA seq=6 ttl=117 id=19857 rtt=11.9 ms
46 bytes from 209.67.181.20: flags=SA seq=7 ttl=117 id=19878 rtt=11.5 ms
--- secure.buy.com hping statistic ---
8 packets transmitted, 8 packets received, 0% packet loss
```

The IP ID fields in both cases show a pattern of steady monotonic increases, which is consistent with trivial packet counting behavior. During this test, the Dell machine sends an average of 208 packets per second (10441 minus 8984 all divided by 7) and secure.buy.com is showing 26 pps. One added complexity is that major hosts like Dell and Buy.Com have many systems behind a load balancer. That device ensures that subsequent packets from a certain IP address go to the same machine. Sendai is able to count the machines by sending probes from many different IP addresses. This step is critical, as the pps rate for a single box will naturally decrease when more machines are added to the farm or vice versa. Against a popular server farm, he may need many addresses, but huge netblocks can easily be purchased or hijacked.

Sendai begins to execute his plan. He writes a simple C program to do the probing and host counting using Dug Song's free libdnet library. It runs via cron a few dozen times a day against each of many publicly traded targets that are vulnerable to this problem. These samples allow an estimation of traffic for each day. Sendai knows better than to jump in with his money right away. Instead he will let his scripts run for a full quarter and count the cumulative traffic for each company. When each company reports results, he will divide their actual revenue for that quarter by his traffic estimate to compute revenue per packet. The second quarter will be a test. He will multiply revenue per packet by his calculated traffic to guess quarterly revenue, and then compare that revenue to the official numbers released later. Companies that prove inaccurate at this point will be discarded. With the remainder, Sendai hopes finally to make some money. He will watch them for a third quarter and again estimate their revenue. He will then compare his estimate to the First Call Consensus. If his revenue estimate is substantially higher, he will take out a major long position right before the earnings conference call. If he estimates a revenue shortfall, Sendai will go short. Obviously he still needs to research other factors such as pricing changes that could throw off his purely traffic-based revenue estimates.

Corrupted by Greed

Although Sendai feels that this plan is legal and ethical, greed has taken over and waiting nine months is unacceptable. He thinks about other market moving events, such as mergers, acquisitions, and partnerships. How can he predict those in advance? One way is to watch new domain name registrations closely. In some mergers and partnerships, a new entity combines the name of both companies. They must register the new domain name before the announcement or risk being beaten to it by domain squatters. But if they register more than a trading day in advance, Sendai may be able to find out early. He obtains access to the .com TLD zone files by submitting an application to Verisign. This gives him a list of every .com name, updated twice daily. For several days, he vets every new entry, but finds nothing enticing. Again, impatience gets the best of him. Sendai decides to cross an ethical line or two. Instead of waiting for a suggestive name, he will create one! Sendai takes a large (for him) position in a small Internet advertising company. A few minutes later he registers a domain combining that company name with a major search engine. The public whois contact information is identical to that used by the search engine company. Payment is through a stolen credit card number, though a prepaid gift credit card would have worked as well. That was easy!

The next morning, the ad company is up a bit on unusually high volume. Maybe Sendai wasn't the first person to use this domain watching strategy. Message board posters are searching to explain the high volume. His heart racing, Sendai connects through a chain of anonymous proxies and posts a message board response noting the new domain name he just "discovered." The posters go wild with speculation, and volume jumps again. So does the price. A company spokesman denies the rumors less than an hour later, but

Sendai has already cashed out. What a rush! If this little episode does not receive much press coverage, perhaps investors of another small company will fall for it tomorrow. Sendai clearly has forgotten the hacker ethic that he used to espouse, and now dons his black hat for profit rather than solely for exploration and learning.

Freed from his misgivings about outright fraud and other illegal methods, Sendai's investment choices widen immensely. For example, his fundamental research on a company would be helped substantially by access to the CEO and CFO's e-mail. He considers wardriving through the financial district of nearby cities with his laptop, antenna, GPS, and a program like Kismet or Netstumbler. Surely some public company has a wide open access point with an identifying SSID. Standard network hacking through the Internet is another option. Or Sendai could extend his domain name fraud to issuing actual fake press releases. Sendai has seen fake press releases move the market in the past. Still giddy from his first successful investment hack, Sendai's mind is working overtime contemplating his next steps.

Sendai has plenty of time to research investments during work hours because pen-testing jobs have been quite scarce now that the dot-com market has collapsed. Sendai is pleased by this, due to the free-time aspect, until one day when the whole security department of his office is laid off. So much for the best job he has ever had. Sendai takes it in stride, particularly because his severance pay adds to the investment pot that he hopes will soon make him rich.

Revenge of the Nerd

While home reading Slashdot in his underwear (a favorite pastime of unemployed IT workers), Sendai comes up with a new investment strategy. A pathetic little company named Fiasco is falsely claiming ownership of Linux copyrights, trying to extort money from users, and filing multibillion dollar lawsuits. Sendai is sure that this is a stock scam and that Fiasco's claims are frivolous. Meanwhile, mainstream investors seem so fixated by the enormous amount of money Fiasco seeks that they lose their critical thinking ability. The stock is bid up from pennies to over $5! Sendai takes out a huge short position, planning to cover when the stock tumbles back down. Since the claims have no merit, that can't take long.

Boy is he wrong! The Fiasco stock (symbol: SCUMX) climbs rapidly. At $9 per share, Sendai receives a margin call from his broker. Being unwilling to take the huge SCUMX loss, Sendai sells all his other positions and also wires most of the balance from his checking account to the brokerage. This allows him to hold the position, which is certain to plummet soon! It rises further. Maybe this is still due to initial uncritical hype. Perhaps the momentum traders are on board now. Maybe some investors know that anti-Linux corporations Microsoft and Sun secretly are funneling money to Fiasco. At $12, Sendai is woken by another early morning margin call and he lacks the money to further fund the account. He is forced to buy back shares to cover his position, and doing so further raises the price of this thinly traded stock. His account value is devastated.

In a fit of rage and immaturity, Sendai decides to take down Fiasco's Web site. They are using it to propagate lies and deception in furtherance of criminal stock fraud, he reasons. Sendai does not consider his own recent stock shenanigans when judging Fiasco.

Web sites are taken down by attackers daily, usually using a brute packet flood from many source machines (known as a distributed denial of service attack). Sendai realizes that much more elegant and effective attacks are possible by exploiting weaknesses in TCP protocol implementations rather than raw packet floods. Sendai has taken down much bigger Web sites than Fiasco's from a simple modem connection. His favorite tool for doing this is a privately distributed application known as Ndos. He reviews the usage instructions.

Ndos Denial of Service Tool Options

```
# ndos
Ndos 0.04 Usage: ndos [options] target_host portnum
Supported options:
-D <filename> Send all data from given file into the opened connection
   (must fit in 1 packet)
-S <IP or hostname> Use the given machine as the attack source address (may
   require -e).  Otherwise source IPs are randomized.
-e <devicename> Use the given device to send the packets through.
-w <msecs> Wait given number of milliseconds between sending fresh probes
-P Activates polite mode, which actually closes the connections it opens
   and acks data received.
-W <size> The TCP window size to be used.
-p <portnum> Initial source port used in loop
```

```
-l <portnum> The lowest source port number ndos should loop through.
-h <portnum> The highest source port number used in loop
-m <mintimeout> The lowest allowed receive timeout (in ms).
-b <num> Maximum number of packets that can be sent in a short burst
-d <debuglevel>
```

Ndos is one of those tools that has no documentation (other than the usage screen) and is full of obscure parameters that must be set properly. But once the right values are determined from experimentation or actual understanding, it is deadly effective. Sendai starts it up at a relatively subdued packet rate from a hacked Linux box. You can bet that the *-P* option was *not* given. The Fiasco Web site is down until the compromised box is discovered and disconnected three days later.

Although his little temper tantrum was slightly gratifying, Sendai is still broke, jobless, and miserable. Only one thing cheers him up—the upcoming annual Defcon hacker conference! This provides the rare opportunity to hang out with all his buddies from around the world, in person instead of on IRC. Sendai worries whether he can even afford to go now. Stolen credit card numbers are not wisely used for flight reservations. Counting the pitiful remains of his checking and brokerage accounts, as well as the remainder of his credit card limit, Sendai scrapes up enough for the trip to Las Vegas. Lodging is another matter. After mailing several friends, his hacker buddy Don Crotcho (a.k.a The Don) offers to share his Alexis Park hotel room for free.

The following weeks pass quickly, with Sendai living cheaply on ramen noodles and Kraft macaroni and cheese. He would like to try more "investment hacking," but that requires money to start out with. Sendai blames Microsoft for his current condition, due in part to their clandestine funding of Fiasco, and also because he is one of those people who find reasons to blame Microsoft for almost all their problems in life.

A Lead from Las Vegas

Sendai soon finds himself surrounded by thousands of hackers in Las Vegas. He meets up with The Don, who surprisingly has sprung for the expensive Regal loft room instead of the standard cheap Monarch room. Maybe they were out of Monarchs, Sendai thinks. The two of them head to the Strip for entertainment. Sendai wants to take in the free entertainment, though The Don is intent on gambling. Upon reaching the Bellagio, Sendai sees a roulette table and is tempted to bet his last remaining dollars on black. Then he realizes how similar that would be to the Fiasco speculation that landed him in this mess. And as with airline tickets, using a stolen credit card at casinos is a bad idea. Instead, Sendai decides to hang around and watch The Don lose his money. Don heads to the cashier, returning with a huge stack of hundred dollar chips. Shocked, Sendai demands to know how Don obtained so much money. The Don plays it off as no big deal, and refuses to provide any details. After several hours of persistence and drinking, Sendai learns some of the truth. In a quiet booth in a vodka bar, Don concedes that he has found a new client that pays extraordinarily well for specialized telecom manipulation, which is The Don's professional euphemism for phone phreaking.

Given his precarious financial situation, Sendai begs The Don to hook him up with this generous client. Perhaps he needs some of the security scanning and vulnerability exploitation skills that Sendai specializes in. The Don refuses to name his client, but agrees to mention Sendai if he finds a chance. Sendai really cannot ask for anything more, especially after The Don treats him to a visit to one of Vegas' best strip clubs later that night. Don says it reminds him of Maxim's at home in Iceland.

The Call of Opportunity

The following Tuesday, Sendai is sitting at home reading Slashdot in his underwear and recovering from a massive Defcon hangover when the phone rings. He answers the phone to hear an unfamiliar voice. After confirming that he is speaking to Sendai, the caller introduced himself.

"Hello Sendai. You may call me Bob Knuth. The Don informs me that you are one of the brightest system penetration experts around. I'm working on a very important but sensitive project and hope that you can help. I need three hosts compromised over the Internet and an advanced rootkit of your design installed. The rootkit must be completely effective and reliable, offering full access to the system through a hidden backdoor. Yet it must be so subtle that even the most knowledgeable and paranoid systems administrators do not suspect a thing. The pay is good, but only if everything goes perfectly. Of course it's critical that the intrusions are all successful and go undetected. A single slip up and you will feel the consequences. Are you up to this challenge?"

Thinking quickly, Sendai's first impression is not positive. He is offended by the handle "Bob Knuth," as it was obviously patterned after the world-renowned computer scientist Don Knuth. How dare this arrogant criminal compare himself to such a figure! "His words also sound patronizing, as if he doubts my skills," Sendai thinks. There is also the question of what Knuth has in mind. He volunteered nothing of his intentions, and for Sendai to ask would be a huge faux pas. Sendai suspects that Knuth may be the vilest of computer criminals: a spammer! Should he really stoop to this level by helping?

Despite this internal dialog, Sendai knows quite well that his answer is yes. Maintaining his apartment and buying food trump his qualms. Plus, Sendai loves hacking with a passion and relishes the chance to prove his skills. So he answers in the affirmative, contingent of course on sufficient pay. That negotiation does not take long. Usually Sendai tries to bargain past the first offer in principle, but Knuth's offer is so high that Sendai lacks the tenacity to counter. He would have insisted on receiving part of the money up front had he not known that The Don has been paid without incident. Knuth sounds extremely busy, so no small talk is exchanged. They discuss the job specifics and disconnect.

Initial Reconnaissance

Sendai first must perform some light reconnaissance against the three hosts Knuth gave him. Given the amount of "white noise" scanning traffic all over the Internet, he could probably get away with scanning from his own home IP address. A chill passes through him as he remembers operation Sundevil. No, scanning from his own ISP is unacceptable. He moves to his laptop, plugs an external antenna into the 802.11 card, then starts Kismet to learn which of his neighbors have open access points available now. He chooses one with the default ESSID *linksys* because users who do not bother changing router defaults are less likely to notice his presence. Ever careful, Sendai changes his MAC address with the Linux command **ifconfig eth1 hw ether 53:65:6E:64:61:69**, associates with *linksys*, and auto-configures via DHCP. Iwconfig shows a strong signal and Sendai verifies that cookies are disabled in his browser before loading Slashdot to verify network connectivity. He should have used a different test, as he wastes 15 minutes reading a front-page story about that latest Fiasco outrage.

Sendai needs only a little bit of information about the targets right now. Most importantly, he wants to know what operating system they are running so that he can tailor his rootkit appropriately. For this purpose, he obtains the latest Nmap Security Scanner[2] from www.insecure.org/nmap. Sendai considers what options to use. Certainly he will need **-sS -F**, which specifies a stealth SYN TCP scan of about a thousand common ports. The **-P0** option ensures that the hosts will be scanned even if they do not respond to Nmap ping probes, which by default include an ICMP echo request message as well as a TCP ACK packet sent to port 80. Of course **-O** will be specified to provide OS detection. The **-T4** option speeds things up, and **-v** activates verbose mode for some additional useful output. Then there is the issue of decoys. This Nmap option causes the scan (including OS detection) to be spoofed so that it appears to come from many machines. A target administrator who notices the scan will not know which machine is the actual perpetrator and which are innocent decoys. Decoys should be accessible on the Internet for believability purposes. Sendai asks Nmap to find some good decoys by testing 250 IP addresses at random.

Finding Decoy Candidates with Nmap

```
# nmap -sP -T4 -iR 250
Starting nmap 3.50 ( http://www.insecure.org/nmap/ )
Host gso167-152-019.triad.rr.com (24.167.152.19) appears to be up.
Host majorly.unstable.dk (66.6.220.100) appears to be up.
Host 24.95.220.112 appears to be up.
Host pl1152.nas925.o-tokyo.nttpc.ne.jp (210.165.127.128) appears to be up.
Host i-195-137-61-245.freedom2surf.net (195.137.61.245) appears to be up.
Host einich.geology.gla.ac.uk (130.209.224.168) appears to be up.
Nmap run completed -- 250 IP addresses (6 hosts up) scanned in 10.2 seconds
#
```

Sendai chooses these as his decoys, passing them as a comma-separated list to the Nmap **-D** option. This carefully crafted command is completed by the three target IP addresses from Knuth. Sendai executes Nmap and finds the following output excerpts particularly interesting.

OS Fingerprinting the Targets

```
# nmap -sS -F -P0 -O -T4 -v -D[decoyslist] [IP addresses]
Starting nmap 3.50 ( http://www.insecure.org/nmap/ )
[...]
Interesting ports on fw.ginevra-ex.it (XX.227.165.212):
[...]
Running: Linux 2.4.X
OS details: Linux 2.4.18 (x86)
Uptime 316.585 days
[...]
Interesting ports on koizumi-kantei.go.jp (YY.67.68.173):
[...]
Running: Sun Solaris 9
OS details: Sun Solaris 9
[...]
Interesting ports on infowar.cols.disa.mil (ZZ.229.74.111):
[...]
Running: Linux 2.4.X
OS details: Linux 2.4.20 - 2.4.22 w/grsecurity.org patch
Uptime 104.38 days
```

As the results scroll by, the first aspect that catches Sendai's eye are the reverse DNS names. It appears that he is out to compromise the firewall of a company in Italy, a Japanese government computer, and a US military Defense Information Systems Agency host. Sendai trembles a little at that last one. This is certainly one of the most puzzling assignments he has ever had. What could these three machines have in common? Knuth no longer appears to be a spammer. "I hope he is not a terrorist," Sendai thinks while trying to shake thoughts of spending the rest of his life branded as an enemy combatant and locked up at Guantanamo Bay.

Shrax: The Ultimate Rootkit

Sendai looks at the platforms identified by Nmap. This is critical information in determining what type of rootkit he will have to prepare. Rootkits are very platform-specific as they integrate tightly with an OS kernel to hide processes and files, open backdoors, and capture keystrokes. Knuth's demands are far more elaborate than any existing public rootkit, so Sendai must write his own. He is pleased that these systems run Linux and Solaris, two of the systems he knows best.

Rather than start over from scratch, Sendai bases his rootkit on existing code. He downloads the latest Sebek Linux and Solaris clients from www.honeynet.org/tools/sebek. Sebek is a product of the Honeynet Project,[3] a group of security professionals who attempt to learn the tools, tactics, and motives of the blackhat community by placing honeypot computers on the Internet and studying how they are exploited. Sebek is a kernel module used to monitor activity on honeypots while hiding its own existence. Sendai revels in the delicious irony of this white hat tool fitting his evil purposes perfectly. A major plus is that it is available for Linux and Solaris.

Although Sebek serves as a useful foundation, turning it into a proper rootkit requires substantial work. Sebek already includes a cleaner that hides it from the kernel module list, but Sendai must add features for hiding files/directories, processes, sockets, packets, and users from everyone else (including legitimate administrators). The syslog functionality is also compromised to prevent intruder activity from being logged. Sendai adds several fun features for dealing with any other users on the system. A TTY sniffer allows him to secretly watch selected user terminal sessions and even actively insert keystrokes or hijack the hapless user's session.

The TTY sniffer makes Sendai smile, thinking back to those youthful days when he would hack university machines just to pester students and professors. Watching someone type rapidly at a terminal, Sendai would sometimes enter a keystroke or backspace, causing the command to fail. Thinking they made a typo, the user would try again. Yet the typos continued! While the user was wondering why she was having so much trouble typing and starting to suspect that the keyboard was broken, phantom keystrokes would start appearing on the screen. That is quite disturbing in itself, but induces panic when the keystrokes are typing out commands like **rm –rf ~** or composing a nasty e-mail to the user's boss! Sendai never actually took these damaging actions, but derived a perverse pleasure from alarming the poor users. He wondered what tech support would say when these users would call and declare that their systems were possessed. Sendai now considers himself too mature for such antics, but implements the terminal reading capability to spy on administrators that he suspects are on to him.

Sendai adds another user manipulation feature he calls capability stripping. Linux process privileges are more granular than just superuser (uid 0) or not. Root's privileges are divided into several dozen capabilities, such as CAP_KILL to kill any process and CAP_NET_RAW to write raw packets to the wire. Sendai's feature removes all these capabilities from a logged-in administrator's shell. He may still appear to be root from the **id** command, but has been secretly neutered. Attempts to execute privileged operations are rejected, leaving the administrator more frustrated and confused than if Sendai had terminated the session by killing his shell.

The infection vector is another pressing issue. Sebek hides itself in the kernel module list, but the module itself is not hidden on disk. Worse, the system startup process must be modified to load the module, or a system reboot will foil the whole plan. This is acceptable on a honeynet, because there is no other legitimate administrator who would notice changes to the start-up process. It does not meet Sendai's requirements so well. Yet Knuth was very clear that the system must be resilient in the face of reboots. Sendai's solution is to inject his evil kernel module (which he has taken to calling Shrax) into a legitimate kernel module such as an Ethernet driver.[4] This avoids having an extra suspicious binary around and modifying startup files. Additionally, Sendai adds an inode redirection system so that the module appears unmolested once loaded. This should protect Shrax from file integrity checkers such as Tripwire, Aide, and Radmind. Of course it is possible that the Linux targets compiled their kernels without module support, as many administrators still believe that will stop kernel root kits. No problem! Sendai has tools for both forcing a module into a running kernel using just /dev/mem, and for injecting a module into a static kernel image so that it will be executed silently during the next reboot.

There is also the backdoor issue. One option is to simply compile and run an ssh server on some obscure port number like 31,337. A trivial patch will bypass the authentication and give root access when a secret username is given. Shrax is capable of hiding the ssh process (and its children) from other users, as well as hiding the socket so it isn't disclosed by netstat and the like. Despite this, Sendai finds the option unacceptable. Even though hidden within the system, an outsider could find the open backdoor port with

Nmap. More importantly, Knuth insisted that he be able to activate the backdoor using a wide variety of protocols and subtle packets. Ssh would require that the target network firewalls permit TCP connections to the chosen port. Such permissive firewalls are unlikely at some of the sensitive organizations Knuth wants to attack.

After further brainstorming, Sendai decides on an in-kernel backdoor rather than relying on external programs such as ssh. For backdoors, this one is pretty advanced. Knuth will be happy that its activation interface is the epitome of flexibility. It puts the system interfaces in promiscuous mode (hiding that fact, of course) and examines every IP packet that comes in, regardless of the destination IP address or protocol. The first data bytes are then compared to an identification string. At first Sendai sets that string to "My crime is that of curiosity," but then he smartly decides to be more subtle and chooses a random-looking string. If the string matches, the remainder of the packet is decrypted using AES and a configurable key. The result is interpreted as a response method description followed by a series of shell commands to be executed as root. There are also a few special configuration commands for tasks like changing encryption keys, activating the TTY and network password sniffers, and disabling Shrax and removing every trace of it. Sendai is particularly proud of the response method description. This tells Shrax how to send back command responses, which are always encrypted with the shared key. Sendai is quite proud of all the transport methods supported. Of course, straightforward TCP and UDP to a given IP and port is offered. Or the user can have responses sent via ICMP echo request, echo response, timestamp, or netmask messages. ICMP time-to-live exceeded messages are supported, too. The data can be marshaled into a web request and even sent through a socks or http proxy. Sendai's favorite Shrax technique is to use a series of DNS requests falling under a domain controlled by the attacker. Shrax can even be set to poll a nameserver frequently for new commands. Unless the system is completely unplugged, Knuth should be able to find a way to tunnel his data back. Of course, one can choose to execute a command without returning a response. This allows the intruder to do so completely anonymously with a spoofed IP packet.

Yet another unique Shrax feature is that it can transparently pass commands through a chain of rootkits. An attacker can configure the client to go through an initial rooted machine in Romania, then to one in China, then to a web server on the target corporation's DMZ, and finally to an internal database machine. The first hops help the attacker cover his or her tracks, whereas the final one may be necessary because the DB is accessible only from the web server.

Sendai goes all out working on Shrax because he plans to use it for several years to come and to share it with his buddies. If it had been written only for this specific task, he would have likely hacked the targets first and written only the most critical features.

After all this work on Shrax, Sendai is itching to deploy his new baby. He wants to start hacking immediately, but knows better. Considering that military and government sites are involved, attacking from his neighbor's wireless connection would be foolish. Sendai remembers how the authorities tracked down Kevin Mitnick based on a wireless connection from his apartment. And if the police ever show up at Sendai's apartment complex, he will be a prime suspect. Sendai suddenly regrets ordering the license plate HACKME for his vehicle. The police might not even notice a more subtle plate such as SYNACK. Sendai has a number of compromised boxes all over the Internet, but he really wants some machine that is unconnected to him, which he can use once and then discard.

Throwaway Account

Sendai decides to venture outside after all these days writing Shrax. Perhaps a day at the theatre, on the beach, or attending a game would be good for him. Instead, Sendai heads for the annual ASR Cryptography Conference. He cannot afford the presentations, but hopes to gain free schwag at the giant expo. He won a Sharp Zaurus PDA the last time, which is wonderful for war-walking to find open WAPs. Sendai brings it along in case they have wireless access at the conference.

Although ASR does offer free wireless connectivity, they attempt to secure it with 802.1X and PEAP authentication. That major hassle causes lines at the free wired terminals. Although Sendai would have checked his mail over ssh (after verifying server's ssh key) from his Zaurus, he certainly will not do so from the terminal pavilion. Even if he trusted the ASR organizers (which he does not), they are totally exposed for any hacker to plug in a keylogger or defeat the software and install a program to do the same. In that instant,

Sendai's expression turns from outrage to a mischievous grin as he recognizes this as a source of throwaway accounts!

The next morning, Sendai arrives early at ASR to beat the crowds. He takes an available terminal and loads Slashdot. Feigning frustration, he turns to the back of the machine and unplugs the PS/2 keyboard cable. He blows on the PS/2 port behind the machine, while his hands are inconspicuously slipping the KeyGhost SX onto the cable. This tiny device stores up to two million keystrokes and supposedly even encrypts them so that other troublemakers at ASR cannot steal the passwords.[5] Sendai plugs the keyboard cable back in with his little addition, turns back to the front, and resumes web surfing. He smiles to complete his little act that the machine had been broken and is now working again. Darn those dusty keyboard ports! Nobody paid the least attention to him during his charade and he could have been far more blatant without attracting any attention, but it never hurts to be careful. Plus it makes him feel sneaky and clever.

Attaching the Keyghost to Terminal Keyboard Cable

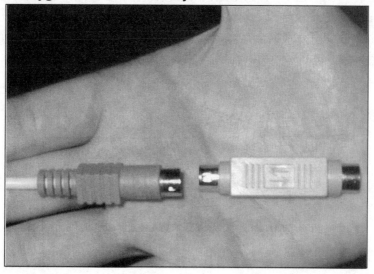

Sendai spends the next few hours at the expo collecting T-shirts, software CDs, pens, a pair of boxer shorts, an NSA pin and bag, magazines, and a bunch of candy treats. After a series of recent Internet worms, many vendors apparently decided that worm-themed giveaways would be clever and unique. Sendai was stuck with gummy worms, refrigerator magnet worms, and a keychain worm. He is tempted to watch the terminals from nearby to ensure nobody steals his $200 KeyGhost. Then he realizes that even if he watches someone discover and take it, he cannot risk a scene by approaching and yelling "Hey! That's my keylogger!" Sendai leaves for a long lunch and then spends a couple hours browsing at a nearby computer superstore.

Late in the afternoon, Sendai returns to ASR, hoping the keylogger remains undetected. He breathes a sigh of relief when it is right where he left it. The terminal is open, so Sendai simply repeats his "broken system" act and 10 minutes later is driving home with all the evidence in his pocket.

At home, Sendai quickly plugs the Keyghost into his system to check the booty. Sendai opens up the vi editor and types his passphrase. Upon recognizing this code, the KeyGhost takes over and types a menu. Sendai types 1 for "entire download" and watches as pages and pages of text fill the screen. Scrolling through, he sees that the vast majority of users do little more than surf the web. Security sites such as securityfocus.com, packetstormsecurity.nl, securiteam.com, and phrack.org are popular. Many folks made the mistake of checking their Hotmail or Yahoo webmail from the terminals. Sendai has little interest in such accounts. There are also a surprising number of porn sites. No purchases with typed credit card numbers, unfortunately. Search engine queries are interesting. One user searched for "windows source torrent," another for lsass.exe, and someone else seeks "security jobs iraq."

Downloading Keyghost Logs

```
                              31337

KeyGhostOpenSesame

Hit 'c' to slow menu

***
KeyGhost SX Std 512KB v8.9
www.keyghost.com

Menu >

1)  Entire download
2)  Section download
3)  Erase
4)  Format
5)  Options
6)  Speed
7)  Password change
8)  eXit

Select > 1

- key to stop -

Keys so far 13456 out of 523744 ...

<dwn>slashdot.org
<dwn><dwn><dwn><dwn>(<dwn>(3x))www.google.com
windows source torrent
<dwn><dwn><dwn><dwn>(<dwn>(45x))w<dwn><dwn><upa><dwn><dwn>www.hotmail.com
katyli81<tab>mysecret
<dwn><dwn><dwn><upa><dwn><dwn><dwn><dwn><upa><dwn><dwn>www.orkut.com
rtelhi<tab>passwdokt
-- INSERT --                                    32,21           Top
```

Sendai starts to worry when he passes over half the file without a single remote login. The few people who open terminal sessions only execute simple commands like **ls** and **cat /etc/passwd**. Seventy percent into the file, Sendai discovers promising data: A user logged in as antonio via ssh to psyche.ncrack.com. Sendai scans through the following commands, hoping the user will run **su** and type the password to become the root superuser. There is no such luck—Antonio simply reads his e-mail with mutt, sends a note to a coworker describing the conference, then disconnects. In all the excitement of reading keystroke logs, Sendai almost forgets to erase the Keyghost and remove it from his system. If he were to be convicted later based on evidence from his own keylogger, Sendai would be the laughing stock of the criminal hacker community. Such a gaffe reminds him of all the hackers who have been caught based on evidence logged from the packet sniffer they installed on a compromised box.

The keystroke logs contain no further remote system passwords, so Sendai tries to make the most of psyche.ncrack.com. He moves to the laptop (which is still associated with the *linksys* WAP) and successfully logs in to Psyche. Now the pressure is on, as he must move fast to avoid detection. His first action is to run the **w** command to see who else is online. He is relieved that the real antonio is not online, but two other users are. Hopefully they do not notice this suspicious antonio login from an unusual IP address. An attempt by them to chat with the imposter antonio could be a disaster as well. Feeling vulnerable and exposed, Sendai focuses on the task at hand. He runs **uname -a** to determine that Psyche is running the Linux 2.4.20 kernel. The distribution is Red Hat 9 according to /etc/redhat-release. Sendai immediately thinks of the brk() kernel exploit for kernels up to 2.4.22. That bug was unknown to the public until it was used to compromise many Debian Project machines. Sendai was a little miffed that he had not been in on it during that pre-publication 0-day period. It is a very interesting bug, and Sendai had spent two days massaging assembly code into a working exploit. It is about to come in handy. He uploads hd-brk.asm and types:

```
psyche> nasm -f elf -o hd-brk.o hd-brk.asm
psyche> ld -o hd-brk hd-brk.o -Ttext 0x0xa0000000
psyche> ./hd-brk
# id
uid=0(root) gid=0(root)
groups=0(root),1(bin),2(daemon),3(sys),4(adm),6(disk),10(wheel)
#
```

Despite the hundreds of boxes that Sendai has compromised in his lifetime (legally or not), he never fails to feel a joyful rush of triumph when he first sees that glorious hash prompt signifying root access! But this is still only a minor victory, as the purpose of Psyche is simply to cover Sendai's tracks. There would be no time for celebration even if it was warranted, as there is now a suspicious root shell that other users might notice.

Sendai turns his attention to rootkit installation. The command **lsmod** shows that the kernel allows modules and that almost 50 of them are installed. This is typical for kernels from major Linux distributions. Sendai injects Shrax into the parport_pc module which, as the name implies, handles PC parallel ports. It is loaded early and unlikely to be changed, meeting the two most desirable attributes. It is also easy to remove and then re-insert the parallel port module without attracting attention. Sendai does so.

With the rootkit seemingly installed, Sendai tests his power. He issues the Shrax *hideall* command against the sshd process through which he is connected. Suddenly that sshd and all of its descendants (including his rootshell) are now hidden from system process lists. Their syslog messages are ignored and sockets are concealed. Sendai wipes the relevant wtmp, lastlog, and syslog records to remove any trace that antonio logged on this evening. He checks up on the other two logged in users with the TTY sniffer to ensure that they are doing their own thing and not suspecting that anything is remiss. Sendai lightly tests a few complex system components including the compiler gcc and emacs. One of the most common ways attackers are discovered is that they inadvertently break something. The generally attentive Debian folks did not notice intruders until kernel crashes began occurring on several boxes at once. Sendai is glad that no problems have yet appeared with Shrax. A feeling of relief rolls over him as he can now relax. His activities on the system are well hidden now that Psyche is securely 0wn3d.

Seeking the Prize

After all this preparation, Sendai is ready to go after the three primary targets. First he must learn as much as possible about them. He starts with an intrusive Nmap scan. Red Hat 9 comes with Nmap 3.00, which is far out of date. Sendai grabs the latest version from www.insecure.org, then compiles and installs it into a directory hidden by Shrax. As for the options, Sendai will use **-sS -P0 -T4 -v** for the same reasons as for his previous scan. Instead of **-F** (scan the most common ports), Sendai specifies **-p0-65535** to scan all 65,536 TCP ports. He will do UDP (**-sU**) and IP-Proto (**-sO**) scans later if necessary. Instead of **-O** for remote OS detection, **-A** is specified to turn on many aggressive options including OS detection and application version detection. Decoys (**-D**) are not used this time because version detection requires full TCP connections, which cannot be spoofed as easily as individual packets. The **-oA** option is given with a base filename. This stores the output in all three formats supported by Nmap (normal human readable, XML, and easily parsed grepable). Sendai scans the machines one at a time to avoid giving the other organizations an early warning. He starts with the Italian company, leading to the following Nmap output.

Nmap Output: A More Intrusive Scan of Ginevra

```
# nmap -sS -P0 -T4 -v -A -p0-65535 -oA ginevra-ex fw.ginevra-ex.it
Starting nmap 3.50 ( http://www.insecure.org/nmap/ )
Interesting ports on fw.ginevra-ex.it (XX.227.165.212):
(The 65535 ports scanned but not shown below are in state: filtered)
PORT    STATE SERVICE VERSION
22/tcp open  ssh     OpenSSH 3.7.1p1 (protocol 1.99)
Running: Linux 2.4.X
OS details: Linux 2.4.18 (x86)
Uptime 327.470 days
TCP Sequence Prediction: Class=random positive increments
                         Difficulty=2325858 (Good luck!)
IPID Sequence Generation: All zeros
Nmap run completed -- 1 IP address (1 host up) scanned in 1722.617 seconds
```

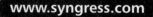

The results show that 22 is the only open TCP port. Sendai is a little disappointed. He was hoping for many more ports, as each is a potential security vulnerability. He notices the line saying that the other 65,535 ports are in the filtered state. That usually means administrators have made an effort to secure the box, since most operating systems install in a default closed state. A closed port returns a RST packet, which tells Nmap that the port is reachable but no application is listening. A filtered port does not respond at all. It is because virtually all the ports were filtered that Nmap took so long (almost half an hour) to complete. Probes against closed ports are quicker because Nmap has to wait only until the RST response is received rather than timing out on each port. A RST response also means that no retransmission is necessary since the probe obviously was not lost. Care clearly was taken to eliminate unnecessary services on this machine as well. Most Linux distributions ship with many of them open. It is also common for small companies to host infrastructure services like name servers and mail servers on the firewall. They do this to avoid placing these public services on a separate DMZ network, but it substantially weakens their security. As a pen-tester, Sendai had compromised many firewalls because they were inappropriately running public BIND nameservers. Apparently Ginevra is smarter than that.

According to Nmap, port 22 is running OpenSSH 3.7.1p1. This is another service that would not be available to the whole Internet in an ideal world, but Sendai can understand why administrators allow it. If something breaks while they are far from home, the admins want to connect from the nearest available Internet service. In so doing, administrators accept the risk that attackers might exploit the service. Sendai intends to do just that. OpenSSH has a sordid history of at least a dozen serious holes, though Sendai does not recall any in this version. Several exploitable bugs in buffer management code were described in CERT Advisory CA-2003-24, but those problems were fixed in 3.7.1. Sendai may have to implement a brute force attack instead. This is often quite effective, though it can take a long time. First Sendai will troll the Internet looking for employee names and e-mail addresses. He will search web pages, USENET and mailing list postings, and even regulatory findings. These will help him guess usernames that may be authorized on fw. He will also try to trick the public company mail server into validating usernames. The username root, of course, will be added to the brute force list.

With a list of users in hand, Sendai will begin the search for possible pass-words. He already has a list of the 20,000 most popular passwords out of mil-lions that he has acquired from various databases. Everyone knows words like "secret," "password," and "letmein" are common. What used to surprise Sendai is how common profane passwords are. "Fuckyou" is #27 on his list, just above "biteme." It is also surprising how many people think asdfgh is a clever, easy-to-type password that no bad guys will ever guess.

Of course, common passwords differ dramatically based on the organiza-tion they are from. So Sendai cannot use just his top password list. He will need to download an Italian language wordlist. Then he will recursively download the entire www.ginevra-ex.it Web site and parse it for new words. Finally, Sendai will whip out Hydra, his favorite open source brute force cracker, to do the actual attack. It may take days, but Sendai is optimistic that he will find a weak password.

Sendai is preparing his plan when he suddenly remembers an obscure vul-nerability that affects only OpenSSH 3.7.1p1, and then only when the Pluggable Authentication Modules (PAM) system is in use and privilege separa-tion is disabled. PAM is often used on Linux boxes, so he decides to give it a shot. The vulnerability is laughably easy to exploit. You simply try to login using SSH protocol 1 and any password (except a blank one) is accepted. No wonder that problem did not last long before being discovered and fixed! Sendai crosses his fingers and begins to type.

```
psyche> ssh -1 root@fw.ginevra-ex.it
The authenticity of host 'fw.ginevra-ex.it (XX.227.165.212)' can't be
established.
RSA1 key fingerprint is 2d:fb:27:e0:ab:ad:de:ad:ca:fe:ba:be:53:02:28:38.
Are you sure you want to continue connecting (yes/no)? yes
Warning: Permanently added 'fw.ginevra-ex.it,XX.227.165.212' (RSA1) to the
list of known hosts.
root@fw.ginevra-ex.it's password:
#
```

There is that happy hash prompt again! Sendai will not have to spend days preparing and executing a noisy brute force attack. He does a little root dance, which is similar to what sports players sometimes do when scoring a goal. Nobody is logged onto fw at the time, and the **last** command shows that people rarely do. So Sendai takes his time cleaning the logs and installing

Shrax. He is exceedingly careful not to crash or otherwise break the box, as that sort of blunder could be ruinous.

With one down and two to go, Sendai moves his attention to the Japanese government box. He launches the following intrusive Nmap scan.

An Intrusive Scan of koizumi-kantei.go.jp

```
# nmap -sS -P0 -T4 -v -A -p0-65535 -oA koizumi koizumi-kantei.go.jp
Starting nmap 3.50 ( http://www.insecure.org/nmap/ )
Interesting ports on koizumi-kantei.go.jp (YY.67.68.173)
(The 65535 ports scanned but not shown below are in state: filtered)
PORT     STATE  SERVICE VERSION
113/tcp closed auth
Running: Sun Solaris 9
OS details: Sun Solaris 9
Nmap run completed -- 1 IP address (1 host up) scanned in 1791.362 seconds
```

Oh dear! This host is even worse (from Sendai's perspective) than Ginevra in that it does not even have a single TCP port open! All ports are filtered, except the identd (auth) port, which is closed. Leaving port 113 closed often is done for better interoperability with some (poorly implemented) IRC and mail servers. Even though Sendai cannot connect with closed ports, they improve OS detection accuracy. The lack of open TCP ports will certainly make cracking in more challenging. There must be another way. Sendai considers wardialing the department's telephone number range for carriers, though so many calls to Japan would certainly rack up the long distance charges. Social engineering might work, though that is risky business. UDP scanning is worth a try, though it tends to be slow as sin against Solaris boxes due to their ICMP rate limiting. So Sendai does a UDP scan with the -F option that limits it to about a thousand common ports. No responses are received. This box is locked down tightly. Another idea is IPv6, particularly since this host is in Japan where that protocol is used more frequently than elsewhere. Psyche does not have an IPv6 interface, so Sendai tests this from his laptop using one of the free public IPv6 tunneling services. They provide an IPv6 address and also conceal his originating IPv4 host. Using the **–6** option to activate IPv6 mode, Sendai takes another shot at scanning the host.

IPv6 Scan against koizumi-kantei.go.jp

```
# nmap -6 -sS -P0 -T4 -v -sV -p0-65535 koizumi-kantei.go.jp


Starting nmap 3.50 ( http://www.insecure.org/nmap/ )
Interesting ports on koizumi-kantei.go.jp
(2ffe:604:3819:2007:210:f3f5:fe22:4d0:)
(The 65511 ports scanned but not shown below are in state: closed)
PORT         STATE     SERVICE           VERSION
7/tcp        open      echo
9/tcp        open      discard?
13/tcp       open      daytime           Sun Solaris daytime
19/tcp       open      chargen
21/tcp       open      ftp               Solaris ftpd
22/tcp       open      ssh               SunSSH 1.0 (protocol 2.0)
23/tcp       open      telnet            Sun Solaris telnetd
25/tcp       open      smtp              Sendmail 8.12.2+Sun/8.12.2
37/tcp       open      time
79/tcp       open      finger            Sun Solaris fingerd
111/tcp      open      rpcbind           2-4 (rpc #100000)
512/tcp      open      exec
513/tcp      open      rlogin
515/tcp      open      printer           Solaris lpd
540/tcp      open      uucp              Solaris uucpd
587/tcp      open      smtp              Sendmail 8.12.2+Sun/8.12.2
898/tcp      open      http              Solaris management console server
(SunOS 5.9 sparc; Java 1.4.0_00; Tomcat 2.1)
4045/tcp  open      nlockmgr          1-4 (rpc #100021)
7100/tcp  open      font-service      Sun Solaris fs.auto
32774/tcp open      ttdbserverd       1 (rpc #100083)
32776/tcp open      kcms_server       1 (rpc #100221)
32778/tcp open      metad             1 (rpc #100229)
32780/tcp open      metamhd           1 (rpc #100230)
32786/tcp open      status            1 (rpc #100024)
32787/tcp open      status            1 (rpc #100024)


Nmap run completed -- 1 IP address (1 host up) scanned in 729.191 seconds
```

Now this is exactly what Sendai likes to see! Many of the services may be unpatched too, since the administrators assumed they were inaccessible. Unfortunately they forgot to firewall IPv6 in the same way they do IPv4. Sendai uses an IPv6-enabled rpcquery command to learn more about the running RPC services, including many that are using UDP. He has several avenues of attack available, but decides on a UDP sadmind vulnerability. Sendai obtains an exploit from H.D. Moore's Metasploit framework (www.metasploit.com), and 10 minutes later is doing the root dance again.

Hacking .MIL

This leaves only one host remaining, and it is certainly the scariest. Hacking Italian and Japanese hosts from the US is one thing. Hacking infowar.cols.disa.mil is quite another. Yet it is too late to stop now. Sendai launches an intrusive scan of the host, and is disappointed to see zero open ports. Not again! This host has no IPv6 address and UDP scans come up negative. Sendai tries some more advanced scan types including Fin scan (**–sF**), Window scan (**–sW)**, and the ultra-sneaky Idle scan (**–sI**), all to no avail. He knows Knuth will not accept two out of three, so giving up is no option. Sendai broadens his search, launching an intrusive scan of every host in that 256-host subnet by issuing the command **nmap –sS –P0 –T4 –v –A –p0–65535 –oA disanet infowar.cols.disa.mil/24** . That trailing /24 is CIDR notation that tells Nmap to scan 256 addresses. Classless Inter Domain Routing (CIDR) is a method for assigning IP addresses without using the standard IP address classes like Class A, Class B, or Class C.

Upon seeing the results, Sendai grins because many machines are not locked down as tightly as infowar is. Unfortunately, they seem to have their patches in order. During the next day and a half, Sendai finds numerous potential vulnerabilities only to fail in exploitation because the hole is already patched. He is starting to worry. Then he begins to investigate webpxy.cols.disa.mil and discovers a Squid proxy.

A Squid Proxy Is Discovered

```
Interesting ports on webpxy.cols.disa.mil (ZZ.229.74.191):
(The 65535 ports scanned but not shown below are in state: filtered)
PORT       STATE SERVICE      VERSION
3128/tcp open  http-proxy Squid webproxy 2.5.STABLE3
Device type: general purpose
Running: FreeBSD 5.X
OS Details: FreeBSD 5.1-RELEASE (x86)
Uptime: 110.483 days
```

Many organizations maintain a proxy to allow internal clients access to the World Wide Web. They often do this for security reasons, so that material can be scanned for undesirable or malicious content before being provided to the client. It can also keep clients shielded on the internal network so that attackers cannot reach them. Performance and site logging are further reasons managers often prefer this approach. Unfortunately these proxies can do much more harm than good when they are misconfigured. Sendai finds that the Netcat utility (nc) is unavailable on Psyche, so he connects to the proxy with the standard Telnet command and manually types an HTTP CON-NECT request.

Open Proxy Test

```
psyche> telnet webpxy.cols.disa.mil 3128
Trying  ZZ.229.74.191 ...
Connected to ZZ.229.74.191.
Escape character is '^]'.
CONNECT scanme.insecure.org:22 HTTP/1.0

HTTP/1.0 200 Connection established

SSH-1.99-OpenSSH_3.8p1
```

Sendai is quite pleased. The proxy allows him to connect to port 22 (ssh) of an arbitrary Internet host and the SSH banner display shows that it suc-ceeded. So perhaps it will allow him to connect to internal DISA machines too! A hacker by the name Adrian Lamo was notorious for publicly breaking into high-profile sites this way. Many companies thanked him for exposing the weaknesses, though the New York Times did not appreciate the unsolicited security help and they pressed charges. Sendai tries to exploit this problem by connecting to port 22 of infowar.cols.disa.mil through the proxy. He had been unable to reach any port on this machine, but through the proxy it works! Apparently he is behind the firewall now. Infowar is running 3.7.1p2, for which Sendai knows of no vulnerabilities. Nor does he have a password, though brute force is always an option.

With the newfound power of his open proxy, Sendai wants to fully portscan infowar and explore the whole department network. He curses the fact that Nmap offers no proxy bounce scan option. Then Sendai remembers a primary benefit of open source. He can modify it to meet his needs. Nmap does offer an ftp bounce scan (**-b**) that logs into an FTP server and then tries to explore the network by issuing the *port* command for every interesting host and port. The error message tells whether the port is open or not. Sendai modifies the logic to connect to a proxy server instead and to issue the *CONNECT* command. After an afternoon of work, he is proxy scanning likely internal IP ranges such as RFC1918-blessed 192.168.0.0/16 and 10.0.0.0/8 netblocks, looking for internal machines. He finds a whole intranet under the 10.1 netblock, with the primary internal web server at 10.1.0.20. That server is a gold mine of information about the organization. Sendai sifts through new employee manuals, news pages, employee mailing list archives, and more. In one mailing list post, a quality assurance engineer asks developers to try and reproduce a problem on the qa-sol1 machine. The password to the qa role account is buserror, he helpfully adds.

Sendai moves quickly to try this sensitive information. He scans qa-sol1 and finds that the Telnet and ssh services are available. It would be simple to Telnet into the proxy and then issue the *CONNECT* command himself to log into the telnetd on qa-sol1, but Sendai cannot bear to do that. He wants to connect more securely, using ssh. Sendai downloads an HTTP proxy shared library to Psyche, which allows normal applications to work transparently through the webpxy.cols.disa.mil proxy server. With that in place, Sendai makes an ssh connection to qa-sol1 and successfully logs in as qa. The system is running Solaris 8 and has quite a few users logged on. Sendai immediately reads */etc/passwd* and finds that the first line consists of "+::0:0:::". This means

the system is using NIS (formerly called YP) to share accounts and configuration information among the whole department. NIS is wonderful from
Sendai's perspective. It makes obtaining usernames and password hashes trivial
using the ypcat command.

Obtaining the Password File from NIS

```
qa-sol1> ypcat passwd
root:lCYRhBsBs7NcU:0:1:Super-User:/:/sbin/sh
daemon:x:1:1::/:
bin:x:2:2::/usr/bin:
sys:x:3:3::/:
adm:x:4:4:Admin:/var/adm:
lp:x:71:8:Line Printer Admin:/usr/spool/lp:
uucp:x:5:5:uucp Admin:/usr/lib/uucp:
smmsp:x:25:25:SendMail Message Submission Program:/:
listen:x:37:4:Network Admin:/usr/net/nls:
nobody:x:60001:60001:Nobody:/:
jdl:mY2/SvpAe82H2:101:100:James Levine:/home/jdl:/bin/csh
david:BZ2RLkbD6ajKE:102:100:David Weekly:/home/david:/bin/tcsh
ws:OZPXeDdi2/jOk:105:100:Window Snyder:/home/ws:/bin/tcsh
luto:WZIi/jx9WCrqI:107:100:Andy Lutomirski:/home/luto:/bin/bash
lance:eZN/CfM1Pd7Qk:111:100:Lance Spitzner:/home/lance:/bin/tcsh
annalee:sZPPTiCeNIeoE:114:100:Annalee Newitz:/home/annalee:/bin/tcsh
dr:yZgVqD2MxQpZs:115:100:Dragos Ruiu:/home/dr:/bin/ksh
hennings:5aqsQbbDKs8zk:118:100:Amy Hennings:/home/hennings:/bin/tcsh
[Hundreds of similar lines]
```

With these hundreds of password hashes in hand, Sendai goes to work on
cracking them. He starts up John the Ripper on every one of his reasonably
modern home machines. Each machine handles a subset of the accounts,
which Sendai has sorted by crypt(3) seed (the first two characters of the hash)
for efficiency. Within five minutes, dozens of the easiest passwords have been
cracked. Then the rate slows down, and Sendai decides to sleep on it.

The next morning, nearly a third of the accounts have been cracked.
Sendai is hoping that at least one of the users has an account on infowar
using the same password. From qa-sol1, Sendai tries repeatedly to ssh into

infowar, trying each cracked account in turn. The attempt fails time after time and eventually he runs out of cracked accounts. Sendai will not give up so easily. After 24 more hours, he has cracked almost half the accounts and tries ssh again. This time, he gets in using the account bruce! This is a Linux box, so Sendai tries the brk() exploit that was so successful against Psyche. No luck. He spends a couple hours trying other techniques in vain. Then he slaps himself on the forehead upon realizing that bruce is authorized to execute commands as root in the /etc/sudoers file. Sendai simply types **sudo vi /etc/resolve.conf**, as if he planned to edit an administrative file. Then he breaks out of vi to a root shell by issuing the command **:sh**. Game over! Shrax is promptly installed.

Bursting with pride and looking forward to a wallet bursting with green, Sendai composes an e-mail to Knuth's e-mail address at Hushmail.com. He describes the systems and how to access them via the Shrax client. An encrypted version of Shrax has been posted on a free Geocities Web page that Sendai just created. He then obtains Knuth's PGP key from a public keyserver and verifies that the fingerprint matches what Knuth gave him. A couple minutes later the encrypted and signed document is waiting for Knuth in his inbox.

Triumph and New Toys

The next morning, Sendai wakes up to find a glorious e-mail from PayPal notifying him of a large deposit. Knuth keeps his word, and quickly too! Sendai browses to eBay, pricing huge LCD monitors and Apple PowerBooks. These are a good way to blow a bunch of money and have something to show for it, unlike his Fiasco investment. Sendai is bidding on a 17" laptop when Knuth calls. He has already tried out Shrax and verified that the machines were fully compromised as promised. Suddenly Knuth drops a bomb, mentioning that it is now time to "start the real work." Sendai is speechless. He spent weeks of nonstop effort to own those machines. What is Knuth saying? Apparently Knuth has no interest in those boxes at all. They were just a test to insure that Sendai is expertly skilled and reliable. "You passed with flying colors," Knuth offers in an unsuccessful attempt to restore Sendai's pride. He notes that those machines would make a great Shrax proxy chain for safely owning the primary targets. Sendai highly approves of that idea. It should allay his constant fear of being caught, and also brings value to all of his recent efforts.

Sendai accepts the next assignment and Knuth starts rattling off the new targets. Unlike the crazy assortment last time, these all belong to banks with a heavy African presence. They include the Amalgamated Banks of South Africa, Stanbic Nigeria, and Nedbank. Knuth wants numerous machines compromised with a covert Shrax install, as well as network maps to better understand the organizations. Knuth will apparently be doing the dirty work, as Sendai need only document the access methods and leave.

"This is so much better than working at that accounting firm," Sendai thinks as he begins his first of many successful and lucrative bank intrusions.

Endnotes

[1] Further information on this technique is available at www.insecure.org/nmap/idlescan.html.
[2] Nmap was written by your humble author.
[3] Your humble author is a Honeynet Project member.
[4] Kernel module injection on Linux and Solaris is described at www.phrack.org/show.php?p=61&a=10.
[5] The KeyGhost is only one of many such products easily available over the Internet. The KEYKatcher is another popular choice.

Aftermath...The Investigation Continues

After "The Don's" heavy involvement with Knuth and his operations throughout Africa, The Don was now under a considerable degree of covert surveillance. As the agent now responsible for the surveillance of The Don's activities in relation to Knuth, it was my task to observe The Don as he made his way to Def Con, the annual hacker conference held at the Alexis Park hotel – Las Vegas. As I arrived at the Alexis Park hotel (supposedly the only hotel in Vegas without some kind of gambling) I reminded myself of last year when an agent from our organization fell foul of the yearly "spot the fed" competition – a fate which I was eager to avoid. This year, The Don was sharing his hotel room at the Alexis with an individual named Sendai – an individual, who our sources inform us, is an extraordinarily skilled cracker, who has written a number of private kernel root kits and exploits codes in his time.

On the Saturday evening of the conference, Sendai and The Don were observed in a secluded vodka bar located in a more seedy area of Vegas, several miles from the strip itself. Thanks to the audio monitoring equipment we had been given for the purposes of this operation, we were able to hear almost every word of their conversation. By then, both The Don and Sendai had had far more than their fair share of flavored vodka drinks and had become considerably more loose-lipped than they would have otherwise been. Although we were unable to pick up all of their conversation, The Don was caught describing a "new client" who had paid him extremely well for "the manipulation of telecommunication equipment". From my studies of the hacker community, I have learned that many crackers/hackers/blackhats/ [insert media buzz word here], call them what you like – have a tendency to be extremely entrepreneurial. Sendai, being no exception, saw the opportunity and enquired about The Don's new client and his need for a highly skilled cracker. In spite of The Don's reluctance to provide Sendai with additional information, a promise was made to Sendai that his information would be passed over to his "client" – "With a good reference". With that, the two disappeared off to one of the few strip joints in Vegas which sold both alcohol and promised a "full" showing.

Although we were aware that Knuth was not the only client that The Don had ever had, we were pretty sure that he was his only current client, leaving a pretty good chance that the new client The Don referred to was indeed Knuth. Given the possible severity of Knuth's projects this information proved more than sufficient to have a covert observation warrant signed for young Sendai. Sure enough, the following Tuesday evening, Sendai received a phone call at his current place of residence (his parent's house) from an individual claiming to be a "Bob Knuth". During the conversation, the two agreed to terms under which Sendai would carry out a compromise of three Internet based hosts – one of which was operated by the Defense Information Systems Agency (DISA). Over the following weeks, our surveillance team made every effort to monitor the activities of Sendai, attempting to monitor the attacks against both DISA and two other systems hosted outside of the United States. Through our monitoring of Sendai and the information which our behavioral science unit continues to send our way, I have written the following capability and motivational analysis of Sendai.

After a careful analysis of the attacks initiated by the individual who is known to his friends as just "Sendai", I have drawn the following conclusions regarding both his capability and motivation to execute tasks, which in this case are contrary to the Patriot Act of October 2001. For the sakes of keeping this report short and to the point, the attack case study I have chosen to use is that of the attack initiated against a system owned and operated by the Defense Information System Agency (DISA).

Attack Inhibitors:

Consequences of attribution given detection (C(A)/D).

Due to the system concerned being the property of the United States government, the consequences of attribution given detection for Sendai could range from 25 years imprisonment to, in extreme cases, the death penalty. Although in previous cases Knuth has made use of unwitting agents, we have no reason to believe that Sendai was an unwitting agent and believe that he was fully aware of his actions and the potential consequences if he were to be detected and attributed to the attack. To this end, after a careful analysis of Sendai's financial history, we believe that a lack of finances motivated Sendai into performing a task which in the past, he may have turned down due to the risks associated with the attack. Further to this, he did not make any attempt to utilize resources to reduce the consequences of attribution given detection – rather neglecting the consequences of attribution given detection due to the significantly influential "attack driver" or motivator – the bounty he would receive on successful completion of the tasks Knuth had assigned to him.

Perceived Probability Of Attribution Given Detection (PP(A)/D)

Although not overly elaborate – Sendai went to considerable lengths to ensure that if his attacks were to be detected, at the worse case scenario, his attacks would be traced back as far as a neighbors wireless internet connection. If his attacks were to be detected they would at very least be traced back to the "psyche.ncrack.com" – a host compromised by Sendai to leverage his attacks against his three primary target hosts. This is a typical example of how adversaries are able to leverage a resource (in this case the resource being another compromised system) to being the inhibitors associated with an attack to an acceptable level. In this context, an acceptable inhibitor level is the point at which an attacker is "happy" that as far as he or she can see the attack conditions are in their favor.

Perceived Probability Of Detection Given Attempt (PP(D)/A)

Leveraging his considerable skill (a technological resource) Sendai wrote a customized "root kit" to install on all hosts compromised during this particular project. The root kit significantly reduced Sendai's probability of detection, again bringing the inhibitors associated with the attack to an acceptable level through the use of resources.

Perceived Probability Of Success Given Attempt (PP(S)/A)

As we have already noted, Sendai is an individual who holds a substantial technological resource and therefore capability, against most target hosts. This resource was used in a measured manner in all observed attacks, utilizing privately written proof of concept codes to exploit flaws in software to achieve his objective – once more, leveraging his resource to bring what may have otherwise been an attack inhibitor to acceptable level. His exploitation of kernel level flaws (an activity which if performed incorrectly can result in the failure of the information system attacked due to the possibility of it being rendered unstable) also demonstrates that he is either highly reckless, or (and I suspect this is the case given that such a flaw was exploited with his own proof of concept code) extremely sure of what he is doing.

Perceived Consequences Of Failure Given Attempt (PC(F)/A)

From an analysis of the intercepted phone call made by Knuth to Sendai, it
is clear that Sendai is somewhat frightened of the possible consequences if
he were to fail in the execution of the tasks given to him by Knuth. This in
itself acts as a motivator, and is worth noting that in this case the value
of PC(F)/A may have resulted in Sendai being more neglectful of other
variables such as the consequences of attribution or a low probability of
success.

To summarize, Sendai is an individual who is so well resourced and under the
correct conditions – motivated that in his mind, no single, conceivable
attack profile will consist of adverse attack inhibitors that are such that
are not counter-able by the resource to which he has access. In laymen's
terms – if motivated to do so, there are few, if any targets that Sendai
will decline to engage due to any adverse conditions which may exist. If now
under the full command of Knuth, which given past actions, I would suggest
he is – Sendai poses a somewhat greater threat than his counterpart The Don
and should be monitored carefully as Knuth's yet-unknown project develops.

Final Words

The topic of cyber adversary characterization is indeed a vast one, with many avenues of which one can venture and many caveats down which one can fall. As we become increasingly reliant upon technology for the day-to-day running of our countries, businesses and lives, this problem will continue to grow, our attack surfaces will increase and with it, the need to understand where the real threats lay and what the true nature of those threats really are.

Throughout this publication, we have introduced a set of principals, methodologies, metrics and how to manage the vast amount of data—all of which have been designed to give structure to the process of characterizing cyber adversaries and determining specific threats to specific assets.

The theories presented in this book were conceived in the hope that they will aid in solving the growing problems which large corporations, government agencies and private users of information technology all face on a daily basis. With the growing use of information systems, the cost of managing the security of those systems will only increase, heightening the importance of understanding where the highest risk threats lay and how to manage those threats in an effective and cost efficient manner.

To this end, efforts to research new characterization methodologies and theories continue. Using the theory established thus far to form a firm foundation; we seek to document and discuss emerging issues surrounding the topic of cyber adversary characterization, analyzing how the established theory can be used to provide practicable solutions to some very real problems. The progress of cyber adversary research has only been possible because of the diverse groups of individuals, from both public and private sectors who have dedicated their time to this topic—something that the authors of this book hope will gain momentum as a result of this publication.

If you feel that you would like to learn more about this topic or feel that you can add to the extensive efforts which have already been dedicated, we would like to hear from you.

The author, contributing authors of this publication and the organizers of the working group responsible for furthering research in this area are available by sending an email to: syngress@characterize.us.

Acknowledgements

On a personal note, I would like to personally thank the following people for making this book possible. Marcus Sachs, Eric Shaw, Matthew Devost and Ed Stroz whose efforts toward this book and dedication to the topic of adversary characterization have made this book a total success.

From Syngress, Andrew Williams for acknowledging the need for a publication on and the importance of the topic of cyber adversary characterization and Christine Kloiber for her editorial skills and guidance throughout the development of this book.

I would like to thank all of those who have been involved in the adversary characterization workshops in the past, all who have contributed to the development of this topic in one way or another, including: Mark Rowe, John Denneny and Dave Watson from Pentest Limited and Dave O'Farrell and Sami Saydjari.

I would also like to thank Jon Harris, Martyn Ruks, Stephen Kho, Christian Angerbjorn, Paul Midian, David Howorth, Chris Ransford, Brett Kells and Cindy Bellefelluille, Nicola Calmeyer and Shaheena Ahmed from NetSEC for supporting my efforts in the development of this publication.

Finally, I would like to thank my fiancée and family for their support over the last six months, while this book became a reality.

Glossary

Attack A set of parameters associated with an offensive act against a target.

Attacker A Cyber Adversary

Attack Technique The systematic procedure through which an attack is launched

Attack Tool A computer program designed to automate the execution of an attack technique

Attack Noise The level of attack noise pertains to the level of anomalous activity created by an attack. High levels of attack noise are typically undesired by an adversary as attack noise often increases the chances of detection.

Adversary Objects A component part of the three adversary properties. Adversary objects consist of multiple "adversary elements." See Chapter 2 for details.

Adversary Elements Component parts of adversary objects that pertain to specific adversary variables, such as the time and finance an adversary has.

Attacker Property A collection of "objects" relating to the capability and motivation of the cyber adversary. These include the attack inhibitor object and the attack driver object (see Chapter 2).

Box An information system

CARC Cyber Adversary Characterization

CERT/CC The CERT Coordination Center (CERT/CC) is a center of Internet security expertise, located at the Software Engineering Institute, a federally funded research and development center operated by Carnegie Mellon University.

Cyber Adversary An opponent or enemy whose attack medium typically consists of computer networks.

Characterization Metric A standard for measuring a variable associated with an adversary, such as an attack tool characterization metric.

Digital Equipment Corporation (DEC) The company responsible for the original version of the VMS operating system. DEC is now a part of Hewlett Packard Corporation.

Dumpster Diving The art of going through the refuse containers in the hope of retrieving computer equipment and sensitive data such as authentication credentials.

Environment Property A collection of "objects" representing the environment surrounding an adversary. These include the association's object and the legal/political object (see Chapter 2).

Host An information system

Intrusion Detection System (IDS) An intrusion detection system will attempt to detect certain types of attack.

Internet Protocol (IP) The Protocol widely used around the world to facilitate the networking of information systems

Insider An individual with an elevated inside level of initial access to an asset such as an organization

Network A structure of interconnected information systems. The Internet is comprised of many interconnected networks (hence "inter-net").

Private Branch Exchange (PBX) A subscriber-owned telecommunications exchange that usually includes access to the public switched network

Port Scan A process that is typically used to enumerate the services available on a specific information system

Sniffer A software program designed to capture data from an information system or network of information systems, such as the "DECNET" sniffer sought by Kevin Mitnick

Target Property A collection of "objects" which represent the properties of an attack target, specifically, the properties that are of most "interest" to the cyber adversary. These include the owner object and the resource object (see Chapter 2).

Virus A computer program that will infect the memory space of other files on information systems

Virtual Address Extension (VAX) VAX systems were a line of mid-range information systems developed by Digital Equipment Corp (DEC).

Virtual Memory System (VMS) An operating system developed by DEC to run on DEC's VAX information systems

Worm Not to be confused with a virus, worms have the ability to propagate themselves between information systems, typically leveraging vulnerabilities in software running on target systems.

Index

A

Active Server Pages (ASP), 120–121
adversarial groups
  conditions for (table), 34
  environment property impacts, 36
adversarial model. *See* cyber adversarial
  model
adversaries
  environment property, 24–25
  political and cultural impacts, 25–28
  types, placement in disclose pyramid,
    68–72
adversary masquerading, 104
adversary object matrix model, 21–22
adversary property
  matrix, 37, 48
  model skeleton, 21–22
  relationships, 23–24
advisories, security. *See* security
  advisories
al-Muhajiroun, 247
al Qaeda
  characterizing threat of, 249–250
  and September 2001 attacks, 214
  as threat group, 223
ALF (Animal Liberation Front), 248
American Registry for Internet
  Numbers (ARIN) and IP
  registration, 78
analog data, 13
anger of disgruntled employees,
  measuring, 150–153
Animal Liberation Front (ALF), 248
anonymous threats
  identifying source of (WarmTouch
    case), 157–158
  and information warfare, 234
antivirus software, 210–211
anxiety of disgruntled employees,
  measuring, 150–153

applications, Web. *See* Web applications
Askit.com, insider threat at, 183
ASP applications, 120–121
assets
  and target property, 108–109
  threat characterization, 116–122
  threat characterization case study,
    122–135
  and variable impact given motivation
    (table), 29–30
  Web application flaw attack score
    tables, 120–121
associations, intelligence sources, and
  impact of attack, 31
AT&T and Bell System breakup, 208
attack deterrents, 122
attack drivers, geographical, physical
  location of target property, 112
attack inhibitors
  and attack techniques, 93–94
  influences on (case study), 124–125
  and partial disclosure, 59–60
  and pyramid metric capability, 67–68
  workarounds, 53–54
attack preference tables, using, 110
attack techniques
  attack inhibitors reduced through use
    of, 93–94
  described, resources required for, 92
  network service, vulnerability
    enumeration, 95–98
  scoring metrics, 94
attack tools
  See also attack techniques
  availability of, 83–84
  characterization metrics, 139–141
  commercial, 90–91
  customized compromise, 252–253
  ease of use, 82–83
  mass rooters, 84–86
  metrics, caveats of, 91–92

313

Syngress: *The Definition of a Serious Security Library*

Syn·gress (sin–gres): *noun, sing.* Freedom from risk or danger; safety. See *security*.

AVAILABLE NOW
order @
www.syngress.com

Zero Day Exploit: Countdown to Darkness

Rob Shein aka Rogue Shoten and Marcus H. Sachs
The Holy Grail for malicious, criminal program and virus writers is the "Zero-Day Exploit." Just imagine the chilling consequences resulting from a "Zero-Day" which exploits critical infrastructure systems falling into the hands of international terrorists targeting the United States. Zero-Day Exploit: Countdown to Darkness provides a fictional, yet realistic and downright scary tale of cyber-terrorism. Written, edited, and reviewed by the cyber security experts who monitor and safeguard the Internet in the real world, "Zero-Day" is a frighteningly realistic story about the elite and undercover world of Internet security. With a special foreword by David Litchfield.

ISBN: 1-931836-09-4

Price: $49.95 U.S. $69.95 CAN

Stealing the Network: How to Own a Continent

131ah, Russ Rogers, Jay Beale, Joe Grand, Fyodor, FX, Paul Craig, Timothy Mullen (Thor), Tom Parker, Ryan Russell, Kevin D. Mitnick
The first book in the "*Stealing the Network*" series was called a "blockbuster" by Wired magazine, a "refreshing change from more traditional computer books" by Slashdot.org, and "an entertaining and informative look at the weapons and tactics employed by those who attack and defend digital systems" by Amazon.com. This follow-on book once again combines a set of fictional stories with real technology to show readers the danger that lurks in the shadows of the information security industry... Could hackers take over a continent?

ISBN: 1-931836-05-1

Price: $49.95 US $69.95 CAN

AVAILABLE NOW
order @
www.syngress.com

AVAILABLE NOW
order @
www.syngress.com

Richard Thieme's Islands in the Clickstream: Reflections on Life in a Virtual World

Richard Thieme is one of the most visible commentators on technology and society, appearing regularly on CNN radio, TechTV, and various other national media outlets. He is also in great demand as a public speaker, delivering his "Human Dimension of Technology" talk to over 50,000 live audience members each year. *Islands in the Clickstream* is a single volume "best of Richard Thieme."

ISBN: 1-931836-22-1

Price: $29.95 US $43.95 CAN

SYNGRESS®